THE RSL BOOK OF
WORLD
WAR I

THE RSL BOOK OF
WORLD WAR I

Edited by John Gatfield with Richard Landels

HarperCollins*Publishers*

HarperCollins*Publishers*

First published in Australia in 2015
This edition published in 2016
by HarperCollins*Publishers* Australia Pty Limited
ABN 36 009 913 517
harpercollins.com.au

HarperCollins*Publishers*
Level 13, 201 Elizabeth Street, Sydney NSW 2000, Australia
Unit D1, 63 Apollo Drive, Rosedale, Auckland 0632, New Zealand

National Library of Australia Cataloguing-in-Publication data:

The RSL book of WWI / editors: John Gatfield with Richard Landels.
   978 0 7322 9966 8 (paperback)
   Includes index.
   Returned Services League of Australia--Archives.
   World War, 1914–1918 – Personal narratives, Australian.
   World War, 1914–1918 – Participation, Australian.
   Mateship (Australia)
   Other Creators/Contributors: Gatfield, John, editor. Landels, Richard, editor.
940.48194

Cover design by Darren Holt, HarperCollins Design Studio
Cover image: France: Picardie, Somme, Amiens Harbonnières Area,
Villers-Bretonneux Area, Villers-Bretonneux, 1 May 1918. A group of the 46th
Australian Infantry Battalion just after coming out of the line in front of Monument
Wood, where they had experienced a period of very severe fighting, showing the
condition of the men after an attack. Taken by an unknown Australian official
photographer. Held by the Australian War Memorial (E02307).
Index by Michael Wyatt.
Typeset in Sabon by Kirby Jones

Contents

Preface

A century after the cataclysmic events of the world war that was thought of at the time as the 'war to end all wars', it is fitting that the Returned and Services League of Australia should commemorate the stories of the men and women who served.

Most often those writing about war focus on the broad sweep of history, or on why one side or the other won a particular battle, or on the actions of political and military leaders. When stories about individuals are included in such histories, they tend to feature specific acts of valour or military consequence.

This history is markedly different. Its focus is on the experiences of individuals, as recorded by the participants themselves. As such it is an authentic reflection of how those caught up in the Great War of 1914–18 saw their involvement. They do not dwell on grand strategy, or on the political implications of their actions. Instead they recount what happened to them and to their mates.

This, then, is a series of stories about Australians going to war, seeing and doing things which prior to August 1914 they could never have imagined they would experience. These very personal accounts provide a rare insight into how Australians – most of them very young – coped when sent in harm's way. From the tropical steaminess of what was then German New Guinea to the challenging terrain of the Gallipoli peninsula and the expanse of the Arabian desert, these stories reach out from the past to remind us what our forebears endured.

They record the excitement and horrors of battle, the extraordinary courage of ordinary men and women, and the irrepressible larrikinism of boisterous young men who, when not face to face with the enemy, found opportunities for fun and camaraderie even at the front.

The RSL was founded by such men in 1916. Having endured the tragedy of war, and looking for a means of coming to terms with its aftermath, they saw a need to bond and to support their mates. They were also determined to look after the families of those who had paid the supreme sacrifice or who had been damaged by their involvement in war.

This bond also allowed them to come together to share yarns and to reflect on their achievements. Many wrote about their experiences for the RSL's various publications. Others had kept diaries or written letters during the war, and it is fortunate that many of these documents survived. This treasure trove of material now allows us to hear from them what they saw, how they felt and what they thought they had achieved.

This is a book of which every Australian can be enormously proud. The members of the RSL hope you enjoy its contents.

Rear Admiral Ken Doolan AO RAN (Retired)
National President
The Returned and Services League of Australia

Introduction

When the first Australian soldiers returned from Egypt, embarking from Suez on the hospital ship *Kyarra* on 5 February 1915, they quickly understood that an organisation was needed to advocate for their welfare and resettlement. From that nucleus grew what we know today as the Returned and Services League of Australia.

While the RSL's priority has always been the care of veterans and their families, another commitment has been the commemoration of those who did not return, the preservation of that spirit of shared experiences, and the pledge that Australia would not forget the sacrifices of the Great War.

In due course RSL state branches established newsletters or magazines to inform members, to entertain them, and to record their histories. These publications evolved through various formats and titles, but their principal incarnations are *The Listening Post* (Western Australia), *Mufti* (Victoria), *Reveille* (New South Wales), *The Queensland Digger* (Queensland), *On Service* (Tasmania) and *The Signal* (South Australia).

From these magazines has come this remarkable account of the Great War, 100 unique experiences by 100 authors. These are factual accounts, most of them written by veterans for one another to read. Published as they were in veterans' magazines, there was no tolerance for errors of fact or opinion. Many were written five, ten or twenty years after the event, sometimes in anniversary years, but it is clear that the emotions are still raw and the memories vivid. These were shared experiences never to be forgotten.

These stories cover the whole of the four years of 1914–18, from the first enlistment of volunteers through to the Armistice. There are contributions from airmen and sailors, nurses and padres, officers and privates, highly decorated heroes and those whose exploits were never recognised publicly.

They are written in the language of the day: these soldiers referred to 'Fritzies' and 'Jacko', 'Gyppos' and 'the Boche'. It would be inappropriate to edit this language, and the stories are printed here as they appeared originally, except for corrections of, for example, the spelling of placenames, the standardisation of certain spellings, and the formatting of numbers and dates. A few stories have been abridged.

Some authors remain anonymous but in each case the context or facts are authentic, and names, units and events were checked against the WWI and embarkation rolls, and in some cases against unit histories. The various magazines sometimes published literary efforts which were clearly fictional or suspiciously close to it, and these were not included.

If there appears to be a geographical bias in the origins of contributors, this is not deliberate on our part. It is simply because some RSL branches encouraged members to write stories for their magazines more enthusiastically than others. The Western Australian branch went out of its way to do this, even producing in 1929 *The WA Digger Book*, from which some stories have been taken.

The explanatory and biographical notes are mine, included to give the reader a sense of context for the events described, and an insight into the author's age, occupation and education.

The RSL and veterans in general do not seek to glorify war, and nor does this book. It does, however, seek to preserve the collective memory of these veterans, as well as the individual accounts, sometimes horrific, sometimes humorous, but always honest. These are their stories, and theirs alone.

John Gatfield

It's war! Enlisting, embarking

'Once accepted, the would-be soldier is re-born into the army. He brings nothing with him into his military world save the mufti he stands up in, and that, as soon as possible, is shed. He has to be clothed, fed, supplied with all a man's toilet necessities, with blankets, waterproof sheet, eating and cooking utensils, firearms, entrenching tools, spades and picks, and diverse other things. Then, too, he has to be sworn in and finally paid.'

— Major J.W.B. Bean

First Angry Shot

By Lieutenant Colin Beszant

An Australian troopship which began its life as a German merchantman, the SS *Pfalz* drew the first 'angry shot' fired by Empire forces in WWI.

The tale of the mixed fortunes of the SS *Pfalz*, later the *Boorara*, began in the Port of Melbourne on 4 August 1914. Rumours of war had been circulating in Australia for weeks and had gained height on 2 August, when the Naval Board set up a Port Examination Service designed to inspect all incoming and outgoing shipping in all major ports.

As early as 1912 the German government had issued a paper entitled 'Instructions in Case of War to Shipping'. This document had been circulated freely and openly to all German merchant shipping; however, in addition to this instruction was a secret supplement issued only to serving Masters.

In part, this supplement stated that 'vessels with all or most of their cargoes on board, which can carry enough coal to take them home via South America, should take that route'. It was because of this instruction that the *Pfalz* delayed her departure from Melbourne until the morning of 5 August, having spent the previous night taking on some 200 tons of extra coal. In an effort to conserve fuel, the *Pfalz*, now under the direction of the pilot, Captain Robinson, steamed slowly up Port Phillip, arriving at the Heads, opposite Portsea, at about 10 a.m. Following the directive of the Port Examination Service, she anchored, awaiting examination by a Service launch. It was this delay which sealed the fate of the SS *Pfalz*.

Ostensibly bound for Sydney, the *Pfalz* was inspected and cleared to proceed. However, during the inspection she had turned with the tide and she was further delayed as Captain Robinson attempted to swing her around. The inspection crew, as they left the vessel, would have become aware of the true destination of the *Pfalz* as a number of German Consul officials appeared on deck and 'they and the ship's captain displayed great jubilation'. This jubilation would prove to be short-lived, because word of the outbreak of war had just reached the battery at Point Nepean.

Immediately the fort raised pennants signalling for the ship to stop. Captain Robinson, busy manoeuvring the ship, did not notice the signal and the first he knew that something was astray was when he heard a report from one of the fort's guns, and seconds later a splash to the stern of the vessel. Captain Robinson immediately ordered 'full astern', only to be countermanded by 'full ahead' by the ship's Master. For a short time struggle ensued between the pilot and the captain, until reason prevailed, and the *Pfalz*, her crew and passengers returned to Melbourne.

The *Pfalz* then began a second life, commissioned by the Commonwealth government for war service, and renamed the *Boorara*. Her first duty was to join the second convoy of December 1914, transporting Australian troops and horses to Egypt. In 1915 she was acquired by the Admiralty to undertake supply runs between Alexandria and Mudros and to transport Turkish prisoners from the battlefields of the Dardanelles.

Despite three collisions and twice being torpedoed, the *Boorara* was extensively repaired, transferred to the Commonwealth government line in June 1919, and completed her service career repatriating Australian troops from England.

Australian Army, 1979

Colin Beszant accepted a Direct Entry Officer appointment in the Royal Australian Army Educational Corps in February 1976, and resigned as a captain in December 1983. He has been a member of the Moss Vale RSL sub-branch since 1991 and branch treasurer since 2013.

The First Away

By Lance Corporal John W. Martin

Germany had based its Pacific Squadron, including the cruiser
Emden, *in the colony it leased at Tsingtao (now Qingdao) in China.*
Britain, Australia and New Zealand shared a concern that this fleet
could ambush troopships and disrupt Allied shipping throughout
the Pacific and Indian Oceans. Germany also held several islands,
including Samoa, Nauru and part of New Guinea. The Australian
priority was to seize German wireless stations in these territories so
as to prevent them from communicating with the German fleet.

The momentous news that we were at war broke in Sydney on
Sunday 4 August 1914. Radio and broadcasting stations as we
know it today were non-existent but special editions of the press
rapidly appeared on the streets of city and suburbs. They created
great excitement, mixed with more sober reflections, on the
implications that Australia was to be involved in a great struggle
for survival.

On 6 August the British government had asked the Australian
government to seize and destroy the German wireless stations in
the South Pacific. The government here decided to immediately
raise a special force, to be known as the 1st Naval and Military
Expeditionary Force, and at the same time to raise and organise the
Australian Imperial Force. The former force comprised 1000 men
divided into eight companies, A to H; and another 500 naval reservists
and seamen to act as infantry under the command of Colonel Holmes
(later to lose his life in France) and Colonel W. Watson as his 2IC
[Second-in-Command].

Men from all walks of life, trades and professions flocked
to Victoria Barracks to enlist; the writer, with a group of twenty

from Mosman, all passed the medical and were drafted to the same company, 'F'.

Surely a record must have been then established in the transformation of civilians to soldiers, for in the brief, hectic space of eight days from enlistment to embarkation, we raw recruits were organised into companies, issued with uniforms and equipment, drilled and given a hasty insight into the basic fundamentals of soldiering; then a battalion parade with fixed bayonets in Moore Park and reviewed by Governor Strickland; on the final day (19 August) to march through the streets of Sydney and excited crowds to Circular Quay and Fort Macquarie, board ferry boats, and be transported to the troopship *Berrima* (also fitted out in a week!); then to sail through the Heads to the traditional tooting of harbour shipping, and full steam ahead for a 'destination unknown'.

On the way north, despite attacks of *'mal-de-mer'*, on the limited deck space, lectures and drill were the order of the day. The *Berrima* anchored later off Palm Island, where troops went ashore in the ship's boats for field training and musketry practice (many to fire the .303 for the first time). After leaving Palm Island a formidable naval escort accompanied the troopship, the flagship *Australia*, cruisers *Sydney* and *Encounter*, submarines *A.E.1* and *A.E.2* (the former later lost, with her crew, presumed to have struck a reef or submerged coral rock), supply ship and coal boats.

The expedition moved on to Port Moresby. On 11 September the ships approached Blanche Bay [in German New Guinea], the *Berrima* to land her troops at Rabaul, but word came through that one of the two parties of naval reservists who had earlier landed at Kabakaul and Herbertshohe had struck opposition and fighting was taking place. Admiral Patey, in charge of operations, ordered the *Berrima* to Kabakaul to land reinforcements and destroy the wireless station at Bitapaka, some miles inland. In the earlier action Captain Brian Pockley was killed after he had taken off his Red Cross brassard and placed it on the arm of a stoker, whom he left in charge of a mortally wounded seaman, W.G. Williams, the first man to be hit. He [Williams] died later in the day. Lieutenant-Commander Elwell fell leading a party of fifty reservists on another trench, where Lieutenant Bowen and several men were wounded.

In the meantime the *Berrima* had landed half the battalion at Herbertshohe under the command of Colonel Watson. After advancing some distance under enemy fire, a runner came back with the news that the Germans had surrendered. The great wireless mast was found destroyed but the valuable instruments were recovered. The acting [German] governor, Dr Haber, had withdrawn to Toma, the seat of government, and refused to surrender. On 14 September the *Encounter* shelled the ridges shown on a captured map to be the enemy's defence line, and two companies, with a naval party pulling a 12-pounder gun, advanced on Toma.

Approaching the objective, several rounds were fired by the gunners; a flag of truce was displayed and Toma was occupied. A few days later the governor surrendered, with his force, after a parley with Colonel Holmes and staff, and granted 'military honours'. Dr Haber was to be allowed to return to Germany on condition he took no further part in the war. German civilians who took the oath of neutrality could remain in their homes, and the native constabulary serving in the German defence force was to be transferred to the new administration. Later Colonel Holmes was to come in for some strong criticism in the Australian press for the leniency of the terms, but his instructions had been to occupy, not annex, the German colony, and his actions were subsequently generally approved.

On 13 September the Proclamation was made, and the British and Australian flags hoisted. A translation into pidgin-English was made for the benefit of the native population. Colonel Holmes then set up a government – officials for the Treasury, Lands and Surveys, Works, Post and Telephones etc. being found among his troops.

Some of the companies then had an interesting month, setting out in small captured German steamers and rounding up enemy officials – New Ireland, Bougainville and Kieta in the Solomons being some of the outposts occupied. Then began – for the troops – the tedious job of garrison and guard duty, a routine that became doubly boring as news came through of the grim struggle in Europe.

One rather sensational interlude occurred shortly after the day of Proclamation – an episode that was probably unprecedented in Australian military annals. Three Germans, after giving their parole, broke it and went bush. In a spirit of revenge, or sadism, they beat up a European missionary and his wife with green canes cut from the jungle. A native escaped and brought the news back to Rabaul. A punitive force was then despatched to round them up, and eventually they were captured and brought back. At a battalion parade Colonel Holmes addressed the troops and assembled German population, condemned the prisoners' actions and announced that they would be punished in the same manner. In turn, they were laid across a huge chest lashed to the ground, and a burly MP [military policeman] administered the strokes ordered with green bamboo canes. Later they were placed on a ship, under guard, and sent to Sydney to a prison camp.

As this expedition was organised so rapidly, attestation papers provided for service of 'six months only', not as in the AIF, for 'the duration'. Consequently, in February 1915, the garrison was relieved by a force of older men, christened the 'Druids', and the ships *Eastern* and *Navua* brought us back to Sydney, where, after a triumphal march through the streets to Victoria Barracks, we were welcomed back by Governor Strickland and discharged.

It says much for the spirit of the men of the Australian Naval and Military Expeditionary Force (AN & MEF) that within a few months 80 per cent had re-enlisted in the AIF, some to get to the [Gallipoli] Peninsula as reinforcements, others to serve in Egypt and France. Some of the remainder were put out of action by malaria, which had been prevalent in the islands.

This expeditionary force was notable for the fact that it was the first to leave Australia under the direct control and command of Australian officers, without Imperial supervision, as in the past.

Though the objective was attained, and men gave their lives, were wounded and suffered sickness, as surely did their comrades on Gallipoli, Palestine and France, no recognition was ever officially bestowed in the form of a medal. This has always been a sad bone of contention with ex-members of the AN & MEF.

Reveille, August 1955

Lance Corporal John William Martin, a 24-year-old hairdresser living at the family home in Mandalong Road, Mosman, re-enlisted on 11 July 1915 and was posted to the 30th Infantry Battalion. He embarked on the troopship Beltana *on 9 November and returned to Australia on 16 October 1916.*

A Doctor with the Australian Forces

By Major J.W.B. Bean

For a year or more I have been medical officer to an infantry battalion – a battalion which holds a magnificent record for dash and efficiency, steadiness and endurance; a battalion which has borne the brunt of the heaviest fighting; a battalion whose casualty list is, alas, a terrible one.

Thirty-two officers we set out from Sydney, and thirty-two officers, still intact, we took part in the great first landing on Gallipoli. Of the thirty-two, not a single one remains intact. About half have been killed, nearly all the rest wounded (some more than once), and one or two not actually wounded, broken down under the terrible strain and remain shaken in health.

I shall try to paint for you something of the life of our splendid men and show you glimpses of their spirit.

I shall never forget that first day, 27 August 1914, when I joined the forces. I was told to present myself at Victoria Barracks, Sydney, at 9 a.m. When I arrived, what a scene of confusion it was. Crowds of men in mufti jostling each other, talking and laughing excitedly, tall men, short men, and youngsters just left school, men in the prime and full maturity of manhood, even a sprinkling of grey heads.

Mostly their faces were bright, attentive and eager. Sometimes one's slow dissecting scrutiny met primitive faces, heavy-jawed, bullet-headed, beetle-browed, small bright eyes with a curious yet pathetic look and fixity of gaze – the undeveloped soul which we call criminal – gazing out through the prison windows of its poor brutal body. How often as the months went on and some of these primitive men came up again for drunkenness and overstepping leave, has one seen that same dumb struggling look, half-sullen, wholly pathetic?

One or two did improve wonderfully and became good soldiers in spite of occasional relapses, and at the front proved brave and trustworthy. One such, in particular, I remember – a Sydney 'docker' of French extraction. He had a long, lean, fierce face, with hard eyes, passionate expanded nostrils, and lips which drew back from his teeth in a perpetual snarl. It was a wolf-face, and he had all the fierceness of a wolf, especially when drunk. He was a manly beast though – always spoke the truth, never made excuses, never grumbled, but took his punishment like a man. He loved the colonel and the colonel loved him. They had a heart-to-heart talk in the colonel's tent shortly before leaving for Gallipoli, and he gave his promise that he would give up drink. He did very well after this and fought most bravely at the front. Eventually he left the Peninsula, either wounded or invalided.

But to return to my beginning. Here and there in the crowd stand men with quiet resolute faces and trim bodies – men with an air of respect and self-control. They are not excited. They wait patiently, not speaking for the most part unless they are spoken to. They are scholars of a grand school of character – the British Army. The steady ex-Imperial men will form the nucleus of our Non-commissioned Officers [NCOs], and the regiment is largely what its NCOs make it. The dissolute ex-Imperial man – called technically 'the old soldier' – will be a constant source of trouble to himself and everyone else. Let the company officer beware of him. He has already become a past master in the special sins of the soldier – certainly a clever shirker, and (beware of him O! doctor) a skilled malingerer.

From this time began our life as soldiers. Quarters were pretty rough for the men – two battalions camped in the Randwick Racecourse and two in the Kensington Racecourse. The grandstand was the men's dormitory. They had no tents at first – just slept in their clothes on the wooden terraced steps, a blanket over them and their civilian greatcoat, perhaps, to cover them. I don't suppose you realise what a tremendous job it is raising a battalion of infantry. A thousand and twenty-three men bodily and mentally fit to a high degree have to be sorted from the still larger number of would-be applicants.

Once accepted, the would-be soldier is re-born into the army. He brings nothing with him into his military world save the mufti he stands up in, and that, as soon as possible, is shed. He has to be clothed, fed, supplied with all a man's toilet necessities, with blankets, waterproof sheet, eating and cooking utensils, firearms, entrenching tools, spades and picks, and diverse other things. Then, too, he has to be sworn in and finally paid.

It was an extraordinarily busy time for me at first, examining men from morning until night – up at six every morning, often not to bed till 1 a.m. next morning, grovelling over interminable lists. Funny fellows these men. They are all secretly terrified that they will be rejected and they look at you with a pathetic feeble smile and twitching lips and heave a huge sigh of relief when it is over and they are safely in. Many of them have thrown up jobs of three and four pounds a week and have travelled hundreds of miles to join us. They have been feted as heroes before leaving their native villages and they would rather die than go back there rejected. Some I have to refuse, and they plead with me and almost break down. Some do go away gulping down their feelings and with tears of disappointment in their eyes. We do the best we can for the rejects – write them a certificate to say why they have been rejected, and pay their railway fare home. This helps them to get taken on again at their work, but it does seem so awfully hard.

One boy I remember, a little, delicate, undersized chap with a gentle girlish face – a regular 'mother's boy', you'd say – and with no physique at all. I had a letter from his people imploring me not to take him. He was going dead against their wish. He pleaded so hard that I gave in, against my better judgment and against his parents' wish. It turned out well, though. He is a corporal now and made a splendid soldier, marvellously tough for his weak little frame, always cheerful and efficient, and never on the sick list – a clear case of mind conquering matter, or rather, lack of matter in his case. Many a time we've laughed about it since.

Poor beggars, they were regular heroes right from the start. Such awful mouths the Australians have, many of them. You couldn't fail them for teeth too rigidly or you'd have never made up your battalion. They used to come to me in squads of forty at a time for black draught and 'Condys' or chlorate of potash as a mouthwash. Up they would stalk with a grin, toss off their potion with a shudder and wry face, give me an involuntary wink, and march off cheerfully with their lozenges to the 'Chamber of Horrors' – in this case a dental pavilion at the Agricultural Ground – where shoals of victims were lined up waiting their turn. In the afternoon they turned up with swollen faces and bleeding, lacerated gums, having had a dozen or more roots dug out. Still cheerful, though, and for the most part, unable to manage their solid tack for some days. The men had to be vaccinated, and inoculated for typhoid too. Altogether they went through a lot with the utmost cheerfulness, just like a lot of happy-go-lucky schoolboys.

Looking back over those days with the light of experience, I can see many mistakes made. Far more care should have been given to the matter of fitting and softening military boots. Oh! What a lot of trouble and pain we afterwards had from sore feet in Egypt. The same can be said of trousers, which chafe badly if not a perfect fit.

It's wonderful how loyalty soon comes with these dear, warm-hearted country lads. Mulcahey was one of the best of my stretcher-bearers, brave as a lion, true as steel. He helped to carry me down to the beach when I was first wounded, and shook hands with me warmly ere he returned to duty and death. He was hit saving a wounded officer under heavy fire. A tragedy – he should never have died, but in the rush of wounded, poor Mul was overlooked. He had no attention but his first field dressing till he reached Alexandria, and then, alas, it was too late. His poor thigh was terribly swollen and septic, and he died a true hero – pure, manly, upright, good.

Smallpox and diphtheria both broke out in the regiment, and we had isolation tents roped off in the most distant parts of the camp before we left. On the voyage we had a great deal of sickness. The men were very crowded, and the heat of the tropics was stifling. We had quite a lot of pneumonia, and two of our poor chaps died of it. Just as we got to Egypt there was a tremendous epidemic of colic – hundreds suffering and many being brought to the hospital in a state of collapse. We made them very sick with soda, gave injections of morphia and atropine, lots of hot-water bottles, and abdominal massage, and nobody died, though some looked rather near it.

It was a mystery. The steam-cooker was found in a very dirty state, much food refuse having silted between the inner and outer jackets. This may have had something to do with it. One of the horses, too, had strangles, and sprayed his nasal discharge over the lines of mess orderlies as they waited by the kitchens with their dixies [food containers]. This was looked on as a possible cause, and the third idea was arsenical poisoning by a spy, but we never knew for certain. I shall never forget the hospital deck though, strewn thick with writhing, groaning men – for all the world like a battlefield.

The Queensland Digger, November–December 1931

John Willoughby Butler (Jack) Bean embarked from Sydney with the rank of Captain on 20 October 1914 on the troopship Euripides. *He was listed as a 34-year-old medical practitioner from South Randwick and posted to the 3rd Infantry Battalion. He was wounded on the day of the Gallipoli Landing and again at Lone Pine, later served on the Western Front, and returned to Australia, with the rank of major on 23 October 1918. He was the younger brother of the official Australian war correspondent and historian, Charles Bean.*

The First AIF Convoy's Narrow Escape

By Rear Admiral A. Gordon Smith, CMG

The departure of the convoy from King George's Sound [in Western Australia] before daybreak on 1 November 1914 was rather impressive. Five miles ahead of us was the *Minotaur*, the *Sydney* to port, *Ibuki* to starboard of us. The New Zealanders formed a separate little fleet, steaming in two columns by themselves, two miles in rear of ours. *Melbourne*, out of sight astern, was our rear-guard.

It was a clumsy sort of fleet. Its total length, including the New Zealanders, should only have been seven miles, but on some mornings it was double that, and sometimes the tail was almost out of sight. Also there was trouble with lights at night. Some ships could not be induced to limit themselves in that respect. If their penchant for illumination had not been checked, they would have made a glow on the sky that could be seen fifty miles off on a dark night. Check, too, had to be kept on the habit ships have of throwing overboard refuse, which would have left a trail on the ocean as plain as any raider could desire. The horse transports, naturally, were the worst offenders.

We had our moments of anxiety from time to time, especially during the first few days and nights. There was one contingency, however, that I dreaded above everything, and for which I could devise no procedure that was feasible. This was an attack by night by a hostile cruiser. Allah only knows what might have happened in such an event. We had to get these soldiers to Europe somehow. As it was, the *Emden* only missed us by a day. She crossed our track 200 miles ahead of us.

When the brief message was received from the *Sydney*, 'Enemy in sight', there was no reason for secrecy and in fifteen seconds everyone in the *Orvieto* knew and came swarming up on deck, craning their necks to see a few inches over the horizon. Finally, after a long wait, during which our passengers – the 5th Infantry – could hardly restrain their excitement, we received '*Emden* beached and done for'. This message was greeted with cheers from every ship in the convoy. It was a red-letter day for the Australian Navy.

At Colombo four officers and forty men – half of the unwounded survivors from the *Emden* – came on board as prisoners of war. Among the officers were the captain of the *Emden*, von Müller, and young Prince Franz Joseph von Hohenzollern, a thin, pale-faced, haughty little man. I had several long talks with von Müller while on our way to Aden [in modern-day Yemen], usually while pacing up and down their playground. He only had the one suit of white clothing, not too clean, that he was wearing during the action, and wore a pair of old gymnasium shoes that were too big for him. Although he was 'high-born' and a friend of the Kaiser, he was a very decent chap all round. He was quite upset when I told him we had heard by wireless that he had been given the Iron Cross.

At Aden, it was learned with great surprise, that the Australians were to be disembarked in Egypt to finish their military education there. It was better so, in some ways; the Queenslanders, particularly, would have found England in the depth of winter, very chilly.

The absence of lights in the southern part of the Red Sea caused a little anxiety. There are a lot of rocks and small islands scattered about near the entrance, and the currents are strong and rather irregular. An unusual route was taken on account of the possibility of mines. Fortunately the weather was clear and the captain of the *Orvieto*, having passed through it regularly six times a year, knew the Red Sea from end to end.

It was a good thing he did. On the first night we sighted ahead shadowy shapes of a group of islands that ought not to have been there, according to our reckoning, and the convoy was steering straight for them. The question was, on which side of them should we go? The captain, fortunately, recognised one of the lumps by its outline, and had just time to signal an alteration of course, which took them clear of the whole group.

It was a bit exciting. He barely cleared them. If he had tried to pass on the other side he should have put the whole convoy on a rocky shoal!

The troops were disembarked at Alexandria, where they proceeded by train to the camps that had been prepared for them near Cairo. The New Zealanders, having been longest on board, were landed first and were the first to proceed to Alexandria. The *Orvieto* troops, after a two days' rest at Port Said, followed, and the others in succession as soon as there was room for them. It was a fortnight or more before all the ships were cleared of men and stores. It was a tedious job and it rained continually.

Reveille, November 1934

Rear Admiral Arthur Gordon Smith (1873–1953) was a Royal Navy officer who was on secondment to Australia as a member of the Naval Board when WWI broke out. He was commander of the fleet from the Orvieto.

The *Sydney–Emden* action

By Paymaster Lieutenant Commander Eric Kingsford-Smith

From mid-August 1914 the Emden *had roamed the Indian Ocean, bombarding oil storage tanks at Madras, sinking a Russian cruiser and a French destroyer at Penang, and in just six weeks sinking or capturing twenty-one vessels totalling 100,000 tonnes.*

9 November 1914! A date for remembrance in Australia – the day on which her young navy had its first taste of war! And what an antagonist was provided by the gods to test the mettle of this hitherto untried arm of Australia's defence! Critics there had been aplenty, to decry this 'foolish experiment', this 'playing about with a so-called Navy'; but on this date they were silenced forever.

The *Sydney–Emden* action was the answer most effectively given by those who believed in our navy and its paramount importance to Australia and the Empire.

The action came to be fought almost by accident. Twenty-eight transports, containing the first of the Australian and New Zealand Expeditionary Forces, assembled at Albany [Western Australia] under the wing of their escorting cruisers, *Minotaur*, *Melbourne*, *Sydney* and the Japanese *Ibuki*. It was understood at first that the route would be via Cape Town, but at sailing time it became known that we would proceed to Colombo and thence to Egypt.

After nine days at sea the three lines of ships were approximately fifty miles to the eastward of the Cocos Islands, when shortly before 7 a.m. on 9 November a wireless message was picked up from Direction Island (the principal island of the Cocos group) saying, 'Strange ship off the entrance.' The message was sent to whoever might pick it up, and was followed by an attempt to say more, but 'jamming' by the ship referred to made it incoherent.

Captain Silver, of the *Melbourne*, was senior officer of the convoy, *Minotaur* having left us the day before for South Africa, and as he considered his duty was to remain with the transports, he detailed *Sydney* to proceed at full speed to Cocos and investigate.

Those who have done any convoying will realise how trying is the monotony and how welcome is any excitement. To say that we in the *Sydney* were delighted is to put the case mildly, and our fond but remote expectations of a scrap were intensified when the islands appeared and a three-funnelled cruiser showed on the horizon, steaming at high speed to intercept our course.

'Who is she?' was the question on everyone's lips. Feverish activity was going on aboard *Sydney*. Guns' crews were closed up, ammunition supply parties were hoisting shells and charges from the magazines, and all preparations were made.

By this time there was no doubt the strange ship was either the *Emden* or the *Königsberg*, as they were the only German cruisers to answer to her description.

At 9.20 a.m. the two ships had closed to 11,500 yards' range, and the stranger opened fire. The first salvo was about 500 yards over, her second short, and her third hit us. We also opened fire, and soon picked up the range.

Our first casualty occurred very early in the action, when a shell demolished our fore range-finder on the upper bridge, taking the leg of the range-finder operator with it. Luckily the shell was a 'dud'. Had it burst it would most likely have accounted for Captain Glossop, the gunnery lieutenant, and about half a dozen officers and men who were within a radius of six feet from the range-finder.

Terrible damage was done on the enemy. Soon one of his funnels went over the side; shortly a mast followed suit, and then a second funnel. Columns of smoke began to appear, and it was soon apparent that she was on fire aft. The *Emden*'s gunfire slackened as gun after gun was put out of action, but with those remaining she still pluckily kept on with the action. Her movements became more sluggish, particularly when altering course, caused, as was ascertained later, by the fact that her steering gear was shot away and all turning movements had to be accomplished with her propellers.

About this time we closed to 5500 yards and fired a torpedo, which, however, failed to hit. While so close we could see huge gaping holes in the *Emden*'s hull, and she appeared to be in a sinking condition. One gun only was in action, and that was being fired at a slower and slower rate. Soon her captain (von Müller), realising the hopelessness of continuing the unequal fight, turned his ship towards North Keeling Island and ran her aground on the beach.

The *Sydney* left him there, *pro tem*, and proceeded to chase a collier that was hovering about, some miles distant. While overhauling her we were able to take an inventory of our own damage. Our casualties were two killed and fourteen wounded, of which latter two died the following day. Damage to the ship was not great. The fore range-finder was demolished, the after control platform badly damaged, and one shell had burst through the mess deck. Another shell had gone through the deck, two bulkheads, across the commander's cabin and out through the ship's side, after considerately passing through the knee-hole of his desk without hurting the desk itself. It also was a 'dud'. In fact the great majority of shells that hit us failed to burst, which accounts for our damage being so slight.

Two shells had hit the ship's side, one slightly penetrating it; one had chipped a few inches of wood from our main mast and one cut through the exhaust steam pipe on the after funnel. Half a dozen or so other hits were registered, including one shell that burst behind the crew of a gun on the disengaged side, killing or wounding most of them.

When we reached the collier we found her to be the British ship *Buresk*, which had been captured by the *Emden* and kept with her to supply the coal required for her Indian Ocean operations.

The writer, another officer, and an armed party went aboard the *Buresk* and ordered the officer commanding the German prize crew to steam with the *Sydney* back to North Keeling Island. He replied that it was impossible as fires had been drawn and a valve opened in the engine-room, which was allowing water to rush in and flood the ship. This was ascertained to be so, and, as the valve had been broken off and could not be closed, there was no alternative but to return to the *Sydney* with the German crew and allow the *Buresk* to sink.

We returned to the *Emden* in the late afternoon and found her with her colours still flying. Captain Glossop signalled by international code, 'Do you surrender?' to which a reply was signalled in Morse, 'Repeat your signal in Morse as I have no signal books.' This was done, but no reply was forthcoming. A second and third time the signal was made, and then Captain Glossop added, 'If you do not reply I will open fire.' Still no reply was made, so he reluctantly gave the order to fire. This had the desired effect, as immediately a white flag was shown aboard the *Emden* and a man was seen going aloft to cut down the German ensign.

An officer was then sent to the *Emden* to formally receive Captain von Müller's surrender and to inform him that the *Sydney* would first proceed to Direction Island (fifteen miles distant) to obtain additional medical assistance, and then return and remove the *Emden*'s wounded and unwounded.

Owing to delays through stopping to pick up several German sailors who had been blown overboard during the action and were still swimming about, it was too dark to proceed to Direction Island anchorage that day, and we lay off till daylight. We then took Dr Ollerhead, of the cable station, on board and returned to the *Emden*, and by evening had transferred her wounded and unwounded to the *Sydney*. There were approximately 200 all told, about 50 per cent of whom were wounded. The numbers killed in the action were about 120.

After the last boatload had been brought aboard (the last person being Captain von Müller himself) we landed a party to search for and bring aboard several German sailors who had managed to get ashore. They were not found until daylight.

With them safely aboard, we returned to Direction Island to land Dr Ollerhead. He and our own two surgeons had been working with the wounded without intermission for the past twenty-four hours and had treated all the most serious cases. It was with great gratitude that we said goodbye to him and headed for Colombo.

Two days after leaving Cocos we passed between the lines of the transports, but continued our course without stopping. The following day we were met by the armed merchantman *Empress of Russia*, to which ship we transferred about sixty of the wounded, as the *Sydney* was greatly overcrowded.

Next day we arrived at Colombo and thankfully got rid of the remaining wounded and unwounded.

There but remained to repair the damage done to the *Sydney*, and this was taken in hand two weeks later at Gibraltar. The last visible sign was thus removed of the action, but to those who participated in it the memory will never fade.

So was fought Australia's first naval action, against a famous ship which had already destroyed over twenty merchantmen and a Russian cruiser. So will our navy fight again should the needs of Empire demand it.

Whether the next action will be victorious or not, of one thing may the people of Australia feel assured, and that is the same spirit which has animated the glorious Royal Navy for hundreds of years will be found in the men composing its youthful offspring – the Royal Australian Navy.

Reveille, August 1927

Eric Kingsford-Smith, born in 1887, was the older brother of the aviation pioneer Sir Charles Kingsford-Smith. Having trained as an accountant, he joined the Royal Australian Navy in August 1912 as an assistant paymaster. He was posted to HMAS Sydney *in January 1914. He also served in WWII and was demobilised in September 1946. He was killed in a light aircraft crash at Mount Hagen in Papua New Guinea in July 1968.*

The Signal That Doomed the *Emden*

By Dover Farrant

Dover Farrant was on the Cocos Islands when the Emden *launched its attack on the Australian communication station. Shortly after his death twenty years later,* Reveille *published his first-hand account of the incident.*

Mr Dover Farrant, who died at Warmley, England, in November 1934, aged sixty-nine, had been superintendent of the cable station at Cocos Island, and in that post, played an important part in putting an end to the spectacular career of the German raider *Emden*. His story is best described in his own letter to his wife, written immediately after the event:

At 5.45 pm on 9 November 1914 I was having my tea when the supervisor reported a strange four-funnelled warship steaming in fast. We had heard about the 'four' funnels of the *Emden* before, and I immediately smelt a rat. I went on the roof and had a look through my glasses, and saw one funnel was a poor-looking dummy, so I put out a wireless call for cruisers. I left the operator calling – the German cruiser jamming his note as hard as he could – and I wired London, Adelaide, Singapore and Perth that a three-funnelled warship was entering the harbour.

The *Emden*, for so it turned out to be, put off two boats and an armoured launch, which came in at full speed with a landing party. The officer said his instructions were to demolish the wireless and cable stations, but to respect private property. He blew up the wireless mast – engines, dynamos, batteries, and instruments were all split to pieces, and a Maxim was trained on to our staff meanwhile.

The launch then went out into the lagoon and I was highly amused to see them get hold of half a mile of spare cable and cut it. I had put it out as a 'blind'. They then raised another cable, which happened to be Perth, but they did more harm to their instruments than to the cable.

Just then there was a recall siren, and I noticed the *Emden* had steamed close in. Then I saw she was signalling frantically with siren and flags to her men to return. The launch whistled up the guards that had been put on all the houses, and they quickly collected, shook hands with us, and put off. But they never reached the *Emden*.

The *Emden*, with the first shell from the Australian cruiser *Sydney* bursting close to her, couldn't wait, and flew as hard as she could. The landing party returned to the island. The whole lot of them stood with us watching the fight, seeing the *Sydney* gradually coming out of the horizon, and, with her well-placed shots, rapidly disabling the *Emden*.

The Admiralty presented Mr Farrant with a gold watch, inscribed: 'Presented to Dover Augustus George de Horsey Farrant, Esq., by the Lords Commissioners of the Admiralty in recognition of the action in signalling the presence of the German cruiser *Emden* off Cocos Island on November 9 1914, which resulted in her destruction by H.M.A.S. *Sydney*.'

Reveille, February 1935

Experiences of an Indian in the AIF

By Private Cass Mahomet

Though anxious to enlist early in the war, I had to think long and hard, because, being a full-blooded Mohammedan Indian, I would have to fight against men of my own faith – the Turk.

Being under the age of twenty-one years, I wrote to my dad for permission to enlist, but he would not think of it. However, I was anxious to do my bit for the country that was giving me my bread and butter, so I decided to join up without letting my parents know.

At the recruiting depot at Port Pirie (SA) the NCO in charge said to me, in a gruff voice, 'We can't accept you.'

'Why?' I asked.

He replied, 'Well, we are already having enough trouble with the Aborigines' Protection Board over you fellows.'

His ignorance in guessing my nationality nearly caused a stink; not because he took me to be an Aborigine, as some of my best mates were Aborigines, but because he would not accept me, thinking I was an Abo. In the end I walked out, disgusted.

Some time later I went to the Currie Street (Adelaide) recruiting depot, and everything was going fine, until it came to my name. The official in charge exclaimed, 'Mahomet you're an enemy subject.'

I retorted, 'And you are a ——.'

Another stink, and I hopped it again. I guess he took me for a Turk.

Time went on. I gave up my profession as an acrobat and left the circus I was with, going to work in the ironstone quarries at 'Iron Knob'. I started an amateur concert party, the proceeds of which went to the All-British League – the sponsors of a fund for farewelling soldiers. Each week I farewelled a mate or two who had enlisted, so I wrote a pleading letter to the Currie Street recruiting depot, which sent back a telegram, 'Come and enlist.'

At Adelaide many of the officials were anxious to see the fellow who was once taken for an Aborigine, then a Turk. During the examination the medical officer said, 'Hop up there on your left leg and back on your right.' I hopped up on my left leg, and then did a round of flip flaps and a back somersault, landing about two feet from the medical officer's table. He said, 'Why didn't you do that at first? It would have saved a lot of trouble.'

Before I had my first meal in camp I explained to the cooks that I was a Mohammedan and did not eat pig. On the *Berrima* for breakfast, the first day out, was bacon; for dinner, stew with the remnants of breakfast bacon thrown in. For the first three days all the dishes had some part of pig in them. I kept alive by eating ginger biscuits.

I couldn't stand it any longer, so I sought the intervention of the padres of the different religions. Their advice was: 'Well, it's war. There is nothing else to do but eat whatever is given to you.' I thanked them and went to the mess table, just in time to see an officer handing out a bottle of beer to every man. I drank a whole bottle of beer on an empty stomach, and then tore into the pork.

On arrival in England we were sent to Lark Hill Camp, Salisbury Plain. The first Sunday on church parade all the Diggers sorted themselves out according to their denominations. I stood stock still. All eyes were on me as the regimental sergeant major came over to me and said: 'What's up with you?'

I replied: 'I'm a Mohammedan and I don't wish to go to any other church but my own. There is a mosque at Woking. So I'll need two days' leave to attend there.'

So I was given a pick and a shovel, told to dig a hole eight feet long, two feet wide and eight feet deep. I was still digging when the mob returned from the parade. They sang out to me: 'Go on, dig away; you'll be on church parade next Sunday.' And so I was. I was out with one denomination or other every Sunday.

I joined that 10th Battalion after it came out of Bullecourt. We 'rainbows' were lined up, and the regimental sergeant major picked out two Aborigines and myself. I thought Fritz had drawn the colour line and that we were to be sent back to Aussie. But the shock was to come – we were detailed off to become snipers!

I said to the instructing corporal: 'Why pick on me for a sniper?'

He replied: 'All you Aborigine boys have a great sense of seeing, hearing and smelling.' Well, this is the limit, I pondered. First, they knock a man back because they reckon he's a native; and when he gets in, they shove him out in front of all the others. I was out for promotion, so I joined the rifle grenadiers.

Arriving in England after the Armistice I accepted an offer to organise a concert party for headquarters, and stayed for seven months on this job. My homecoming was sad. My mother had died and my father was killed in an accident. Our home had vanished. Still I will always remember my experience with the AIF – the finest chaps on God's earth. Colour or creed made no difference in the AIF. At all times I have proudly worn my Australian soldier's badge. I've got a soft spot in my heart for the good old AIF. And if it goes la guerring again, you can count on the Indian Digger.

Reveille, November 1935

Private Cassim ('Cass') Mahomet was described as a 21-year-old vaudeville artist from Iron Knob, South Australia, when he embarked with the 10th Battalion, 23rd Reinforcements in December 1916. His next of kin was recorded as his mother, living in East Sydney. After the war he resumed his vaudeville career, performing as 'the Indian Digger' and writing patriotic songs with titles such as 'Australia for Mine' and 'Anywhere in Australia'.

How Two Light-Horsemen Got to Gallipoli by Bluff

By J.D.

When the 2nd Light Horse was in training at Heliopolis – six months of it – we were fed up to the teeth. Talk about monotony! We did not know what to do with ourselves, and we envied the infantry battalions when they were suddenly moved off, no one knew where.

But when hundreds of wounded started to come back to the Palace hospital, we knew at last that there was a war on. It was rumoured that they were fighting in trench warfare, and we felt pretty well out of it; fed up to the eyes, messing about training in the desert with horses, while our foot-slogging cobbers were going their hardest stoushing the enemy. To make matters worse, a furphy went round that the light horse would not be wanted at the front, and it looked to us as though we would be left there for the duration, doing mounted parades.

You can imagine the excitement, then, when one day orders suddenly came that the 2nd L.H. was to go up to the front as infantry. It was 'Hooray!' for most of the mob, but not for yours truly. A few days previously I came the proverbial gutzer through being crimson fool enough to have a bet on with Eric Raff as to whose horse was the fastest over half a mile. I never found out which was the fastest; what I did find out was that my horse could fall down the quickest. For my faithful steed took it into his head to come a purler when he was flat out. Down I went, head over turkey, my horse using me as a cushion, and rolling me out as if I was a lump of dough and he was the rolling pin.

There I was, hobbling on crutches, when the rest of the mob was getting ready to set out for the front, and I was to be left behind, moaning my luck, with one other, Mick McGreevy, the shoesmith, who had the job of feeding and watering the horses.

I was so disappointed that I paraded before Major Glasgow (Sir William Glasgow) and pleaded to be allowed to go with the baggage. I told him I would be as right as ninepence in a few days. But of course I was knocked back.

That night the mob set out for the fighting, and with all my cobbers gone I was as miserable as a lousy cuckoo. McGreevy and I talked the situation over. We decided we had got to get to the fighting somehow, crutches or no crutches, and horses or no horses. So we agreed that I should pop off by train to Ma'adi to see Colonel Cameron (now Sir Donald Cameron) who was commanding the 5th Light Horse there. He and I had served together in the South African War and I thought, being an old Boer War cobber, he could help us get to the front.

When I reached there I found the 5th Light Horse under orders to leave for the fighting. I ducked along to see the Colonel and implored him to let us go with his regiment somehow or other. He told me that if I could get permission from the officer left in charge of us he would take me – not otherwise. That was a knock back. For I knew we wouldn't stand a dog's chance of getting permission from the O.C. So I returned to the camp at Heliopolis a very disappointed man.

But I have found out in life that if you want a thing very badly, there is always some way of getting it. I discovered that Colonel Cameron's mob were to rail to Alexandria to board a troopship there.

A day or so later, McGreevy and I pinched a couple of helmets and infantry packs from the store, and planted our felt hats and bandoliers. My injury was a little better and although I was still a bit lame, I dumped my crutches, and after dark, dressed as infantrymen, we set out for Cairo. We had to bluff the Arab tram conductor because we had no money for our tram fares. Having bluffed our way through to Cairo, we reached the railway station, walked boldly on to the platform, and hopped into a first-class compartment labelled 'Ladies only'. In real careless Gyppo fashion, we found that a key had been left in the carriage door, so we locked ourselves in, the train started, and we had survived the second stage of our plan to get to the front.

The train stopped alongside the platform at Alexandria, and by a bit of dodging we escaped the attention of the rather lax railway officials. Our next job was to find the troopship. But we found that every wharf entrance was guarded by French troops. We questioned some of the Froggies about the ship, but they all gave us the same answer, 'Non compree.'

Well, we hung about those wharves till daybreak and finally we came across a wharf with a lot of troops in marching order sitting about on their kits inside the gate. A troopship was tied up alongside the wharf. We were stopped at the entrance by the Frenchies, but we managed to make them understand that this was our regiment and we'd miss the boat if they didn't let us in. We got through. The mob turned out to be the 5th L.H. all right, and we quietly mixed in, yarning with some of them as though we belonged to the mob. When the order came to fall in, we fell in too, and marched up the gangway with the others.

It was too risky to stop with the troops so we ducked along and stowed away forrard near the quarters of the Dago crew and almost on top of the anchor. Next day I sneaked down between decks and was lucky enough to pinch a big lump of cheese and some biscuits without being seen. That kept us from perishing altogether. For three solid days we were stowed away on that troopship, and after what seemed three weeks, we knew by the noise and commotion that the ship had arrived at its destination. Then McGreevy and I mixed in again with the troops, and we went over the side into pontoons. We had reached Gallipoli! And we stepped on to the beach, which was under fire!

Almost at once we met a bloke of the 2nd Light Horse coming down to the beach for water. He told us the regiment was resting in

Monash Gully, just behind Quinn's Post. They had been in very hot fighting and had lost a lot of men.

We went back with him, feeling very dubious, as desertion is a most serious charge in wartime. We made up our minds to take the bull by the horns, and make a clean breast of it. We went and found Major Glasgow and walked up to him.

'Here I am, Major,' I said, braving it out. 'Come to report, and I've brought reinforcements with me.'

He laughed, and said, 'Righto! Get into one of the dugouts!'

So that was that. (But later on we were charged with desertion and admonished.) We had a great feed of bully beef and biscuits – I don't think I ever enjoyed a meal so much. We found our 'A' troop mates terribly thinned out – all in one week. A couple of hours later they were at it again, and I got my first taste of fighting on Gallipoli. The Turks attacked Quinn's Post. I found myself with a couple of mates, Birch and Weller, in a T-shaped trench pushed out into no-man's-land from the main trench. Somehow or other we held on to that little trench by the skin of our teeth till night came, and the attack was repulsed.

In the fighting I got separated from McGreevy. But when I saw him a few hours later, he did look a scarecrow. He must have been up to his neck in it.

'Square and all,' he went crook. 'We must have been a couple of silly b——s to leave Cairo!'

But McGreevy and I came safely through the whole issue, and eventually got home to Australia.

The Queensland Digger, October 1937

The author was identified only by his initials, 'J.D.' A search of the records suggests he was Corporal James Durham, a 32-year-old married billiard maker from Yarraman, Queensland. He was a member of A Squadron, 2nd Light Horse, as were the other men he mentions. *Two Queenslanders named James Durham also served in the Boer War. He enlisted on 21 August 1914 and returned to Australia on 28 January 1916.*

Shoesmith Michael McGreevy, a 26-year-old carpenter from Brisbane, enlisted on 28 September 1914, embarked from Sydney on the Boorara *20 December 1914, and returned to Australia on 2 May 1916.*

Gallipoli

'I shall never forget as long as I live, seeing the 4th Battalion coming out of the trenches when it was relieved either during or after the fight. The men looked like a thin line of spectres. One officer who knew me well stared at me with glassy eyes, and failed to recognise me. We only realised how great the cost had been when we began to bury the dead.'

—The Very Reverend A.E. Talbot

Memories of the Landing after Seventy Years

By Private Mervin H. Spencer

I was born at Waratah on the west coast of Tasmania on 20 January 1891. I was one of a family of thirteen: nine girls and four boys.

The First World War broke out in 1914 between England and Germany. Two weeks later they were calling for volunteers to go away to fight. My brother Tom and I journeyed to Hobart to join up.

One had to have certain qualifications to join, such as some military experience, rifle club etc., and we both belonged to a rifle club. The 12th Battalion Brass Band was being formed and we both played a brass instrument, so we had no problems.

The 12th Battalion of 1000 consisted of 500 men from Tasmania, 250 from South Australia and 250 from Western Australia. We all trained together at Brighton Camp, Tasmania. We left Hobart on 20 October 1914 on the troopship *Geelong* and sailed to Egypt. We joined the rest of the Australian contingent, 20,000 in all, at Mena Camp, ten kilometres from Cairo at the foot of the pyramids. All bandsmen were made stretcher-bearers and we were trained by a well-known Hobart surgeon, Dr V.R. Ratten. I had my twenty-fourth birthday in Cairo.

After three months' training we left on the troopship *Devanha* and sailed to the Greek island of Lemnos about 100 kilometres from Gallipoli. We sailed into Mudros Harbour [and] lived on the ship for three months training, practising rowing and handling – I was made a rower, being one of the strongest in the 12th.

We were the first ship in here, and as we leave now at 3 p.m. on 24 April 1915 the harbour is a forest of masts. Warships have been going out at dusk every night since we came here and returning at daylight, after blasting the forts at the Dardanelles, but not with much success. Lemnos had plenty of spies posing as Greeks, so the enemy knew as much about our plans as we did ourselves.

It is now 11 p.m., a lovely bright moonlit night and not even a ripple on the water. The ship drops anchor, the destroyer *Ribble* comes alongside and in a few minutes 300 of us climb down the rope ladders on to the destroyer's deck. She then moves off, manoeuvring slowly through the early hours of the morning, keeping just far enough from land not to be detected.

We have been given 'Kye', a hot chocolate drink, every two hours by the *Ribble*'s crew while sitting on the cold steel deck. The moon is slowly disappearing, the engines are stopped, there is a deathly silence in the atmosphere. I see a searchlight track across the sky, then a flash goes up on the horizon as daylight is starting to appear.

Then a rifle shot like the crack of a whip, and they start to come faster and faster around the ship. Adjutant Hawley from Ross, Tasmania, was the first man to get hit and he was paralysed for life. Now the skipper hurried down the ladder from the bridge and said, with words I shall never forget: 'Come on boys, there's dirty work.' We took our places in the lifeboats which held fifty and with eight rowers in each of the six boats, three strapped to each side of the destroyer.

Dozens of warships are now firing salvos over our heads, including the *Dreadnought* and *Queen Elizabeth*, the largest warship afloat with 18-inch guns hurling its thousand-pound shells into the enemy positions in front of us. Thousands of rifles are cracking and all Hell is let loose. A mate of mine, George Wright from Western Junction, Tasmania, sitting between me and the edge of the boat facing the shore, was hit in a vital spot and I felt a weight come over my oar. He cried out 'ooh' and never breathed after that.

Now I was in trouble, catching crabs – I could not get the blade in the water. The coxswain was shouting, I knew it was meant for me, so much noise, then he was silenced. I half stood up, lifted the 12½-stone dead weight up, got the blade in the water and after that never missed a beat.

Bullets are whistling past us, zip-zapping in the water in front and around. I am now straining every nerve and muscle to keep the blade in the water. I glance along the boat and everyone except the rowers is crouching flat along the bottom like mussels on a rock.

I glance down at George lying on his back, across my oar going back and forth, his white face looking up to Heaven and only the whites of his eyes showing – looking so peaceful and not a care in the world. How do you think I felt? Terrible. What a nightmare row, now my strength is starting to give out, wondering if I can make it and saying to myself: 'Oh God, when will we touch?'

Seconds later we touched. I dropped the oar. It fell with my mate over the seat. I picked up my rifle and pack with two to three days' rations etc. and 200 rounds of ammunition strapped to my shirt. I jumped overboard up to my waist in water. I did not see a soul around. I just remember falling on the beach, exhausted, for a short time before I heard a call: 'Stretcher-bearers!'

I got to my feet. My brother Tom was standing near with a stretcher and his first words to me were, 'Look, poor Mitch has got it.' He was a stretcher-bearer with us from Mitcham, South Australia. He was lying dead between us and the water. We soon got into action carrying in the dead and wounded. Calls for stretcher-bearers were coming from every angle. Snipers were everywhere. Colonel Clark was hit by one, leading the troops into battle, half an hour after landing.

We worked hard until near midnight, the shouting easing down. I lay down just where I stood, so tired I was beyond being tired, and did not care what happened to me. After a few hours' repeat of the day before I just carried one more to the beach. Now there were hundreds and hundreds lying strapped on stretchers, some moaning, others silent and bewildered and so brave.

Then a shrapnel burst right overhead and one man started screaming. I made my way over the stretchers to help him but could do nothing as he had a piece of hot shrapnel buried in his groin – his agonising screams became lower and lower, then I knew he had passed on and thanked God for that.

He was just one of the many thousands that suffered the same agony and horror at Gallipoli. This is what I went through and saw in the first two days of Gallipoli. I have been reliving Anzac Day for seventy years and I know I will continue to do so until I join those brave Anzacs who gave their all for their country. Lest We Forget.

Reveille, July–August 1985

Private Mervin Spencer, 12th Battalion 3 Brigade AIF, returned to Australia in November 1915. In 1984 he was invited to the opening of the Gallipoli Gallery at the Australian War Memorial, and a year later was one of nine original Anzacs who visited Gallipoli for the seventieth anniversary of the landing. It was at this time that he wrote this article. He died in Hobart in 1987. His brother Tom also survived WWI, serving in France after Gallipoli and returning to Australia in September 1918.

A Queensland Anzac's Letter, Written Home in 1915

By Lieutenant D.M. Gillies

We left Lemnos on Saturday 24 April and at 4.30 a.m. next day, woke up at the sound of guns. We rushed up on deck, and saw the warships bombarding the fort at the entrance to the Dardanelles. We could not see very much for a while, but by 7 o'clock it was clear, and we could see the shells bursting on shore.

The *Queen Elizabeth* (or 'Lizzie', as she is called by the troops) was making a terrible mess of things on the shore. One fort on a small hill replied to her fire once, and she sent four shells at the hill. When the smoke cleared away there was nothing of fort or hill left. When you consider she throws a shell weighing 2000 pounds, you can form some idea of the damage she does. We were about a quarter of a mile from the warship, and it was a terrible sight.

Meanwhile our first, second and third brigades of Australians and New Zealanders were landing about twenty miles further up, and our ships moved there. We could hear the firing of our troops. We could see wounded men being brought from the shore to the hospital ships, and our fighting blood rose.

At 8 o'clock at night we got the order to land, and boarded a couple of destroyers. On nearing the shore we got into big pontoons and pulled in. We were ordered to advance to the firing line at once. We had to go up over high hills, and when we were halfway we got the order to fix bayonets and clear the ridges on our right. But the Turks had left before we arrived, and we were ordered to entrench ourselves just behind the firing line.

We did work, I can tell you, with bullets flying all around us, but fortunately none of us were hit. How we escaped them I can't tell. We soon had our trenches down in the soft ground, and after daylight we were ordered into the firing line.

The Turks were well concealed, and were led by German officers. I will give the Germans credit, and say that some of them are very brave. At times they came close to our trenches and gave our men orders in English. When the mistake was noticed, a score of rifles cracked, and the offenders were no more. The Turks' rifle-fire is very poor, on the whole, and most of the damage was done by shrapnel.

About 4 o'clock in the afternoon of Monday 26 April, we got the order to fix bayonets and charge a trench. We took it all right, and then the shrapnel started. The trench was only dug down about six inches and it was no protection against shrapnel. We were under this fire for about half an hour, and the only thing that beats me is that any of us were left. With shrapnel you hear the scream of the shell, and then – bang! – and bullets come down like hailstones. Fortunately the shrapnel was exploding a bit high, and most of it passed over us.

One shell exploded just in front of me, and I got a bullet through my forearm and a piece of shell caught me just below the shoulder. I thought my arm was broken, but luckily my bones are tough, and although it stiffened my muscles and turned my shoulder and arm as black as tar, it is nearly right again.

I waited till the shrapnel eased off, and then made my way back to the dressing station, and that was the worst part, as there was no cover and bullets were plentiful. However I reached the beach safely, and got my arm dressed, and was sent on board [a ship] and brought to Alexandria.

I must say that the doctors and the RAMC [the Royal Army Medical Corps] deserve the greatest praise for their work. I saw Dr Luther and Dr Butler right behind the firing line, and even in it at times, dressing wounded men. On reaching Alexandria, we were taken in motors to various hospitals. I was in hospital twelve days and am now at Mustapha Convalescent Camp. It is about seven miles from Alexandria and right on the sea shore. So we are very comfortable.

To go back to the first part of the Australians' landing. I don't know how ever our boys got ashore at all. They had to land under fire from rifles, machine-guns and shrapnel. They jumped out of the boats up to their waists in water, fixed bayonets, charged straight up a hill nearly as straight as a wall, and drove the Turks on to the next ridge. Then they went over the gully and took the next hill at the point of the bayonet. It was a grand deed, and Australia, I am sure, is proud of her men.

The Queensland Digger, April 1938

*The writer of the above letter was **Lieutenant David Martin Gillies**, a 34-year-old stockman, who left Australia a private (No. 893) in the 15th Battalion. After recovering from his wounds, he returned to Gallipoli. He was seen to be wounded a second time, staggered and fell. From that moment he was never seen again and he was listed as killed in action on 7 August 1915.*

Eerie Armada's Approach

By Brigadier General W. Ramsay McNicoll, CB, CMG, DSO

The 6th and 7th Battalions, which had left Australia on the same transport (SS *Hororata*) were again shipmates on the *Galeka* from 4 April till 25 April.

We were as proud of that ship and its captain, Burt, as we were of our own units. Burt was imbued with the true British bulldog spirit, and his conversation – if such a civilised word could rightly be applied to his fiery utterances – had a most stimulating effect. His crew was equally belligerent – a great contrast to the *Hororata*'s men, who, on our arrival at Alexandria, had refused to unload ship because it was Sunday!

The approach of the fleet to Anzac Cove was an eerie experience. No noise, no lights, no smoking, half speed – steaming towards a hostile, unlighted coast; and our captain dropped anchor 600 yards closer to the shore than any other boat. There is a fine official photograph showing the ship's boats containing the 6th and 7th Battalions leaving the *Galeka* just as the sun rose over Chunuk Bair.

A small 'Snottie' straight from the Royal Naval College was in charge of the steam pinnace which towed our string of boats as close as possible to the beach. The men then took to the oars until the bows grounded. Picks and shovels were thrown ashore and the men jumped out. I was at the stern and the water came breast-high. I can remember holding my Webley [revolver] clear, but have no recollection of feeling wet nor of getting dry again. Later in the afternoon, when a hunger pang made me seek some biscuits from the haversack, their salty and sodden condition brought with a shock the first realisation of the morning's dip.

While the companies were hurriedly forming on the beach, Colonel (later Major General) Sinclair-Maclagan came up with the first definite news. His brigade had landed further north than intended, and we were asked to go in on his right (south), instead of left, as had been planned. So it was half-right for us, and up the hills to another new experience on top of the first ridge – the feeling that we were the definite target of some first-class marksmen not very far away.

When we reached the second ridge a voice behind me asked, 'Where do you want the telephone, sir?' and there were two of the toughest Diggers one would wish to meet – Larkins and Wilkinson. As fast as my headquarters moved forward they were there with the field telephone, time and again having to run back to repair breaks. Men on these and similar jobs – such as stretcher-bearing – had more strain to carry than those who were able to expend their energies in active fighting.

One met small parties composed of men of half a dozen different units. 'Give us someone to lead us and tell us where to go.' The request was an indication of the reliance placed upon leaders, and of the heavy losses of officers and NCOs. It was a case of a quick search for a man with 'that narsty fightin' face that all nice people 'ate'. A sharp order, 'You take charge!' and they were off to join Major (later Brigadier General) Bennett, who was with the forward line until his second wound put him out of action for a while.

About midday, the adjutant, Yeoman, and I were both hit by the same shrapnel burst. My pellet merely ripped the web equipment; his passed clean through the fleshy part of his upper left arm, necessitating a brief withdrawal for treatment. Keiran was hit but in the excitement did not realise the fact. A few days later when he stripped his shirt to have an apology for a wash, one saw a livid welt around his torso. The bullet had entered at his shoulder, probably struck bone, and run round across his chest. It lay just below the skin and was easily removed.

Colonel (later Major General) H.E. Elliott, on the 25th having been shot in the ankle, the 6th and 7th Battalions were placed together, under my command, with Captain Finlayson of the 7th as adjutant. On the fourth night, things having quietened down a bit, Fin and I hollowed out a small space on a hillside and lay down on one spread-out greatcoat to snatch a little sleep. Some slight discomfort woke us in the small hours. A gentle rain was falling, and our hollowed out space was fast filling up. But sleep, as long as it was possible, had the first claim, and we lay in the growing pool until daylight.

Reveille, March 1931

Sir Walter Ramsay McNicoll (1877–1947) was a Melbourne teacher and major in the military forces. In 1914 he sailed for Egypt with the 7th Battalion and before the Gallipoli landing was appointed to command the 6th Battalion. After recovering from wounds he commanded the 10th Infantry Brigade, which took part in the Battle of Messines, the 3rd Battle of Ypres and the Battle of Amiens.

McNicoll returned to Australia late in 1919 and became principal of Presbyterian Ladies' College at Goulburn, NSW. Turning to federal politics he was elected in 1931 as the Country Party candidate for Werriwa. In 1934 he was appointed administrator of the Territory of New Guinea; he retired in 1942. McNicoll died in Sydney in December 1947, survived by his wife and four sons, of whom Ronald became a major general, Alan a vice admiral and David a prominent journalist.

The Landing: First Clash with Turks

By William Cridland

How many pause to give thought to that gallant band who landed on the shores of the Aegean Sea on 25 April 1915, placing Australia in such high esteem throughout the world?

The transports and convoys of the Anzac Armada concentrated at Albany, whence they sailed on 1 November 1914, and the troops were landed in Egypt early in December.

All troops were assembled at Lemnos, the advanced base, and on the evening of 24 April, the assaulting units were taken on board transports and warships to the Gulf of Saros. On arrival they were transhipped on to barges to be taken inshore. 'A' and 'B' Company, of the 9th, 10th and 11th Battalions, were chosen as a covering party, and twenty sappers, NCOs and an officer each from Nos 1, 2 and 3 sections of the 1st Field Company Engineers were chosen to go in as a demolition party.

I had the honour of being one of the chosen of No. 1 section, and we had to go in with A and B of the 9th Battalion. My section and the 9th Battalion were very fortunate in that we went from Lemnos to the hopping-off place in HMS *Queen*, the flagship of the Mediterranean fleet. All ranks aboard treated us with the usual British naval hospitality, and we were all able to get a decent sleep in bunks, and, on waking, a hot bath and a jolly good feed. Then, to cap all, the canteen was thrown open to us, and the sailors packed us with their issue of chocolate.

In the early hours of the morning came the clear but low order to fall in. All lights were out and the night was pitch-black. Each man's load was evened up as well as could be, so I'll mention what I had – the usual full marching order, not forgetting rifle and bayonet,

250 rounds (the dinkum stuff too), emergency rations, pick, shovel, wire-cutters, one dozen sandbags, and a case of guncotton. How we managed to go down the rope ladders into the barges, then through the water and up the sandy beach, God alone knows, for I don't, as each barge had its full complement.

At last all barges were ready and we were taken in tow by steam pinnaces. The moon had disappeared prior to our leaving the ship, but, looking back, we could see the black forms of the battleship following in our wake ready to cover our attack. Here we were at last launching out into the unknown, but it was a long looked-for event, after over eight months' hard, rigorous training at home, on board ship, in Egypt, and at Lemnos. However, our thoughts were suddenly checked by the report of a solitary rifle shot away up in the hills.

Every man realised that the supreme moment had arrived, and presently Hell was let loose, but so far there was only one side having a go. Full speed ahead raced the pinnace towing the barges, then, swinging clear, left us travelling inshore. Now, the little middies [midshipmen] standing erect, grim, determined and heroic, directed the barges, swinging them clear of one another.

Lieutenant Mather, realising that the barges afforded no protection from the murderous rain of lead from rifles, machine-guns and artillery, told us to go overboard and make the beach. His advice was promptly followed.

We were, of necessity, compelled to gain what cover was offering, in order to take a spell, for, after struggling through forty yards of water and then up the beach with our load, we were somewhat blown. This, as near as I can remember, was in the vicinity of 04.20 [hours.]

After a very short breather Colonel Lee reminded us of the job on hand. Now was our turn, and, with fixed bayonets (not forgetting the one in the tunnel), we started off up the hill, dragging ourselves up with the assistance of the undergrowth in places. Eventually we gained the top, and became subjected to fire from all directions, and I think all our casualties there were caused by snipers and shrapnel. There were about seven of us in a group, and we decided to move with caution, for some of our own cobbers coming up behind could very easily take us for Turks, for we were more like ragged tramps than anything else.

Our decision proved a blessing, not only to ourselves, but to those coming up, for, lying hidden as we were, we began picking off the Turks – some at very close range too. As our numbers increased we began to move forward, till a messenger came up with an order that all engineers had to report back and commence the establishment of a line of defence, and cut steps up the cliff so that travelling would be made easier.

It is difficult to remember the position of the job I had to carry out, that of cutting steps in the hill, but, as near as I can judge, it was that steep portion leading to Russell's Top. Whilst engaged on this task, General Birdwood stood talking to me for a while, and was nearly sniped. Later he informed me that it was an occasion he would never forget.

From this job I went up the hill to assist in some trench running, and as soon as I got there a sniper got busy from across the gully; but he did not reign long, as one of our chaps sent him to Allah. That evening my section, in charge of Lieutenant Mather, had a job of trench running somewhere up Shrapnel Gully, and, considering the incessant blaze of rifle and machine-gun fire all night, it was a wonder that any of us were left.

When one considers the geographical formation of the country, it is amazing to think that we ever got a footing on the Peninsula at all. To some people the landing at Gallipoli is merely something that happened in the distant past, but to many it is the most sacred day of the year.

I know many who took part in the landing who travel hundreds of miles for the memorial service on Anzac Day, and then spend the rest of the day with their old unit cobbers. That is the Anzac spirit, and it will last while ever there is an Anzac living.

Reveille, March 1930

William Charles Cridland, a 24-year-old mechanic from Marrickville, Sydney, enlisted on 18 September 1914, and sailed a month later as a sapper, with the 1st Field Company Engineers on the troopship Afric. *He returned as company quartermaster sergeant on 20 November 1918, became president of the T.B. [tuberculosis] Soldiers' Association, and was awarded an MBE in the New Year Honours List of 1936.*

The NZ in Anzac: We All Remember

By Lieutenant Colonel J.M.A. Durrant, CMG, DSO

When Australians commemorate Anzac Day they are inclined to talk and write about the Anzacs as though they were all Australians. Of course, the majority of the original Anzacs at Gallipoli were Australians, but there were many soldiers there who came from another dominion. I refer to the gallant New Zealanders.

The happenings of the landing and subsequent days in April 1915 had a most important effect on the present good will and understanding which exists between Australia and New Zealand, the ties, in fact, upon which the unity of our Empire is based. During the first few days all the little jealousies and lack of understanding were swept away. Common trials, suffering, dangers and interests made Australians and New Zealanders realise that they were brothers-in-arms.

The original Anzac Corps (under General Birdwood) was composed of two divisions, of which the 1st Australian Division (Major General Bridges) was wholly Australian. The other division was made up of New Zealand and Australian troops, and designated the NZ & A Division (Major General Sir Alex Godley). Its divisional troops (artillery, engineers etc.) were nearly all New Zealanders, and there were four brigades: NZ Infantry (Colonel F.E. Johnston), 4th Australian Infantry (Colonel J. Monash), NZ Mounted Rifles (Brigadier General A.H. Russell) and the 1st Australian Light Horse (Colonel H.G. Chauvel).

This organisation was an experiment and there must have been misgivings about it. Would the Australians and New Zealanders co-operate sufficiently well to produce the smooth-working fighting machine upon which success in battle is so dependent?

It must be admitted that the Australian officers and men did not display any marked enthusiasm for their New Zealand kinsmen when they first came in contact with them in Egypt. The plain truth is that we did not understand each other, and I cannot recall that we even made any serious efforts to effect a good understanding. There seemed to be little in common between us.

We afterwards discovered that the New Zealanders' opinion of us was similarly constrained. Their general knowledge of Australians was based largely on newspaper reports of Australian confidence men, cracksmen and such-like unpleasant gentry who had left Australia for their country's good, and emigrated to New Zealand. There was no friction, but there was no real comradeship or trust.

Such were the conditions prevailing between the representatives of these sister-dominions prior to 25 April 1915. Then came the landing, and how changed it all was after that. Within a few hours both Australians and New Zealanders were fighting desperately, side by side. In many parts of the firing line the rugged nature of the country caused such unavoidable confusion that the men of many units of both dominions became intermingled. Then, as various points in the line were seriously threatened, Australians would be sent to support New Zealanders, and vice versa. Age is a matter of experience, not of time, and within a few hours we lived together through many years.

The events of those first few days, when we struggled to secure a footing, and fought so hard to retain what little grip we held, are burnt into our minds. Some impressions are more vivid than others, but to most of the survivors of the 4th Australian Infantry Brigade there was nothing more wonderful than the realisation forced upon us amid scenes of tragedy and death that the NZ Infantry regiments and NZ Mounted Rifles were now joined with us in an indissoluble brotherhood. It all happened so suddenly, but the speed of its accomplishment had no detrimental effect upon its reality. 'The Aussies will do us!' cried the men of Canterbury, Wellington, Otago and Auckland.

The Australians re-echoed this sentiment and were quite content when they had New Zealanders on their flank or in support. I shall never forget the thrill with which I heard some of the Canterburys describe their enthusiastic appreciation of the fighting qualities of my own unit. It seemed too wonderful to be true, but all their subsequent actions proved the depth of their convictions, and so we learned to respect and admire the gallant men of New Zealand, led by brave and efficient officers such as Colonel Johnston, General Russell, Lieutenant-Colonel Stewart of the Canterburys, Lieutenant Colonel Malone (Wellingtons) and Lieutenant Colonel Bauchop (Otago MR), to name only a few. We deplored the loss of Sergeant Wallace, NZ Engineers, a Rhodes Scholar, who was killed while working with the 13th Battalion in front of Pope's Hill.

The relationships of the soldiers of the two great Southern Cross dominions were changed in a day, and that day was Anzac Day. Australians and New Zealanders shared all the dangers, the sorrows and the glories of Anzac, so let all Australians remember New Zealand on all future Anzac Days, and may the experience of this brotherhood, forged under fire, be cherished and handed down as one of the priceless gifts of Anzac.

Reveille, April 1936

James Murdoch Archer Durrant (1885–1963) was born at Glenelg, South Australia, and enlisted in 1907. In December 1914 he was appointed Captain Adjutant 13th Battalion and embarked from Melbourne on the troopship Ulysses. *Service on Gallipoli and the Western Front saw him promoted to lieutenant colonel and appointed staff officer in charge of repatriation and demobilisation. He rose to the rank of major general with senior commands within Australia during WWII, and retired in April 1944.*

Stretcher-Bearers at Anzac

By Lance Corporal Andy Davidson

Our small crowd of stretcher-bearers, under the command of Captain McWhae, had a lively entry into the war. We left Lemnos in the *Devanha*, and, under the shelter of [the island of] Imbros, transferred to the destroyer *Ribble*, on which also were two companies and headquarters of the 12th Battalion. Before daybreak we got into the boats, to be towed and rowed ashore by naval ratings.

Intense rifle and machine-gun fire was opened on us. 'Bow' was the first rower to get hit, and as he fell forward, his place was instantly taken by Ernie Gaunt, who pushed Frank Gill out of his way in his hurry to pick up the oar.

I think none of our men would have been left alive but for one of the queer caprices of war. Two boatloads of 8th Battalion men, well ahead of their time, and a long way out of their course, came across our stern. Fire was instantly turned on them, and their casualties were 100 per cent. Their boats drifted ashore about 300 yards to the left (north) of where we landed.

This respite allowed us to get near the shore before fire was again directed on us. I had to jump ashore and hold the boat on the beach until the unwounded of the bearers climbed out. Eccles was one of the early ones to jump, and fell by the bow of the boat – shot through the head. Following him was his boon companion, Hudson, who shared the same fate. Steve Sheath was next, and gave a queer twist and lay helpless half in the water, shot through the spine. Syd Rosser later went back under heavy fire to help him. His help was of no avail; but for this brave act he was awarded the Distinguished Conduct Medal.

We witnessed many brave acts during the years when heroism became the rule, not the exception, but this one, during our first few minutes of war, will be to most of us an unforgettable memory. Those of us who were left unwounded carried on, but as body and mind became more and more exhausted, the picture, for most of us, lost its clarity. On Tuesday 27 April, at the top of Shrapnel Gully, our gallant captain was severely wounded, so severely, in fact, that to our sorrow and great disappointment he was not able to join us again in the field.

Reveille, April 1936

Andrew Rhind Davidson, a 33-year-old married tailor from Kalgoorlie, embarked on the troopship Medic, *at Fremantle on 2 November 1914, as part of the 3rd Field Ambulance. Another stretcher-bearer who accompanied Davidson on the* Medic *and survived the landing at Gallipoli with the 3rd Field Ambulance was 22-year-old British-born John Simpson Kirkpatrick, who had enlisted under the name of John Simpson, and who, before being killed in action on 19 May 1915, achieved legendary status as 'Simpson and his Donkey'.*

Digger Sister Tells of First Anzac Day

By C.M. Pennefather (previously Sister Connie Keys)

I shall try to tell you what I can remember of that April 1915, when the Australians and New Zealanders (the Anzacs) attempted, and achieved, the almost impossible.

We sisters, of the No. 1 Australian General Hospital, were stationed at Heliopolis Palace [in Cairo], that magnificent structure built by the Belgians to outrival Monte Carlo. The Australian authorities requisitioned this palace for a base hospital, and when we took over, it had been stripped of most of its glory. But well do we remember coming down those gorgeous staircases to meals, carrying our kit – enamel plates, cups etc.

Life for the troops in the desert must have been pretty awful at times, especially when those Khamseens [hot, dry, sandy winds] were blowing. Only a tent for protection, sand in and on everything. In April, after months of training, of which they'd grown weary, they marched away, destination unknown, but to the real thing this time. To all those departing we waved goodbye. So many, many goodbyes.

Far into the night we heard them, company after company, singing as they went, 'Don't Take Me Home', 'Tipperary', 'Who's Your Lady Friend', cheering, coo-eeing again and again. Grand to hear but, oh, so sad. Alas! How many would come back? Their destination was kept secret; but later came news that the troops had gone to Lemnos, with the taking of the Dardanelles as their objective.

On 28 April, all leave at the hospital was stopped, and that night two hospital trains with 200 sick patients from Lemnos arrived, and late the next afternoon, Thursday 29 April, four days after that remarkable landing, the first train of wounded from Gallipoli arrived.

The train drew up right behind the palace, long white carriages, with the Egyptian star and crescent painted in red on the side. Then the work of unloading commenced, walking cases being directed across to the hospital, stretcher cases conveyed by motor ambulance.

The sight of those wounded men, walking, and stretcher cases in endless procession, was one never to be forgotten. No noise, no bustle, no sound, only footfalls. Poor worn-out souls, almost too weary to smile, with only a few rags of clothing (mostly bloodstained) left to them. So quiet, so brave, but their eyes (like those of dumb animals) betrayed their suffering.

We were so ill-prepared for such numbers that the work of getting those men to bed, washed, fed, wounds dressed, seemed a hopeless task; but somehow it was accomplished. Never before did we appreciate to the full the value of the Army Medical Corps [AMC] men. Everyone worked on till all hours of the night, and the night staffs carried on as best they could till morning.

Next day more trains came in with more serious cases, fewer walking, and more stretcher cases. For weeks the work was appalling. Medical men, Australia's best, sisters, AMC men, working to their utmost limit. Work in the operating theatre (formerly the King of the Belgians' suite) never ceased, day or night. Relief staffs carried on. And I write only of one hospital.

The stories the patients told were terrible; of how they landed on that memorable morning of 25 April, how the country was so hard to scale, great hills and cliffs, and how often ropes had to be used for climbing, and all the time under heavy fire. We were so busy, though, we only heard snatches of the tales.

Every article sent, and every article of sewing done, by the women of Australia was now of the greatest value. Every handkerchief and every pair of pyjamas worth its weight in gold. For most of the men came back clad only in a few bloodstained rags, having lost all their possessions.

We should never cease to be grateful to the women of Cairo for their wonderful kindness to those sick and wounded men. How we sisters would have managed without them during those terrible weeks I cannot imagine. They came daily, laden with dainties: fruits, custards etc., and delicious cool drinks for every man, and fed those unable to feed themselves.

Memories flood in. That base hospital, the troops training in the desert, their gallant marching away, their pathetic return, the heartbreak of the numbers who did not come back. And through it all ran the golden thread of bravery and endurance through hardships and suffering untold.

'Their Name Liveth For Evermore.'

The Queensland Digger, April 1936

Constance Mabel Keys (1886–1964) trained at Brisbane General Hospital and enlisted in the Australian Army Nursing Service (AANS) on 21 September 1914, embarking on the Omrah *three days later, attached to the 1st Light Horse Brigade. In Egypt she was posted to a British military hospital at Abbassia and then to the 1st Australian General Hospital at Heliopolis. On 4 December she joined the hospital ship* Themistocles *which was filled with wounded, and after arriving in Sydney re-embarked on 1 March 1916 for Egypt, then went to England and served in hospitals there until November 1917 when she was transferred to the 3rd Australian General Hospital at Abbeville, France. By this time she had been promoted to head sister, AANS. In February 1918 she went to the front line as sister-in-charge of the 2nd Australian Casualty Clearing Station near Bailleul, and remained on active duty on the Western Front until after the Armistice.*

Sister Keys was one of the most highly decorated nurses in the AANS. She was twice mentioned in despatches, received the Royal Red Cross, second class and first class, and was awarded the Médaille d'Honneur des Epidémies for her work with French refugees. After returning to Queensland Miss Keys became matron of a convalescent hospital for returned soldiers at Broadwater, Brisbane. While there she met and married Lionel Hugh Kemp-Pennefather, a Gallipoli veteran. The Pennefathers lived in Brisbane until the 1950s when they moved to Southport. Survived by her husband, a son and a daughter, she died there on 17 March 1964.

Finding Cover at Gallipoli

By Colonel W.W. Giblin, CB

The skirl of the pipes of the Melbourne Scottish (5th Battalion) as the *Novian* sailed out of Mudros Harbour; the deadly quiet as the fleet approached the shore before dawn and we waited for the first sign of Turkish alarm; the eager enthusiasm of the men awaiting their turn to land; the first shells falling around the ships; the crowded beach with the wounded already pouring in; the indomitable cheerfulness of the wounded who seemed to regard the whole affair more in the light of a football match than a battle – all these are indelible memories of our first Anzac Day.

One cannot forget the stretcher-bearers and other ambulance workers who carried on till they dropped from exhaustion, but had the satisfaction of knowing that the last of the wounded had been shipped from the beach.

Only those who were at Anzac during the first few days can realise the difficulty of organising a clearing station on that narrow strip of beach, which also served as a thoroughfare for troops, supplies and guns. No adequate shelter was available for the wounded, who were under constant shell fire till we could ship them off to the hospital ships and transports.

Three months later, just before the Suvla Bay landing, a very high medical authority landed at Anzac Cove and inspected the medical arrangements. After he had finished he turned to Colonel Howse and me, and said: 'You two are to blame for the muddle in evacuating the first wounded and overcrowding the hospital ships.'

I asked him to explain in what way.

'You did not carry out the routine laid down in the RAMC Manual,' he said. 'You had three field ambulances and one clearing hospital. Open up the tent sections of the field ambulances, and with the beds of the clearing hospital you could have kept 800 wounded on shore, and drafted them on to the hospital ships gradually.'

'How about cover?' I asked.

'Cover!' he replied. 'Cover! You can always find cover! I have done a lot of big game shooting and could always find cover!'

His remark was so priceless that it ended the discussion.

Reveille, April 1936

Dr Wilfred Wanostracht Giblin was a prominent Hobart surgeon who was appointed director-general of medical services in Tasmania at the outbreak of WWI, before embarking on the troopship Kyarra *in December 1914 with the rank of lieutenant-colonel. He was then aged forty-two. After commanding the 1st Australian Casualty Clearing Station at Gallipoli, he was posted to London as medical adviser at Australian HQ, promoted to colonel and made a Commander of the Order of the Bath (CB). After returning to Australia in March 1917 he returned to practice in Hobart. Dr Giblin died in 1951, leaving two sons and two daughters.*

Cut of the Cards Decides Patrol

By Lieutenant Colonel J.M.A. Durrant, CMG, DSO

After the landing on Gallipoli, the 13th Battalion was defending portions of what were known later as Quinn's Post and Pope's Hill, and there was great speculation among all ranks as to when the advance was to be resumed. The wonderful spirit of the men made a lasting impression on my mind, and the following story illustrates the typical *sangfroid* of the Diggers.

On the sixth day battalion headquarters received orders from General Godley that the ground in front of our trenches was to be reconnoitred with a view to locating the exact position of the Turks.

The commanding officer (Lieutenant Colonel Granville Burnage, of Newcastle) decided to send out a patrol of three non-commissioned officers to do this work, which was dangerous in the extreme, for it meant crawling through the scrub on Dead Man's Ridge, and the Chessboard, in daylight.

As adjutant, I sent to three of our companies, calling for volunteers for the mission, and in due course they reported, although by some means there were four of them. Such splendid fellows too!

The colonel said, 'I only want three, so one of you must drop out.'

Not one would do so, and there was a delay. Then one, a sergeant, coolly produced a pack of cards from his pocket, and said to the others, 'We'll cut for it!'

This they did, and I can never forget the calm and casual way these brave Aussie soldiers cut the cards for the honour of representing the battalion on a patrol which meant almost certain death.

Two were killed, and one, Sergeant Cotterill, was badly wounded, but returned and made his report of the reconnaissance.

Reveille, March 1930

James Murdoch Archer Durrant (1885–1963) was born at Glenelg, South Australia, and enlisted in 1907. In December 1914 he was appointed Captain Adjutant 13th Battalion and embarked from Melbourne on the troopship Ulysses. *Service on Gallipoli and the Western Front saw him promoted to lieutenant colonel and appointed staff officer in charge of repatriation and demobilisation. He rose to the rank of major general with senior commands within Australia during WWII, and retired in April 1944.*

Spy's Release: He Knew His NSW

By Colonel Granville Burnage, CB

After the Gallipoli landing, when our firing lines were so thinly held, our troops were keenly on the alert for spies. One night I was awakened in my dugout (just an open excavation about six feet square and eight inches deep, cut out by the Turks) by a corporal saying, 'We have got a spy, sir. Caught him trying to get through from the beach to the firing line.'

I got up and found, in the charge of a file of men who had captured him, a dilapidated individual with scrubby hair on his face, dressed in a much-worn Australian uniform jacket, a pair of navy trousers, a black civilian cap, and around his waist a leather belt and sheath knife.

When asked to explain his presence in the fighting area, he said, 'I am an Australian and want to get up there and have a shot at the Turks.' He repeated this with more emphasis on the 'am an Australian' each time, and then told me he was one of the shore working party from the *Triumph*.

The story was plausible, but not satisfactory, and being unable to get further enlightenment from him, I got back to his starting point and asked what towns he knew in Australia. His answer was 'Oh, lots', and named Sydney, Newcastle and other places.

In all Australian ports in the days of sailing ships there were certain hotels very much frequented by seafaring men, so I shot at him, 'Give me the name of your favourite pub at Newcastle.' He gave me several names, the first two being the Black Diamond and the Blue Bell – the former a prominent sailors' house and known to all English-speaking men before-the-mast who had sailed out of Port Hunter. A lonely sailor in a foreign port could always rely on meeting a cobber by making a few remarks about the Black Diamond at Newcastle.

I further got from him that he was born at Milson's Point and went to school there. He gave the name of the schoolmaster and the names of some schoolmates in his class, when one of his captors burst out, 'That's right, sir. I come from Milson's Point and Jack —— (I have forgotten the name) is my brother.'

With that, the firing party at dawn faded from my mind! I complimented our spy on his grit, gave him a few words of advice about keeping away from other people's jobs, and had him escorted back to the beach and released.

Two days later a delightful loaf of ship's white bread was sent to my headquarters from the *Triumph*, which was, by the way, with one exception, the only bread I tasted on the Peninsula.

Reveille, October 1930

Lieutenant Colonel Granville John Burnage (1858–1945), a wine and spirits merchant from Newcastle, NSW, embarked in December 1914 as commanding officer of the 13th Battalion. He was then fifty-five and had considerable military experience, having served in the Boer War. His leadership and concern for his men at Gallipoli earned him great respect and his unit became renowned as 'The Fighting 13th'. Burnage was severely wounded on 29 May 1915 at Quinn's Post, when a bomb shattered his left elbow. He was invalided home and spent the rest of WWI as a commander of various troopships.

A Hectic Night at Quinn's Post, 9 May 1915

By No. 451, 15th Battalion

As a young sergeant, I had carried out an extra day's duty with the Royal Marine Light Infantry in Quinn's Post and had been relieved that morning, Sunday 9 May 1915. I had a doze in my louse-infested dugout and about 15.30 hours, Lieutenant Les Collin, my platoon commander (No. 12 of 'C' Company, commanded by Captain Quinn) called at my dugout.

I was cleaning my rifle and Lieutenant Collin said: 'Bob, the Colonel (at that time Lieutenant-Colonel J.H. Cannan) wants a sergeant to go out with a raiding party from "C" Company. The number will be forty and there will be other parties on right and left, the object being to raid the Turkish trenches. Stop out if possible all night, fill in any mining they might be doing, and return at dawn through communication trenches that would be dug during the night.'

The way Lieutenant Collin said it led me to believe that I would be detailed, so I promptly volunteered, and away he went to Battalion HQ with the information, and came back later to discuss the suggested plan for reaching the Turks' trenches, which were only approximately twenty yards away at the shortest point.

I definitely made the suggestion that we crawl out at least fifteen yards before rising and charging, and that I would lead them in if I was still alive. Lieutenant Collin just smiled, as both of us had had a fair amount of good luck by this time. He told me we were to move out at 9 p.m. and that a machine-gun on Walker's Ridge would give the signal with a burst of fire. I did not like this and told him so, as I preferred the silent way, but was overruled at HQ.

Later Lieutenant Fred Youden, who had just been promoted, was selected to go with this centre party, but my plans were not altered, although we knew we would have to crawl through some decomposed bodies. Just before 9 p.m., the time was altered to 10.45 p.m., as the powers-that-be thought Jacko had smelt a rat and was very quiet and waiting for us.

I scrounged around and got my crowd a tot of rum. Then it became a little more serious to me as Les Collin asked me for my pay book etc. as it was thought there was very little hope of any of the first lot getting back. I then scribbled my note to Mum. 'Dear Mum. This could be it – all the best.' This was put in my pay book.

Eventually the gun opened fire and over we went, crawling over and amongst the bodies and stumps, and some of our fellows were hit. But I could faintly see a fair line as I looked to the right where Lieutenant Youden was supposed to be. I think he had been hit by this time, and as we were about eight yards from the Turkish lines and their forms in the trenches could easily be seen, I jumped to my feet and it was certainly on.

I hope no one ever asks me how I got into the Turks' trench because no one would believe it, but my luck was in, and most of the great lads I had with me also got into the Turks' trenches. We carried bags around our waists to change the parados to the parapet when we had a chance to fill them, and I put every alternate one filling the bags whilst his mate carried on shooting at the Turks.

I began to make my way to the left but the casualties began to come and we had to go canny. We found one mining hole and we killed the miners as they came out, but I desired to join up with the left party. The going was heavy as the Turks had not all left their trenches, and being dark, one had to make sure you were not getting stuck into your mates. I got a bayonet jag in my left hand, and the scar is still there, and then my luck came good again. I heard a voice calling my name, so I got out of the rear of the trench, and it was Lieutenant Frank Armstrong (a great little soldier) who told me Lieutenant Youden was wounded.

He said to me: 'A great effort, lad, we never gave you a hope. I will take over. You return to the original front line. Don't let anyone send our troops unless I ask for them.'

I arrived back where I started from, but, gee, my job was only starting and it certainly was a hectic night. Casualties were now coming thick and fast. I made numerous visits to the Turks' trench with grenades and ammo. But my luck still held. Lieutenant Collin came up to me and said he had been instructed to go out with a few men and try and get the junction with the group on the left, but he was never heard of again. Will always consider Les Collin one of the greatest young officers I ever had the pleasure to serve with in my thirty-four years' army experience.

Captain Harry with Lieutenant Mundell also tried to get this gap filled but Captain Harry was killed. Young Percy Toft (later Major Toft, MC and bar, MM) was a runner this night and what a great job he did, but was wounded in the arm and ribs and was sent away.

The 16th Battalion were brought into the fight and Major Margolin's company were in it before dawn. Lieutenant Armstrong was still going strong and getting messages through to me. Captain Sampson (later lieutenant colonel and a Tasmanian Senator) did a great job with the centre trench and got through. Eventually the withdrawal was carried out. Gee, but what a sacrifice – fourteen officers (ten killed) and 193 other ranks, mostly killed.

Not long afterwards Lieutenant Armstrong saw me and said: 'Hell, you still here? What a great job, laddie.' He did not live much longer as he put his head between two bags to look for some of his wounded men, and he was shot through the head. Later in the day the 15th was relieved – except No. 451, who received a message from Captain Quinn that I was to remain in with the 13th Battalion owing to my knowledge of the post.

In the attack on 9–10 May the losses of two Turkish regiments amounted to 600 killed and 2000 wounded. It certainly was some night, and I don't think I will ever forget it.

The Queensland Digger, April 1957

*The author preferred to be identified only by his regimental number, 451, 15th Battalion. He was **Lance Sergeant Robert Alexander Hunter**, a 22-year-old miner from Maryborough, Queensland, who had enlisted on 17 September 1914. His actions won him the Military Medal.*

*   **Lieutenant Leslie Norman Collin**, who was killed on 9 May, was a twenty-year-old student from New Farm, Brisbane. **Lieutenant Frederick Charles Youden**, a 33-year-old musician, survived that engagement but was killed in action on 8 August 1915.*

The Man with the Donkey

By 'Paleface'

The story of 'The Man with the Donkey' is not new, but it is worth preserving, it being a record of one of the finest examples of courageous and unselfish sacrifice known to the war.

Private W. Simpson was a true son of Erin and had a decided brogue. For the same incomprehensible reason that a dark man was invariably called 'Snow', and a ginger one 'Bluey', Simpson was known to the troops as 'Scotty'.

Scotty was in at the beginning of the Australian offensive at Gallipoli and was attached to a Western Australian unit, the 3rd Field Ambulance, being a member of 'C' Company. Although attached to a unit, like most stretcher-bearers he was allowed much latitude, and very soon his work won him a complete roving commission.

After a few heavy-laden trips from the forward positions back to the dressing stations, Scotty displayed initiative by helping himself to a couple of apparently ownerless donkeys. These animals he christened 'Duffy I' and 'Duffy II'.

It was Scotty's custom to proceed with his donkeys to the furthest point where cover could be found, then leaving his dumb assistants in comparative safety, he would worm his way into no-man's-land until he was within striking distance of the wounded soldier. He would then make a smart rush, and lifting his human freight with a powerful and swift swing on to his broad shoulders, would beat a hasty retreat to cover.

There he would dress the wounds with 'a touch like a woman's' and then, with his donkeys carrying the human freight, he would make his way through some two miles of danger zone to the beach hospitals.

One day 'Duffy I' was hit, and it became necessary to replace him with another donkey. This donkey Scotty called 'Murphy' and the popular joke of the sector was Scotty's droll comment as he hit 'Duffy' or 'Murphy' on the rump with a little switch he always carried to keep them jogging along: 'Git along, ye lazy baste! Ye'll be ladin' me into danger wan o' these days.'

A peculiar feature was the extent of Scotty's roving commission. He came and went as he pleased, and was most welcome everywhere. All could spare rations for this kindly hero. He was responsible for the recovery of many wounded, and would save as many as sixteen in a day.

Then came the fateful day at last – 19 May 1915. Scotty was carrying a wounded comrade on his back and 'Murphy' was by his side bearing his quota. The animal was so tiny that a tall man had to bend his legs to avoid scraping the ground with his feet.

At one particularly vulnerable part of Shrapnel Gully the Turks had trained machine-guns to prevent communication. Scotty's turn came. He was shot through the heart, and as he lay lifeless, 'Murphy' quietly walked on into safety with the burden that he carried in trust for his mate.

His sudden passing cast a deep gloom over the Anzac Sector, and perhaps the sequel is unparalleled in the war.

Upon the grave in the gully where this hero, who saved so many lives, was buried, on the highway to the inferno of battle, bouquets of wild flowers were laid – solemn tributes from hardened comrades: men who would have blushed to hold a flower for any less worthy cause, gathered blooms in this man's honour.

Over the mound of earth which marked the resting place of 'The Man with the Donkey', the little wooden cross bore the simple inscription:

W. SIMPSON
3rd Field Ambulance
19/5/1915

(The writer is indebted for corroborative evidence made by one of the field ambulance men present throughout the period and thanks others who were present with Scotty.)

The Listening Post, November 1925

Later research identified 'Scotty' as **John Simpson Kirkpatrick**, *born in 1892 at South Shields, County Durham, in north-east England. He joined the merchant navy aged seventeen and deserted at Newcastle, NSW, in May 1910. He worked variously as a cane-cutter in Queensland, as a miner in NSW, as a gold-digger in WA and on coastal shipping. Under the name John Simpson, he joined the AIF at Blackboy Hill Camp, Perth, on 25 August 1914, expecting to be posted home to England. He embarked for Egypt on 2 November, and landed at Gallipoli at dawn on 25 April 1915.*

Sniper's Bullet Broke Turkish Plans

By Major General H.E. Elliott, CB, CMG, DSO, DCM

The following incident, which occurred about the end of June 1915, may be taken as an illustration of the great keenness which animated our snipers and observers on Gallipoli, and also of the great value which attaches to the trained and picked riflemen in position warfare such as then prevailed.

At this period the 7th Battalion was holding Steele's Post, on the eastern side of Monash Valley; and owing to the configuration of the ground and the peculiarities of the position, the rear of Steele's where the cookhouses, latrines etc. were situated came in for unpleasant attention and many casualties occurred at the hands of Turkish riflemen who were firing from the Chessboard and the Nek – from the left rear of Steele's. To cope with this nuisance, a sniper's post was constructed one night facing the danger zone and carefully camouflaged.

Amongst the permanent garrison told off for its occupation were Carne, a Bendigo ex-King's Prizeman; Young, formerly the crack shot of the St Arnaud Rifle Club, who still comes from his home at Werribee to take an occasional prize at Williamstown; and Fisher, another well-known militia shot.

They were supplied with field glasses, telescopes, verniers, telescopic and peep sights, and all the other gadgets favoured by the target rifle shot, and speedily proved their value by gaining complete mastery over their opponents.

At earliest dawn they were alert, and remained there until the last gleam had faded from the western sky, sweeping with their glasses backwards and forwards across and again the Turkish lines. Among other things, they remarked, at this time, that every morning a smartly dressed officer visited the enemy's position at the head of the valley. He wore a soft Turkish helmet with a blue uniform with gold braid upon it, and when he arrived at the trenches opposite Pope's he daily went through the following routine: He nodded to the men (the Australian observers noted that through their telescope, they could even see his white teeth when he smiled and shook hands with another officer in the trench), borrowed a rifle from a sentry, rested it on the parapet, and fired a shot or two down the valley or across the hill at the New Zealanders on Russell's Top.

Such a procedure made him an obvious object for attention by our snipers, and after carefully observing him for several successive mornings and noting the time and place of his visits, those of the 7th made special preparation for him.

As the time approached Carne lay, motionless as any Indian brave, with his rifle covering the spot at which his enemy was expected to appear, whilst his comrades explored all approaches with their telescopes. A whispered word, 'He is coming,' caused Carne to nestle his cheek closer to his gun stock and draw a deeper breath as he lined his sights anew.

The Turkish officer halted, took up and placed a rifle on the parapet, and, as he leaned forward for his first shot, Carne's bullet, aimed somewhat low, raised a puff of dust a foot below him. He glanced around for a second and then again bent to his aim.

A second bullet whizzed by just above his helmet and struck dust from the parados behind him – the bracket was complete – but he still dwelt upon his aim, reckless of his danger.

A third shot from Carne echoed across the valley, and his gallant foe threw up his hands and collapsed into the trench.

Much commotion and running about were observed in the enemy trenches, and about half an hour afterwards a blizzard of shell fire of unusual severity descended upon Steele's and Courtney's posts, causing much loss and incidentally obliterating the 7th's cherished sniper's nest. It was duly recorded in the 7th's diary along with the facts that someone of considerable importance to the enemy had evidently been made a casualty, and this was the Turkish revenge.

Our careful and painstaking historian, Captain C.E.W. Bean, has given us in *Volume II* the full explanation that was hidden from us at the time, and it is full of interest.

It appears that the Turkish Commander, Mustapha Kemal Bey (now President of the Turkish Republic), whose division lay across the northern half of the Anzac Front on Baby 700 and the end of Monash Valley, had resolved to capture that part of Russell's Top nearest the Nek. He realised rightly that this was the key to the Anzac position, and if he could seize and hold that key the Anzacs would be forced to withdraw, if they could, from the Peninsula, and would probably be crushed in making the attempt. This plan had been partially suggested, states the historian, by the arrival of an especially fine regiment which he believed might be capable of carrying it out.

This was the 18th, commanded by a particularly brave and distinguished officer, who was idolised by his troops. On reaching Anzac it had been attached to the 19th Division under Kemal, who thought that the high spirit of both the men and their leader justified him in throwing it into a difficult but vitally important operation. He accordingly placed it in the line on Baby 700 and the Chessboard with the object of launching it a few days later from the Nek upon Russell's Top.

But shortly after his arrival it is recorded that the gallant commander of the 18th Regiment was killed while visiting his line. His loss was seriously felt, and although arrangements for the attack went on as before, when the attack was launched the plans for it went sadly askew. Time, place and date fixed his identity, and while we may deplore the loss of a very gallant foe thus obscurely and untimely slain, we may nevertheless congratulate ourselves upon the results which flowed from the untiring watchfulness and deadly skill of our own men, which saved us from a possible disaster at the hands of the enemy.

Reveille, March 1930

Major General Harold Edward 'Pompey' Elliott (1878–1931) was born and educated in Ballarat, Victoria, served in the Boer War, and at the outbreak of WWI was a prominent Melbourne barrister and solicitor, while serving as lieutenant colonel in the Commonwealth Militia. As commander of the 7th Battalion Elliott fought with distinction at Gallipoli, and was promoted to brigadier general and given command of the 15th Infantry Brigade during some of the fiercest battles in France. He was wounded on more than one occasion in battles which included Polygon Wood, Messines, Bullecourt and Villers-Bretonneux, and was mentioned in despatches no fewer than seven times. After the war he was elected to the Senate for Victoria, and promoted to major general in 1927.

Timber and Tat-tat-tat-tat

By Brigadier General C.H. Foott, CB, CMG

Fortunately, many of the events at Gallipoli which remain clearest in our minds are the amusing ones. It was when that ration barge ran ashore near Brighton Beach that a certain officer got a brainwave.

We were very short of timber for dugout roofs, and so on, and the barge had a splendid deck of real timber – stuff about six inches by two inches. No one seemed to want the barge, this chap wanted the timber, but the catch was that anyone working on it in daylight was a 'sitter' for Johnny Turk.

But a small charge of guncotton under the deck, after dark, would do the trick. The timber could be salvaged before it drifted away. So a plan was made, and like all war plans, was kept a secret, save to those in the know.

The demolition party met at the barge, the charge was laid, connected up, and fired. The decking leapt into the air, but before it could be salved, a burst of machine-gun fire over the heads of the working party in the water made them change their minds. Apparently the Turk was very alert.

Every attempt to salve a plank led to the same result. Unwilling to lose men, and feeling sure that the timber would drift ashore with the tide and wind, the boss timber-getter damned Jacko, withdrew his lads, and early next morning returned to the scene. Not a splinter was to be found; but it did not require a black-tracker to see that there had been plenty drifted ashore, that it had been salved, and that it had found a home with a certain unit of the AIF, which was occupying the ridge a few hundred yards distant. They had done the firing!

Fancy the blighters wasting all that good ammunition on the blue Aegean, just for the sake of some measly timber! And they got it, too. That's what hurt.

Reveille, April 1936

Cecil Henry Foott (1876–1942) was born in New South Wales and educated in Queensland. An army officer and engineer, he was attached to the British Army in England as a major when WWI started. He joined the 1st Division AIF and served at Gallipoli, in Egypt and on the Western Front, being mentioned in despatches seven times.

Portrait of a Soldier: Famous Sniper's Death

By Lieutenant Colonel Stephen Midgley, CMG, DSO

Trooper William 'Billy' Sing was born in 1886 to an English mother and Chinese father, and was raised in Clermont and Proserpine in rural Queensland. Sing was one of the first to enlist in 1914 and was sent to Egypt in December 1914 and then to Gallipoli in May 1915. He earned the nicknames 'the Murderer' and 'the Assassin' for his skill as the Australians' best sniper. He was mentioned in despatches and awarded the Distinguished Conduct Medal in 1916. After the Evacuation Sing was posted to the Western Front with the 31st Battalion, and was again mentioned in despatches for gallantry and awarded the Belgian Croix de Guerre. He died in Brisbane of heart failure in 1943, aged fifty-seven.

All 5th Light Horse men will be sorry to hear of the passing away of William Edward Sing, the 5th's famous sniper. After his sniping exploits on Gallipoli I don't think there was a man better known or respected and liked throughout the regiment, and he deserved it all. He was a good-hearted, well-behaved fellow, and a braver soldier never shouldered a gun.

When he volunteered to take on the job as sniper for certain reasons, I asked him how he felt about shooting men in cold blood, so to speak.

His reply was that shooting the illegitimates would not rob him of any sleep. So he got the job and it was not long before he proved himself the right man in the right place. Very soon a site was chosen and a sniping 'possie' built.

He has been credited with a bag of 150, but I think if another thirty were added it would be nearer the mark, as only those verified by a second party were recorded. His strong suit was his excellent eyesight; he could see as well with the naked eye as the ordinary man could with a telescope.

Sniping is a dangerous game, and Sing had many escapes. On one occasion he and his observers got a bad mauling; a bullet went through the telescope used by one of the latter, reducing it to scrap and injuring both his hands, then entering his mouth and coming out his left cheek, and finally ending up in Sing's right shoulder. The observer, Trooper Tom Sheehan, was of course evacuated, but Sing was able to carry on, but after the shaking up it took him quite a week to get back to his old form. Sing seldom left his possie during the day time, but was never lonely as he had many visitors. Even the GOC [General Officer Commanding] could find time to pay him a call.

Towards the end of October 1915 his possie was, unfortunately, located by the foe. The first shot from a fairly heavy gun got the range, but luckily did little damage. Sing took the hint and got out while the going was good. It was just as well he did, as the second shot, which was not long in coming, wiped his possie off the map.

At night when there were no opportunities for sniping, he always took part in raids, if there were any on the list. At the taking of Wilson's Lookout, which I think was the last operation that took place on the Peninsula except the Evacuation, he played a prominent part, and did all the throwing of 'Labinia bombs', which consisted of a slab of guncotton lashed to a piece of deal board and a time fuse. They had a most devastating effect, but required careful handling. They were used only when we were hard pressed. Sing's prompt action when called on to play his part saved us from disaster more than once.

Sing's DCM was nobly won and richly deserved.

The Queensland Digger, July 1948

Lieutenant Colonel Stephen Midgley (1871–1954) had served in the Boer War, and embarked with the 5th Light Horse Regiment in December 1914, as a 43-year-old captain. He gave his occupation as 'mine owner' along with his mother's address at New Farm, Brisbane. He was promoted to major, and then lieutenant colonel, and returned to Australia on 16 December 1917.

Recollections of Anzac

By Lieutenant Eric Henry Best

Life in the trenches is at times monotonous, and any little incidents which tend to amuse are eagerly seized upon by the men. On a warm sunny day at Chatham's Post the men were idly looking out over the sea and taking occasional pot shots at the trenches opposite, when from somewhere appeared a black and tan smooth-haired mongrel. He trotted down towards Brighton Beach to the accompanying whistles of our men and cries of 'Here boy! Get away back there! Good boy, Towser, come behind! Sit down!'

On he trotted and took a paddle in the water when someone fired a shot just behind him. One startled look and he was off along the beach. Crack! And his pace was accelerated, and presently he was all out towards Gaba Tepe, with every now and then a bullet zipping just behind him. I don't think anyone took his time, but it was just 1100 yards from our trenches to Gaba Tepe, and we estimated that he had done it in even time.

Simple as they seem to an outsider, these little happenings all help to while away the weary hours of watching and waiting.

* * *

Our little friend the destroyer, which each night crept in to within half a mile of the beach, must have caused Abdul many a sleepless night. Regularly, just after darkness had set in, from our trenches could be discerned a dim shape in the offing – it seemed to come from nowhere, but just to arrive as a matter of course.

Then suddenly a long beam of dazzling light would shoot out from her searchlight, and after sweeping along the beach, would perhaps settle on the old fort at Gaba Tepe, then on to Twin Trenches and gradually sneak along to the Green Knoll [and]

Balkan gun pits, and so on right along the Turkish position, as if seeking something. The suddenly it would stop and concentrate on some new work or new trench, and presently, bang! crash! A high explosive shell would land with wonderful accuracy, and up in the air in dust and smoke would go some work that had cost poor old Abdul hours of shovelling and toil to complete.

Then the beam of light would shift and another target would be found and treated in the same summary manner. We loved that little destroyer like a brother, and if she did not come along at her usual hour, we would feel quite disappointed at being deprived of our nightly fireworks.

No doubt the Turks felt differently.

* * *

Major Midgley, of the 5th Light Horse, was a splendid officer and game as a pebble, but he dearly loved his 'stunts' and we often wondered what he would do next. Our great aim was to make the Turks waste ammunition, and one well-engineered stunt which I recall must have cost them many thousands of rounds.

At 3.30 a.m., thirty men of the 5th and 11th under Captain Wright and Lieutenant Munro crept out from the beach post, and entered along the beach opposite the Turkish lines running towards Gaba Tepe. At 4 a.m. the thirty men fired five rounds rapid, then stopped and crouched under the ledge of earth which ran along the beach. All along the line rippled the Turks' fire and grew in intensity, they evidently thinking an attack was contemplated. When they were well going and must have had their front trenches well manned, suddenly in quick succession came ten rounds of shrapnel from the little destroyer which hitherto had been lying quiet and unsuspected off shore. With wonderful accuracy the shrapnel hailed down on the front enemy trenches and must have done great execution.

Strangely enough the Turks would never fire their big guns at night if it could be avoided, as they did not wish to give away their cunningly concealed positions, so the destroyer had a free hand. At daybreak, in came our thirty men, after expending about 150 rounds of ammunition, and causing Abdul to expend some thousands of rounds, and probably to lose a number of men.

The Queensland Digger, April 1937

2nd Lieutenant Eric Henry Best embarked with the 11th Light Horse Regiment on 16 June 1915, on the troopship Borda, *at Brisbane. He was listed as a married 32-year-old grazier, his address being 'Woollahra', The Alice Central Queensland Railway. He returned to Australia in May 1916.*

Smalley: A Hero of the 3rd

By Major J.W.B. Bean

I wonder how many today remember Smalley, of the 3rd Battalion, who was so exactly the opposite of his name? Small he was not, in any way. He had the physique and constitution of a giant, and in his great hairy chest there beat one of the bravest and biggest hearts in the AIF. Rough he was, certainly, in some ways; a queer mixture, not a drawing-room man in any wise, but gentle as a woman before weakness and pain in others, though ruthless to his own sufferings and weariness.

He became a byword in the battalion for 'ever-ready help in trouble'. Was someone limping and wilting on a broiling desert trudge, then Smalley would shoulder his pack and take his rifle. If some extra 'fatigue' had to be faced, Smalley would do it cheerfully and take on more than his share if he could thus help some weaker mate.

Doubtless his big-heartedness was taken advantage of at times, but he was never heard to growl about it. He wasn't a stretcher-bearer, but he was an ex-railway man, and well trained in first aid, and constantly on the lookout to put his skill at the disposal of all and sundry during, or immediately after, 'stunts'. He could 'go on the bust' pretty thoroughly at times when drink was handy and plentiful, but I am sure, however drunk as he might be, he was always, in essence, a gentleman 'in his cups'.

A queer perversity in this grand-hearted man was his apparent callousness and crudeness towards the after-death fragments of his mates.

Probably because the job was painful and hateful and shirked by others, it fell to Smalley to go round with his sandbags and collect what he could find of anyone blown to pieces by a shell. I have known him come into my dugout, which was an annexe of our regimental dressing station, lugging along his dreadful bundle.

'All that's left of Bob Anderson of "A" Company, sir. Direct hit! By Gawd! His mother wouldn't know him now, poor b——. He is in a bloody mess. Like to see him, sir?'

'No, Smalley,' I would reply. 'For God's sake take it away and bury it. No, I don't want to see it.'

Whether this was a sort of 'bluff' in Smalley – a 'pose' whereby he was able to camouflage the whole thing to himself, and dodge its awfulness, I cannot say, but anyhow, there it was! I can see him now, when two men had been buried by a shell, working like a fiend to dig them out before they suffocated. His great frame, bare to the waist, sweat dripping off him, standing on top of the shattered trench, well exposed to enemy fire, his shovel working with rhythmic force and fury of a great piston; the knotted muscles starting out on his mighty arms and shoulders.

Just before our 'hop-over' at Lone Pine, Smalley came to me for a supply of bandages and dressings. 'Soon as I've done with the Abduls I'll get busy with these, sir, and give some of our poor ——s a chance!'

He never did! Kind, gallant help and comrade of all, he was found lying dead in that narrow stretch of no-man's-land not far from the Pimple. There the bullet took him, and there he handed in his checks and passed on, out of our sight but not out of our hearts – to active service 'in Another Place'.

Reveille, September 1930

John Willoughby Butler (Jack) Bean embarked from Sydney with the rank of Captain on 20 October 1914 on the troopship Euripides. *He was listed as a 34-year-old medical practitioner from South Randwick and posted to the 3rd Infantry Battalion. He was wounded on the day of the Gallipoli Landing and again at Lone Pine, later served on the Western Front, and returned to Australia, with the rank of major on 23 October 1918. He was the younger brother of the official Australian war correspondent and historian, Charles Bean.*

Shooting Geese over Gallipoli

By Corporal T.W. McNamara

Anzac, early in May 1915, that small strip of territory recently discovered by Australia. The soft warm sun of early morning dispersing the mists around Imbros, which loomed to the west as a dark threatening cloud, and casting a glistening sheen on the glass smooth waters of the Aegean sea. The brightly coloured hospital ship, catching its searching beams, rides serenely at anchor, and a little way towards the flanks, two destroyers are making a leisurely inspection. Farther out the sun's rays pick out the transports and the warships.

On the beach the ration parties are assembling, having made their tortuous way thither down steep hills and deep gullies, the sides and bottoms of which are thickly clothed with short prickly scrub and wild thyme on which dew drops still glisten.

The first shell of the morning bursts with a crash and a whine of shrapnel, whilst the white acrid fumes float away on the morning breeze like a fleece of freshly scoured wool, and the smell of wild thyme and dead men is borne on the air.

All is quiet save for an occasional shot at the periscopes which we are using as our only means of inspecting the landscape. No shots are sent in return – what is the use of needlessly fouling our rifles, considering the arduous task involved in cleaning them again.

Suddenly, about 500 feet in the air, appears a flock of wild geese on their annual migration, flying in V-formation, and giving forth wild honks as though startled at the evidence of man's imbecility. Immediately our line springs into life, and the rattle of firearms hastily snatched up disturbs the quiet, a bedlam to which Jacko adds his portion.

The geese fly leisurely out of range, except one, which falls with neck and wings outstretched between the lines. One of our men incautiously puts his head above the parapet to watch its fall, and almost immediately falls back with a groan, as a bullet pierces his head, to lie quivering at the bottom of the trench as though the spasmodic movements of his poor tortured body were responding to the call for stretcher-bearers.

Reveille, April 1936

Corporal Thomas William McNamara, of the 11th Battalion, 3rd Reinforcements, was a 24-year-old hairdresser who enlisted in September 1914 and embarked from Fremantle on the Itonus *on 22 February 1915. His next of kin was given as his mother in Sheffield, England. He returned to Australia on 19 October 1917.*

Monash Valley

By Major R.O. Cowey

It was the first Anzac Day.

We had set out to occupy Hill 971, whence we intended to observe and dominate all local enemy movement. But a gap on each flank and deference to superior rank delayed us, and saved us from being permanently lost 'in the blue', as must have happened if we had continued to advance.

Then followed enemy rifle-fire, from concealment that cut down the surrounding scrub almost as a scythe would have done. We replied in kind. The 'overs' from the Turks apparently caused those some distance in the rear of us to think that we were the Turkish firing line. Our casualties were very heavy, and included two out of the three officers present. Ammunition ran short.

We began to wonder if there were other than enemy troops left on the Peninsula, for we had seen none of our force.

Towards evening the few survivors of our party straggled back to the head of Monash Valley, leaving too many good friends lying dead. Things were better here until the Turks again connected with us. We had a short respite during which to look at and think about things.

We could now look down that long valley which led to the sea, and the ships – and in those ships was safety. To stay seemed to make certain of death, of oblivion, of the loss of all those earthly things one had looked forward to.

But to cede our position to the Turks meant that no living thing could enter that valley without being shot to death.

We appeared to be occupying a key position. To leave it surely meant the loss of the whole enterprise.

We stayed.

Robert Orlando Cowey was a 26-year-old lieutenant when he embarked from Sydney on the Euripides *on 20 October 1914, posted to the 3rd Infantry Battalion. In May 1916 he was assigned to the 55th Battalion and promoted to major. He returned to Australia in May 1919. When he enlisted he was employed in Wollongong but he had grown up at Monbulk, in the Dandenong Ranges of Victoria, and after WWI went back there to manage the family farm, 'Weardale'.*

Lone Pine: 1st Brigade in Epic Fight

By Captain J.J. Collingwood, MC, MM

The commanding officer at Gallipoli, Lieutenant General Sir Ian Hamilton, planned a major offensive for early August 1915, based on Suvla Bay. The 1st Australian Infantry Brigade was assigned to a diversionary attack at Lone Pine. Reinforced by other battalions of the 1st Division, the attack was launched at 5.30 p.m. on 6 August. Within half an hour they had captured a maze of underground trenches and then held on to them for four days, despite savage Turkish counterattacks involving hand-to-hand fighting and bombing. Lone Pine forced the Turks to send reserves from other sectors. Seven Australians won the Victoria Cross in this battle, two posthumously. Success at Lone Pine cost the six Australian battalions eighty officers and 2197 men; the Turks are thought to have lost about 5000 troops.

The 1st Brigade AIF for many months had taken a great interest in Lone Pine and its surroundings, as the brigade had been in the trenches, opposite or in the vicinity, since May. As we had been improving and extending our trenches, the Turk had been doing likewise, though, as we discovered later, he had made a much better job of his being able to obtain material, which we could not get.

At the landing, the troops were in excellent physical condition. They had trained hard and had for the greater period been on good food. This condition enabled them to stand up to it for quite a while, but after the landing the food was unfit for troops who were continually under a heavy strain. Salty fat bacon, bully beef, rock-like biscuits, jam that poured out like water, constituted the ration for three months. (There were no canteens on Anzac.)

This deficiency in food, together with the lice and flies, brought the troops to a low state of health. The flies were extremely bad. After the attack by the Turks in May, the dead lay out in no-man's-land until the Armistice, some days later. During the Armistice parties of men went out to assist in burying the dead. During the afternoon they became sickened by the stench and gruesomeness, despite the cotton wool plugged in their nostrils. A staff officer came along, however, and urged them to stick it out, as time was getting short.

A man reached down to a body near him to drag it away, but as he did so, it came in half. Those who have seen sheep lying out dead for a few days, with flies swarming round the carcass, may guess what battlefield burial is like. It was too bad for the staff officer. He hurried away. The dead were mostly buried under a few inches of soil, which to a certain extent smothered the smell, but did not check the flies from breeding and coming over the parapet; these dropped into our food.

During the period between May and August, the troops were either in the front line or in close support – about fifty yards in the rear; those in support being on fatigue, bringing up rations and water, or sapping, with each battalion doing its own pioneer work.

By July the health of the troops was in a very low state – 75 per cent had diarrhoea, and many had sores breaking out on them due to bad food. Sick parades were big. The medical officers did what they could, but very few of the sick were ever evacuated. When word was passed that an attack was to be made on Lone Pine, feelings were mixed – the spirit was right, but could the troops do it? But it seemed the news, when it was drunk in, acted as a tonic. The men forgot to curse the fatigues and war, and the listless air was thrown off. This was what they needed.

By this time the men knew one another; they had lived and worked together for close on four months; and they felt, given an even break, they could do the job. If an incentive was needed, it was the thought that only a few hundred yards in the rear was the sea.

It was frequently discussed among the troops as to what would be the position, should the Turks break through at any point. Such a possibility was always to be reckoned with, so the opportunity of placing more distance between themselves and the sea was welcomed.

Preparations for the attack now became advanced. Bayonets were sharpened, calico patches for back and arm of tunics were sewn on. The secret firing line – about forty yards in front – was practically completed. Keen interest was taken in the destruction of the enemy's wire. At first the artillery did not get on to it too well; but on the day of the attack they got their range, and practically destroyed it, to the great relief of the troops, as they knew how well the Turks' machine-guns had the front ranged. The Howitzers at the same time were firing on the trenches to keep the Turks down; also to destroy overhead cover, but very little damage was done to the overhead cover.

The day before the attack the 6th Reinforcements of the 2nd Battalion joined up and we were very pleased to see them, though they met with very heavy casualties in the attack. At 5.30 p.m. on 6 August, three companies of three battalions hopped over practically simultaneously; one company from the secret firing line, and two from the old firing line. Nearly all who went over in the attack expected to find trenches something like our own – a little head cover here and there but mostly open, but to their surprise nearly the whole of the front line was wired with very solid timber. This checked things a bit and upset the organisation a little. Some of the attackers went straight over the top; others endeavoured to pull the head covering off; while others looked for openings which they found here and there – sally ports probably used by working parties.

This check caused many casualties, for, while men were endeavouring to enter the trench, a number were shot through the loopholes, and others were caught by machine-guns from the flanks. Eventually the Diggers got into the trench to find numbers of the Turks in tunnels which led towards our front line. Some of the enemy resisted for a time but others surrendered right away. Those of the troops who went straight over the top caught a number of Turks in the communication trenches, and they were mostly shot down.

The Australians were greatly handicapped in that very little was known of the system of the Turks' trenches, so that when they happened in to the communication trench, they only had a vague idea of where they were. Consequently they had practically no touch with their flanks. These parties formed themselves into posts, and consolidated their position by erecting sandbag barricades, and fire-stepping the trenches.

It appeared at this time – about dusk – that had a trained brigade been available to go through, a lot of enemy territory could have been won. We were not aware at the time that the attack on Lone Pine was just a demonstration.

The trenches were now in a bad state – full of dead and wounded, and no chance of getting the wounded away, as there were no men available; all were kept busy in securing the position. The saps running back to the old front line were about full of wounded. This meant that as the trenches had to be cleared, the dead and wounded were placed anywhere out of the road. During the night some of the posts were kept busy repelling counterattacks; others were fairly quiet, though all hands realised that the morning would bring the general counterattack.

When dawn broke, to the surprise of the troops they saw Suvla Bay full of transports, while in the valley west from Lone Pine, the Turks could be seen in large numbers moving towards Suvla. We then realised that somebody else must be having a busy time.

The counterattacks commenced shortly after dawn before the posts were connected up. At first the attack was not pressed strongly; the organisation of the enemy did not seem to be too efficient. He would attack, but then let up for a while; probably he was not certain what trenches we had occupied.

Later on, after his artillery had shelled the trenches without doing a great deal of damage, he made several counterattacks, coming over the top in fairly large numbers, but the rifle and machine-gun fire stopped him before he got far. He then resorted to severe bombing attacks, but that is where he had us.

In most of our posts not a bomb was to be had. Despite that our men were smothering enemy bombs before they burst; others catching them and throwing them back; casualties became too heavy, and the remnants had to get back to fresh positions. If there had been a sufficient supply of bombs (jam tins at that) available, very little, if any, of the ground just captured would have been lost. It was poor consolation to know afterwards that bombs were available in the rear.

The Turk continued the counterattack throughout the day but by now a few bombs were available and the Turk was well held. Still our casualties mounted up and the same position arose – the trenches again became impassable and it was impossible to get rid of the badly wounded. Some of the dead had to be put over the top to make room. Wire netting had been sent up and erected in places and this eased the situation somewhat. The cooks had managed to get some tea through during the day and it was very acceptable. The troops, however, were more weary than hungry.

Finally the position was consolidated and held. At no time was there any talk of retiring from the Pine, and had a supply of bombs been kept, many casualties would have been avoided. In many posts the men were without officers for long periods, and carried on.

Lone Pine was an example of frontline discipline of the AIF – an example that was emulated throughout the rest of the war.

Reveille, July 1931

Joseph James Collingwood, MC, MM, service number 147, embarked with the 2nd Infantry Battalion in October 1914, aged thirty-two. At Gallipoli he was promoted to sergeant and ultimately commissioned as a captain. At Lone Pine he was engaged continuously for forty-eight hours in hand-to-hand fighting and throwing bombs at the enemy; he survived the battle unscathed. 'Joe' Collingwood was decorated for bravery on the Western Front and returned to Australia as a major in August 1919. London-born, he had served with British forces in the Boer War, came to Australia in 1909 and took up mining around Inverell, NSW. After WWI he became a farmer at Forbes, NSW and president of the RSL sub-branch there. He died in Sydney, aged eighty-two, in August 1965.

Lone Pine: A Padre's Memoirs

By the Very Reverend. A.E. Talbot, MA

The initial attack on Lone Pine was made on Friday 6 August, at daybreak. The previous night we held service in the dugout church behind the lines at the head of Shrapnel Gully. The church had been an ammunition dump, and though improvised, it possessed a Holy Table, on which rested a wooden cross made by one of the pioneers.

The church was circular in shape, like a miniature amphitheatre, and the seats rose one above the other. The roof was the sky overhead, and we looked down the gully to the Aegean. That Thursday evening we knew, or we guessed, that a move was imminent, and so we celebrated the Holy Communion, the church being crowded. About 100 received the sacrament, and I still treasure the chalice that I used on that memorable occasion. About half the men who communicated must have fallen the following day.

I well recollect the morning of 6 August, for I accompanied a party of batmen, carrying provisions to the front line. I had my pockets full of biscuits, a pudding in a tin in one hand, and a bottle of something or other – it wasn't ginger beer – under my tunic, under each arm. I don't know what happened to the party or the provisions, for a Turkish bullet grazed me as we crossed an open patch, and I crawled the rest of the way, until I dropped into a hole that was filled with wounded. We could scarcely see one another for the smoke of the continually exploding shells.

It was a deadly fight at Lone Pine and we lost many fine officers and men. Our men, in the face of great odds, and with deadly losses, held the trenches they had captured. I shall never forget as long as I live, seeing the 4th Battalion coming out of the trenches when it was relieved either during or after the fight. The men looked like a thin line of spectres. One officer who knew me well stared at me with glassy eyes, and failed to recognise me. We only realised how great the cost had been when we began to bury the dead.

Padre McAuliffe and I went together to say a prayer over the dead who had been buried, in some cases many together, nearby where they had fallen. As in many cases we had no idea to which religious flock they belonged, and the members of different flocks were all mixed up together, the good priest in such cases blessed the grave, and I, with solemn prayer, committed the bodies to the earth. I remember burying about nineteen in one long trench at Brown's Dip.

A young officer, just arrived on the Peninsula, was in charge of the burying party. I asked him for the list of the dead, and when he showed it to me I recognised the names of several I knew well. One was that of Dr Digges La Touche, one of our leading Sydney clergymen, who, when he could not get an appointment as a chaplain, enlisted as a combatant, holding the rank of 2nd lieutenant; and on being discharged for some physical defect, enlisted a second time as a private, rose to be a sergeant, and landed on the Peninsula just in time for Lone Pine, as a 2nd lieutenant. He fell, I understood, just after he had leapt over the parapet. Some days later a man gave me his prayer book, which he had picked up at the spot where he fell and died.

Another name on the list was that of Major C.D. Austin, a fine soldier who was always found at his post in the frontline trench. I went down into the grave and took a last look at the faces of my friends who had paid the supreme price of their loyalty to Australia and the Empire.

Reveille, August 1932

The Very Reverend Albert Edward Talbot (1877–1936) was Dean of Sydney for twenty-four years from 1912. After service at

Gallipoli he returned to Sydney in February 1916 and retained an association with the Australian military for the rest of his life.

The Reverend Dr Everard Digges La Touche is commemorated by a stained-glass window in St Luke's Church, Dulwich Hill, and by a plaque in St Andrew's Cathedral, Sydney.

The Remarkable Mr Digges: A Gallant Conscientious Objector

By Private Desmond Irvine Tomkins

As there were no positions [available] as padre in either the army or the navy, Digges La Touche enlisted in the infantry, the roughest and toughest part of the army. He and I were in the same tent at Liverpool camp. It was very rough on him, not being used to living under the conditions in a partly organised camp.

A lot of the men were also rough, both in speech and actions. When they found out that Digges was an ordained minister of the church, he was baited and insulted by many. I was only a country kid, and like Digges, I had no worldly experiences to boast about, while neither of us drank, smoked or used bad language, so this seemed to forge a bond between us.

One night when we were saying our prayers, which we always did, the 'bully' of the lines came into the tent and insulted both of us in a very filthy way.

Digges immediately got up and asked the bully to withdraw the remarks. The bully then said, 'If I slap one side of your face, will you turn the other cheek?'

Digges said, 'Yes' and the bully did slap Digges's face.

Digges turned the other cheek and the bully said, 'You'll remember this one!'

It never landed. I never saw Digges hit him, but there was the bully flat on his back, gasping for breath. There were no more insults or rude remarks passed.

Digges said it was wrong for him to strike the man, but he said, 'I'll apologise and tell him I'm sorry I hit him.'

'He was going to hit you very hard,' I said. Digges replied that it was not what he was taught, nor was it what I taught in my classes.

When I asked him why he was in the army, where he may have to kill, or he himself be killed, he said, 'I will never kill any man or beast, even though I may lose my own life. The Commandment "Thou shall not kill" will never be broken by me, but I may be able to help in other ways.'

As I was under age and in the army with a forged consent, I took the first opportunity of getting away, while Digges joined an NCOs class. On the morning of 6 August 1915, imagine my surprise when I saw my friend Digges, now a lieutenant of my own unit. Two officers and 136 other ranks landed during the night to join the battalion.

That evening we were to attack the Turkish defences at Lone Pine. We were out of the line, resting and getting ready for the attack, the place being Brown's Dip. Seeing a revolver on his hip, I said, 'You are carrying arms – has your attitude about killing changed?'

'No,' he said. 'When the time comes I'll lead my men forward but I will not use the gun. I do not think I will have to. I feel my time has come to meet my maker. Ask the men if they would like to say any prayers with me.'

About eight men did join us. I remember reciting the 23rd Psalm, finishing with the Lord's Prayer. Digges then said, 'In a couple of hours we will be in the Valley of Death. Fear no evil, do your duty as you must. I know you will.'

As the men were leaving, Digges said, 'Would you mind leaving me alone for a few minutes?' He joined me later, saying he had made peace with God.

He then said slowly, 'I know I'll be killed. I am prepared and not afraid. Do not grieve for me my true friend. I strongly object to war. I object to the killing and maiming of all God's creatures. I love my God, my King, my Country and my fellow man. I'm a conscientious objector, but I believed it was my duty to come and help those who needed it.'

The attack was timed at 5.30 p.m. We were in our positions waiting for the whistle blast that would send us on our way. Digges handed his revolver to one of his men. Holding up a small stick, he said, 'This is all I need.' When the whistle blew, Digges led his platoon forward into a hail of rifle and machine-gun fire.

Seconds later Digges was dead, and so died a good and gallant man. So good that in St Andrew's Cathedral, Sydney, you can see a plaque, 'To the gallant memory of Lieut. Digges La Touche, 2nd Battalion, killed in action 6/8/15.'

Reveille, February 1969

Private Desmond Irvine Tomkins, of Surry Hills, Sydney, was a clerk and aged only eighteen when he enlisted in February 1915. He was posted to the 2nd Battalion, 4th Reinforcement, and embarked on the Argyllshire *in early April. He returned to Australia on 25 January 1919.*

Providence Good to 'Cutsie'

By Captain Dal Cummins

Digger F.W. Cutts, of Lagoon Pocket, Queensland, can thank Providence for having at least on two occasions intervened to save his life.

'Cutsie', as he was known to the old hands, enlisted just after the outbreak of war, in the 15th Battalion. He was a Boer War veteran and a bit of a wag. During the early Peninsula days the 15th had many torrid times in and around Quinn's Post, and on 15 May, if my memory is true, Jacko was particularly hostile. The trenches were only a few yards apart, and the number of cricket-ball bombs which came over kept the Diggers hopping and cursing.

Many of the bombs were thrown back for Jacko to sample, but for us more often it was a case of duck, or a job awaited the stretcher-bearers. Then quite a number came over together. When we'd got to comparative safety, Cutsie could be heard shouting, 'It's a fizzin', it's a fizzin'.' When the dust and smoke cleared we found Cutsie pinned down by a fall of sandbags, with a dud bomb resting against his head. He couldn't move his body nor free his hands to throw the bomb away.

He was pretty shaky when pulled out, but a good 'double header' from the SRD bottle [emergency supply, probably of rum] put him fairly OK, though it took him some time to recover his nerve. Later on he was promoted to the Sanitary Squad, and it was with it that he had his second narrow escape from death – an experience which still lives with him, and very vividly so when he meets any of the old hands. Their greeting is, 'It's a fizzin'.'

About 23 August the 15th Battalion had advanced its position slightly, and Cutsie had the job of digging a latrine. The day was hot and he was showing signs of wear. The going was hard and water was scarce. A Digger who, with a number of others had been pulling Cutsie's leg, jumped into the hole and said, 'Hop out and I'll give you a spell.'

Cutsie had hardly climbed out when there was a thud and a groan, and the fellow who had relieved him dropped dead – skittled by a couple of stray machine-gun bullets from a Turk gun on Hill 971.

Reveille, March 1931

William ('Dal') Cummins was an eighteen-year-old butter factory hand whose address was given as Canal, Ballina, NSW, when he enlisted in September 1914 and was posted to 15th Battalion, 'F' Company, to embark on the Ceramic *in Melbourne in December. By August 1915 he had been promoted to lieutenant and in the following March, to captain. He was discharged in February 1918 and died in 1974, aged seventy-eight.*

Private Frederick William Cutts survived the war and returned to Australia in 1918. At the time of his enlistment in December 1914 he was listed as a 34-year-old labourer and a British veteran of the Boer War.

Heroism Plus Modesty

By Major General the Honourable Sir T.W. Glasgow, KCB, CMG, DSO

Among the many acts of heroism which one observed at Anzac, the two described below have appealed to me as typical of the strong sense of mateship which was one of the most admirable and valuable qualities of the men of the AIF.

On 7 August 1915, as one of the subsidiary operations undertaken with a view to helping the main offensive against Sari Bair, a party from the 1st Light Horse Regiment attacked the Turkish position opposite Pope's. They succeeded in reaching the third enemy trench. The operation proved very costly, and the Australians were so reduced in number that they were hard put to it to keep the enemy off, especially as, being in an angle of the trench, they were being bombed from all directions.

Their situation was rapidly becoming extremely desperate, as they were running out of bombs, so they signalled to their comrades in the old front line, acquainting them of their difficulties. In a very short time a light-horseman was observed to jump out of the old trench and run across no-man's-land with a sandbag full of bombs for his mates in the captured enemy trench.

No-man's-land was covered by the enemy with both rifle and machine-gun fire, and had a bullet struck one of the detonators in the bag, the man would have been blown to pieces. His clothes were practically shot away, but fortunately he escaped unhurt. His action was one of the most gallant I have seen.

On the same day, in an adjoining section – Russell's Top – a man was wounded, and fell down the precipitous side, lodging near the foot. His mates at Pope's noticed he was moving. Accordingly one of them rushed down Pope's Hill, along the gully, up the side of Russell's Top, and picked him up. Then, noticing the wounded man's hat on the ground beside him, he put him down, thrust his hat on his head, picked him up again, and carried him to safety.

All this happened within 200 yards of, and in full view of, the enemy. For some reason the Turks – either because they were so surprised that any man should have the audacity to attempt such a daring feat, or else that they recognised his gallantry, and were chivalrous – did not fire.

Reveille, March 1930

Sir Thomas William Glasgow (1876–1955) was a teenager when he joined the Wide Bay Regiment, Queensland Mounted Infantry; while serving in the Boer War as a lieutenant, he was mentioned in despatches and awarded the Distinguished Service Order. When WWI broke out he was appointed major in the 2nd Light Horse Regiment and landed at Gallipoli on 12 May 1915. He became acting commandant of Pope's Hill and on 7 August he led 200 New South Wales light-horsemen in an attack on Dead Man's Ridge. All but forty-six were killed or wounded. Glasgow was among the last to retire, carrying with him one of his wounded troopers.

In 1916, promoted to brigadier, Glasgow led the 13th Infantry Brigade at Pozières, Messines, Passchendaele, Mouquet Farm and Dernancourt. On 25 April 1918 the 13th and 15th Brigades recaptured Villers-Bretonneux, a feat described by Sir John Monash as the turning point of the war. Glasgow was promoted to major general and appointed commander of the 1st Division, which participated in the massive offensive in August and September.

Back in Queensland, Glasgow was elected to the Senate in 1919 and from April 1927 until October 1929 was minister for defence, before losing his seat in 1931. In 1939 he was appointed Australia's first high commissioner to Canada. He returned to Australia in 1945.

Indian Mule Driver: Sublime Heroism

By Brigadier General Cunliffe-Owen, CB, CMG

In May 1915 the beach at Anzac was a crowded mass of men, stores, carts and all the impedimenta of a large army. At short intervals, bursting shells stirred up this moving mass and made momentary gaps.

Oblivious of the danger to life and limb, boats' crews continually landed and pushed off. Australians bathed, while the shells blew the water up in showers of spray. There were occasional shouts of 'Stretcher-bearers!' when men were badly wounded. The slopes of the hills rising from the beach were covered with dugouts, hospital tents, ammunition dumps and moving figures. In the trenches further up the hills, the Australians and New Zealanders were face to face with their enemy – the Turks – and the roar of rifles, machine-guns, bombs and other warlike noises went on day and night.

I had climbed up Plugge's Plateau – a rough plateau with a precipice on the sea face, about 400 feet above the beach – to watch the fire of a New Zealand battery engaging the Turkish artillery firing from 'Baby 700'. Our guns were concealed on the top of the plateau, and the gunners, stripped to the waist as they served the guns, bent double to escape observation. This battery had been in action since the first landing.

As I left the battery a storm of shells all round made me run to such cover as I could get. I reached an overhanging rock, from which I could see the beach. Below, in a gully, was one of the tanks in which was stored water, brought each night by lighters from Imbros – an island fifteen miles off. There was no water to be found inside our holding. Every pint of water had to be carried up the heights nightly, to the thousands of men in the trenches. We luckily had two Indian mountain batteries, and their mules spent their nights taking water up the mountains. What they could not carry had to be brought by hand.

As I was watching the beach, I saw many bullets hitting the ground near the tank. It was late in the afternoon, and I saw an Indian native driver leading his mule down the gully. The mule had 'puckals' (water bags) on its back. Just as the tank was reached, so many bullets fell near that the mule became uneasy. The driver spoke to the mule, quieting it, and then led it back about fifty yards to safety under a bank. He then took a leather bucket and, utterly oblivious to the danger to himself, he went backwards and forwards fourteen times, between the tank and the mule, till the water bags were full.

He was evidently seen by the Turks, as a perfect hail of bullets followed his steps, knocking up the sand all round. On his last trip he was hit in the foot. He sat down near the mule and talked to it for some time, then, tearing off a strip from his puggaree [turban or scarf], bound up his bleeding wound and limped off, leading the mule up the heights again. The native driver never knew anyone was watching his bravery and self-sacrifice. I was too far off to recognise his features, but made careful note of the markings on the mule, and I felt sure I could identify it.

Next morning I visited the Mountain Battery's mule lines on my way back from the trenches. A native officer, a fine old Sikh, told me they had just been heavily shelled and many killed. Among the debris I recognised what was left of the mule I sought. The driver was lying dead and mutilated beside it.

His name, I found, was 'Mutto', and he was of low caste. He and his mule had been inseparable for eight years. They had been through two campaigns on the Afghan frontier before coming to Gallipoli. 'Mutto' never said he was wounded, as then another driver would have taken his mule. 'Mutto' and his companion lived and died together. Who knows but in 'Mutto's' low-caste Paradise they may be still together!

Brigadier General Charles Cunliffe-Owen (1863–1932) was a Royal Artillery officer who had served in the Boer War and was posted to the Anzac headquarters staff as the senior artillery commander.

How Kitchener Landed:
A Secret History

By General Sir John Monash, GCMG, KCB, VD

The following narrative – not, so far as I know, previously published – may be found interesting. Late in the evening of 12 November 1915, I received a signal message in the following terms: *Meet Corps Commander foot of Mule Gully 11 tomorrow morning. Service dress, belts etc. Leave your ADC* [aide-de-camp] *and armed escort at least quarter mile from meeting place.*

It was difficult to guess what such a mysterious message could mean. Proceeding to the rendezvous, after a tramp of over two miles, mainly in trenches, I found a number of brigadiers assembled, including Sir Andrew Russell and General Johnston, and also divisional generals, among whom was General Godley, and we were presently joined by General Birdwood.

We all stood on the beach gazing out to sea, when, at precisely 12 o'clock, a tiny picket boat was seen threading its way unobtrusively between the throng of lighters, barges, punts, destroyers and submarines lying in Anzac Cove.

General Birdwood went along by himself to the foot of the little jetty, and welcomed a very tall officer in plain service khaki, who had with him a very small retinue. When the party approached us it was seen to consist of Field Marshal Earl Kitchener of Khartoum, General Sir John Maxwell, and Sir Henry McMahon, the high commissioner for Egypt.

The Field Marshal came over to our little group and was introduced to each of us in turn. I happened to be the first Australian to whom he spoke. He said, 'I have brought you a personal message from the King. He wants me to tell you how much he admires the splendid things you have done here.'

There followed a long and intimate discussion, and the party then went into Monash Valley and climbed Walker's Ridge, and K. of K. had a good look for himself.

What he thought about it all he did not say, but after a couple of hours on shore he slipped away into the mists of the Aegean Sea as quietly, as unobtrusively and as secretly as he had come.

Reveille, March 1930

Sir John Monash (1865–1931) was trained as a civil engineer and rose to be considered Australia's finest military commander and one of the best generals in the Allied forces of WWI. Initially he commanded the 13th Infantry Brigade, then became commander of the 4th Brigade in Egypt and at Gallipoli. In July 1916 he was appointed to head the new Australian 3rd Division in France and two years later was given command of the Australian Corps. He planned the August 1918 offensive, in particular the successful Allied attack at the Battle of Amiens, which hastened the end of WWI.

Gallipoli Cheeses

By 'Paleface'

In a sequestered portion of the beach on the Gallipoli coast a field hospital was established, and the wards were contained in marquees. There were two patients in the dysentery ward, who began to realise that the system of starvation then in vogue made the cure worse than the complaint. These two Diggers got their heads together and launched an adventure likely to remedy the situation.

At some little distance from their ward a stack of cases of cheese was guarded by Imperial troops – one sentry only being posted. To this dump Fred Rawkins and Tony Griffiths departed in the still watches of the night, after having previously reconnoitred the position, both intent on doing a bold stroke for what they deemed a deserving cause.

They stealthily approached the objective, and saw that, although dog tired, the youthful Tommy sentry was keeping his watch fairly well. Now to capture a case of cheese under those conditions required some strategy, and they decided that one should keep watch on the sentry whilst the other lifted the case.

Fred Rawkins was the scout, and he stole round to the side of the dump on which the sentry was resting on his beat – the latter, however, was far from asleep, and Fred found himself looking along a glittering bayonet faintly visible in the starlight.

'Halt! Who goes there?'

'Oh, 'salright, cobber – just blew along for a yarn,' was our Digger's reply, and soon a quiet conversation was going on. In the meantime Tony had approached the ration dump from the reverse side, and was expecting to be able to carry out his venture undetected.

All went well until Tony eased the top case over and prepared to lower it to his shoulder, and at that critical moment, the hoop-iron, with which the cases were bound, caught on a nail in the lower case and set the whole column in motion. There was a startling crash as the cases reached the ground, and the sentry rushed towards the sound.

'No,' said Rawkins. 'It's all right, ole man. That's only me cobber, liftin' a case o'cheese for the pore starvin' chaps in the trench,' and with that he handed the Tommy a half-crown piece.

'But it'll be missed,' said the sentry, without omitting the action of pocketing the coin.

'Not it!' responded Fred. 'D'you think they knew what was here when you took over? Not a bit of it. They'll never jerry.'

By this time Tony had regained his breath, and had steadied his frantic heart sufficiently to permit of a hasty departure with the goods. At the appointed rendezvous Fred re-joined Tony, whom he found with the opened case gorging the cheese.

'This beats Fray Bentos!'* said Tony with mouth filled and a smiling face. Fred Rawkins was not long in following suit, and when they had both satisfied themselves they cut the cheese up into large pieces of about two pounds weight and carried them back in an overcoat slung over the shoulder.

At the marquee all was peaceful, and these adventurers stole softly inside and quietly went round to each bed, and, after waking the patients, handed to each one of these a huge slab of cheese. Needless to say, these Diggers were heroes forthwith, for only those who have been so very unfortunate as to suffer from dysentery with no other food than tinned dog and hard biscuits, can realise how welcome was the change.

---

* The 'Fray Bentos' referred to was a processed meat which in the hot climate became runny and greasy and was described officially as 'very, very salt and very stringy bully'. Bread was always in short supply, and many Australian soldiers had poor dental health and were unable to chew the hard biscuit rations. The prevalence of flies, which fed on both human and animal corpses, created terrible health problems, and as many as 1000 men a day were evacuated sick, including those who needed urgent dental treatment. Statistics suggest that at any given time, at least 18 per cent of Australian troops were sick or wounded, reaching a peak of 32 per cent in September 1915.

All would have been well if it had been left at that, but success breeds daring, and these two foragers set out for the quartermaster's marquee and succeeded in pilfering some bread. A glorious night was spent by the patients, and the remnants of the cheese were placed under their pillows for safety.

On his rounds the next morning the medical officer said: 'Orderly, what's the strange smell? The place seems clean enough. Open up the flaps and let some fresh air in.'

Later on the quartermaster missed the bread, and a thorough investigation was made, but not a trace could be found. The only man who seemed to get wise to the happenings was the orderly, and a piece of the cheese bought his silence.

This diet had its effect on the patients, and whereas they had been going from bad to worse before they took a hand in feeding themselves, they were now able to be discharged from hospital for duty in about two or three days.

The Listening Post, August 1922

The names of **Fred Rawkins** *and* **Tony Griffiths** *do not appear in the nominal roll but we suspect the names were changed for the purpose of this article to mask their identities.*

A Useless Digger

Author unknown

The Anzac troops were under the command of Lieutenant General William Birdwood, a very popular leader who made a point of touring the frontline trenches and positions and was in the habit of taking a daily swim off the beach, despite the danger of enemy fire.

It happened one fine morning at Anzac Cove, when 'Birdie', after his usual morning dip, was drying himself vigorously, with his back towards the sea and his thoughts on the front line.

A Digger was floating a punt in from one of the boats and seeing a fellow on the beach, he heaved a line alongside him and yelled for the supposed Digger to give him a pull in. 'Birdie' sidestepped a pace or two and went on with his drying, the line slipping back into the water.

With a flow of profanity about people rearing useless children, the impromptu punt man coiled up his line and heaved it on the other side of the bather, but a bit closer. Still not connecting the 'Wake up, Dig, you stupid blank, and give us a tow' with himself, and being deep in thought of bigger things, the 'Little Chief' sidestepped a bit the other way.

Then followed a flow of the choicest 'Billingsgate' while another Digger came to the rescue and the punt was stranded. Bouncing off at once, the ignored punt skipper approached the bather who was too proud to help, informing him as he approached in the 'choicest Barcoo' what he thought of him and his parentage.

By this time 'Birdie' had come back to earth and astonishment was writ large on his face, when the other Digger got the ear of the irate punter, and whispered in his ear that he was addressing the commander-in-chief!

With an exclamation that only added to the general's bewilderment, our hero beat it at his best pace up the beach. When No. 2 Digger gave a full explanation to Birdwood, the latter's hearty laugh could be heard up at Army HQ.

The Listening Post, August 1926

Captain W.C. Scurry: The Inventor Who Saved the Gallipoli Evacuation

By W.L. Paterson

'I would rather have him with one eye than a dozen others with two. In my opinion, he is a military genius of a type unfortunately only too rare.'

That is what Brigadier General 'Pompey' Elliott wrote in September 1916 from 15th Brigade headquarters of a man who, at his home in Silvan, Victoria, is now just barely able to distinguish night from day. Fate, and the war, have indeed dealt unkindly with this man – a man who is deserving of the best his country can offer him, for he it was who, with a couple of bully-beef tins and a piece of string as his inspiration, undoubtedly saved the lives of thousands of the AIF at Gallipoli.

Then a stripling just turned twenty, Lance Corporal William Charles Scurry fooled the whole Turkish Army and enabled a force of 100,000 to sneak away from the Peninsula under Abdul's very nose without a casualty, and to such effect that a firing front of about twenty miles was completely empty for half a day before the ruse was suspected. Scurry it was who invented the automatic firing device which kept rifles popping long after the troops had departed.

This splendid soldier was born at Carlton, Melbourne, in 1895 and was employed in his father's firm – Wardrop, Scurry & Co., architectural modellers. Soldiering was his hobby. He was commissioned in the 58th Infantry, Essendon Rifles, in 1913, and immediately on the outbreak of war, offered his services, but was considered too young for an AIF Commission. He was for a time engaged at the AIF Depot at Broadmeadows but deserted while on leave and enlisted in Melbourne. Lieutenant-Colonel Hart winked at the desertion and allowed young Scurry to sail with the 8th/7th Battalion Reinforcements in August 1915.

His part in the Evacuation is now history. His automatic firing device was almost laughable in its simplicity. Its principle was that water should drip from a tin into another one below, which was attached to the trigger of a rifle. When sufficient water was in the bottom tin it fell with a jerk, and off went the rifle.

To help fool the Turks, a three days' silence was observed about three weeks before, scarcely a shot being fired during that time. After those three days, men were gradually slipped off the Peninsula, until only a skeleton army was left. These, too, quietly faded off, with Scurry among the last party of the 7th to leave – and long after the last man had gone, those rifles were still popping at intervals, completely pulling the wool over Abdul's eyes.

Scurry was mentioned in despatches, awarded the Distinguished Conduct Medal and promoted sergeant, and in the following month he was given his commission. He was transferred to the 58th Battalion, with which he went to France in June 1916, and a few days later 'Pompey' sent for him and asked if he could make a trench mortar battery. Scurry admits he had no idea what a trench mortar looked like, but nevertheless he agreed.

'Pick three officers and sixty other ranks, any you like in the brigade,' directed Elliott. So the 15th Light Trench Mortar Battery came into being under the command of Scurry, with the temporary rank of captain. Exactly a fortnight later, Scurry used his eight guns with such success in action at Fromelles that he was awarded the Military Cross.

Disaster was in store, however, for this brilliant young officer. It was part of his job to examine and report on any enemy trench mortar projectiles of a new pattern. He was given the fuse of a German 'Rum Jar' which had failed to explode, and finding the fuse of unusual pattern, he stripped and reassembled it. In it was a small safety block which was supposed to fall out during flight. This block became displaced, without Scurry noticing it, as he was replacing the detonator, and as he turned the fuse over, the striker dropped and up went the whole concern. Such was the grit of this youth that the soldier and scientist in him made him forget his pain, and while his wounds were being dressed he was busy explaining the working of the fuse to the battalion major – information that proved particularly valuable.

A couple of fragments in the right eye, a shattered right index finger, later amputated, and several other wounds in the chest and face were Scurry's portion, and a long spell in the 3rd London General followed. His right eye useless, Scurry was boarded for Australia but he was eventually allowed to re-join his battery. After a couple of weeks, however, the wound on his hand broke out again, he was found out, and sent back to the 3rd General. This time he looked a certainty for Australia, but once again he had his own way, for Sir Neville Howse VC, after a heart-to-heart talk, let him go back to his battery in time for the Bullecourt affair. Owing to his defective sight he was sent to the 1st Anzac Corps School at Aveluy in June 1917 and emerged as chief instructor for the 5th Divisional wing.

Arriving back in Australia in May 1919, Scurry joined his father in the old firm and married Sister Doris Barry of Semaphore, South Australia, who had come back in the same ship after service in France and Italy. In September 1920 Scurry's left eye failed, but a strong lens gave him some sight in the right. In 1923 his eyes compelled him to give up his work as a modeller. Scurry then bought a property at Silvan with the intention of growing passionfruit, but eventually he was driven to realising that to save what little vision he had left, he must give up all exertion.

And so, for the last three years, this great-hearted soldier has had no occupation, with little but his pension to keep him, his wife, and four bonnie little girls. But does he complain? No! Scurry has lost none of the spirit which made him an outstanding figure among men who were real men!

Reveille, December 1932

*During WWII, **William Charles Scurry** re-enlisted and, with the rank of major, was posted as commandant of the Tatura Internment Camp. After being discharged in 1945 he retired to Croydon, where he died on 28 December 1963.*

The Last Shot on Anzac

By Major J.P. Caddy, MC

On Thursday 16 December, most of the 5th Field Company embarked, leaving me with Sergeant Conran and Corporal Penny in charge of engineering operations on Russell's Top, which was to be the last spot evacuated. The 17th and 18th were spent in completing arrangements for firing the mines, finishing the defence system, setting traps for the Turks, and a mine was laid under the road to the beach near the 20th Battalion headquarters.

About 1 a.m. on 18 December the supply dump on North Beach caught fire. As this dump contained a number of drums of oil, it made a big blaze, and it then seemed that the Evacuation must be discovered, and that those of us in the rear party had a very poor chance. The enemy artillery opened fire, but nothing else happened, and the fire was soon extinguished.

Right up to the last, men were left in the faces of the tunnels tapping with picks so that the enemy would think that mining operations were being continued. The morning of Sunday the 19th was quiet, and although our planes were in the air all day, when an enemy plane came over it appeared that the rear party would have no chance of getting away, although as the day wore on and nothing happened we were more hopeful. The day was spent waiting for the end and testing the connections with the mines to ensure that they would explode when required.

The Evacuation proceeded smoothly and by 7 p.m. there were only 140 men left on Russell's Top. About 11.30 p.m. we again thought it was all up when Sergeant Vince of the 20th Battalion, who was on watch up Malone Gully, reported that 100 Turks had come down the gully towards the beach. It was afterwards ascertained that this was only an ordinary working party.

The evening was occupied in telling yarns while the last parties checked off. Major Fitzgerald was quite calm and collected during the whole of the night and kept us cheerful throughout the rather trying time of the final stages.

At 1 a.m. the four officers left at the Rear Party HQ – Major Fitzgerald, Captain Hutchinson (the medical officer), Lieutenant Broadbent and myself – decided to have supper. During the last few days plenty of good food, the like of which we had never had before on the Peninsula, was available, and the meal consisted of sardines, biscuits, pineapple and mock cream, and soup! After we had finished the table was left laid for the Turks, with a note written by Major Fitzgerald, which read: '*Good-bye Jackie, will see you later. You are a good fighter, but we don't like the company you keep.*'

It was still doubtful whether the mines would be fired or not, so we fixed up an arrangement which, if necessary, would fire the mines some hours after we had left. This consisted of a sandbag suspended by a string and a candle, which, after staying alight for about two hours, would burn the string, causing the sandbag to fall on the exploders and fire the mines.

At 3 a.m. Russell's Top was the only frontline post held, and the last party withdrew from there at 3.15 a.m. At 3.25 a.m. the machine-gunners of 'P' Post, the last party on the inner line of defence, got away and there was still no sign of the enemy, who was keeping up the normal rifle-fire that went on every night. Everyone was now clear of the trenches and Major Fitzgerald, having received permission from Colonel Paton by telephone to fire the mines, instructed me to do so.

At 3.30 a.m. Sergeant Conran pushed down the exploder connected with the mines in L.8 and L.11, and immediately afterwards I fired the mine in Arnall's tunnel. The ground vibrated, there was a dull roar, and two large craters were formed, seventy Turks being killed by the explosions. Immediately heavy rifle-fire opened up along the whole of the enemy line.

After slabs of guncotton to destroy the exploders had been set off, and Corporal Penny had lit the fuse of the mine on the track leading down to the beach, we made as quickly as possible down the hill and embarked on the last lighter, which at 4 a.m. conveyed us to the transport standing by a short distance from the shore.

As we steamed away about 5 a.m. and had our last look at Gallipoli there was still no sign of anything unusual except the dumps burning near Suvla Beach. Our feelings of surprise and relief at the successful accomplishment of this operation without the loss of life were mingled with a feeling of 'going back': on the many good pals lying in the graves on the narrow strip of land which was now left to the Turks.

Reveille, December 1932

James Pascoe Caddy was a 33-year-old mining engineer from Beecroft in Sydney who had served for two years in the St George's Rifles, Citizen Military Forces, when he embarked as a lieutenant with the 17th Infantry Battalion, 3rd Reinforcement, in August 1915. He was promoted to Captain in March 1916 and to major with the 5th Division Engineers in February 1918, and returned in July 1919, having been awarded the Military Cross.

The Desert

'Our horses were for one period without water for sixty-three hours. It says volumes for the staying power of the good old Waler that in this engagement we did not lose a single horse, except by enemy action. Besides being without water, our horses were compelled to stand with the saddles on, linked up in the blazing hot sun, tormented by the flies, and had very little to eat except barley.'

— S.J. Barrow

The Original Battle of the Wazza

By Lieutenant F.E. Trotter

The first (or original) Battle of the Wazza was fought in the Derb el-Wassa, at the Wassa Karal. Hundreds of Australian and New Zealand troops participated in the fight to free their comrades-in-arms from unjust arrest, and as a protest against the overbearing arrogance of the native police. I am in a position to give you a very fair idea of the various happenings of this particular battle, not only because I was blamed for beginning it, but because I was actually one of the chief actors in it. I will tell you the full authentic story, and you shall judge as to whether the lack of discipline and the atrocities attributed to the Australians were correctly described.

It was a leave day for our battalion. I had lunched leisurely at a small Italian restaurant in the Bazaar el-Meureur. From there I went to the Brasserie du Mirroir in the Sharia el-Genaieh and partook of shrimps and a tankard of *birah*. Then, hiring a *gharry*, I was driven to the Wassa in the native quarters of old Cairo. I strolled along the narrow laneway, looking with interest at the mats and souvenirs, at native dancers and hire-women lying prone upon their mats.

Presently I came across a large crowd of natives, laughing, and jabbering with excitement. In their midst were three Diggers who belonged to my platoon. They had been imbibing too freely and were disporting themselves in comic fashion, fraternising with the Arabs, and dancing to some native music. They were the cause of much amusement to a large crowd of filthy denizens of the Wazza.

Presently a Shawish – native police – tried to manhandle and arrest them, which they naturally resented. The biggest man of the three was about to strike the policeman, when I pushed through the crowd and held his arm. I had taken pains to learn something of the Arabic language, and I told the policeman to leave my comrades alone, and that I would be responsible for them, if he would guide us out of this maze of native lanes. I gave him a couple of piasters to do the job. So away we went.

After some distance, my beery pals began to demand a '*mahal raha*'. I explained their wants and the policeman piloted us through an open doorway. No sooner had we stepped into a large room than the doors clanged behind us. To my surprise I found we were in an office with what appeared to be a chief police officer seated at a table. It then dawned upon us that this must be a police station. The officer was a young, smart-looking man, whom, later we learned, was of Turco-Egyptian descent. I began to back out of the room, apologising, and saying that I had made a mistake.

'Oh, no,' said the officer, speaking perfect English. 'There is no mistake. It is according to plan. Please give me the names and battalions of yourself and your companions.'

'Why?' I asked. 'Please tell your men to open the doors and let us go on our way.'

'No,' he said. 'You will stay here. I want your names and particulars.'

'You be damned!' I roared.

'Hush!' he remonstrated. 'You are not allowed to swear here.'

'I'll use any language I like,' I bawled. 'Don't you try to run the rule over me, old cock. I demand that you have those doors opened for us.'

'It cannot be done,' he said. 'You are in my power. The walls are strong and the windows are barred. I have many policemen here. It will pay you to submit and give me your names.'

No matter how much I argued, he would give no reason for his action. He just had us there, arrested, an easy victory. I thought he could frame up any old yarn about us, and get a feather in his cap for our arrest. In the meantime my three companions began to spar and wrestle with half a dozen policemen.

He gave a sign to our erstwhile guide, who began to rush out to fetch the irons, but I stopped him with a punch in the mouth, then, thoroughly mad, I turned and drew blood from the nose of that autocratic officer. I yelled to my pals to go their hardest, and to fight their best. They did. The office was soon a whirlwind of battering fists, writhing bodies, overturned tables, flying chairs, scattered papers, with grunts and curses, as four Australian soldiers fought a squad of blue-uniformed Arab police.

Somehow the fighting mass surged through the doors into a courtyard, where more police joined in. We were overpowered by sheer force of numbers, and eventually pushed into a dark cell. I shouted to the others not to let the police out of the cell, so they would not be able to shut the cell door. A bottle of kerosene stood in the corner. One of my mates picked it up and crowned a policeman with it. One of our lads picked up a bucket from another corner and he slugged a couple of Arabs on the head with it, before it was torn from him.

Suddenly a loud hammering came on the main door, and an Arab guard opened it a crack to tell some Diggers that there were no Australian soldiers within. An Arab woman had told these Diggers that some Australians had been locked up in the Karal.

The moment I saw the door ajar I shouted to my pals to rush it. I knocked down my chief adversary (the officer), ran for the door, bustled the guard to one side, and slipped through before the door slammed shut again, with the other three still inside, fighting like demons.

The group outside was much too small to force an entrance to rescue the others, so we ran in different directions to bring up reinforcements. By coincidence, the three enquirers at the door were members of my own battalion (my own company, in fact), and one of them was a crack fist-fighter.

A New Zealander I met blew a whistle, and in little or no time a goodly collection of New Zealand soldiers were rushing to the spot. Before long hundreds of troops, Australians and New Zealanders, were attempting to force an entrance to the building to rescue the three prisoners.

Some of the attackers had confiscated axes and sledge hammers, and finding the doors and window bars giving way under the onslaught, the police officer threw the doors open and ordered his police to attack, at the same time shouting in Arabic to the hundreds of natives watching the affair: 'Come on, Mussulmen. Death to the Christian dogs!'

Thus exhorted, a seething mob of natives rushed the soldiers from the rear. Knives flashed, axes were splitting heads, and NCOs were thrusting with bayonets with good effect (privates were not permitted to carry them on leave). I saw an Arab corporal fell one of our fellows with an iron bar; another Arab downed at least one Digger with an axe; fisticuffs were going strong.

At length we gained the interior of the prison and dragged our three companions to freedom. Then the police lost heart and gave up the fight. The civilians began to fall back. I shouted, 'The boys are out! Fight through and get away!'

But our men stayed on to punish the offenders. A chaotic mass of struggling soldiers and Arabs were strangling, chopping, striking and stabbing. Then several Shawish grabbed me from behind, pulled me down and dragged me into the prison. The doors banged and I was a prisoner again in the hands of the Arab police.

The chief leered at me in triumph. Then, at his command, one of his men punched me in the stomach, and winded me. They dragged me into the same cell that I had previously occupied with my three companions. I was thrown onto the stone floor. The door was shut and locked.

The irony of it! To come to the assistance of comrades in trouble, to settle the dispute for them, then to be tricked into this Wassa Karal. I had fought my way out, organised the storming of the Karal, had my mates released, and now, at my own command, the Diggers who could have helped me were gone. And I, innocently enough, was imprisoned in a cell with filthy, slimy walls and floor, and with the prospects of a court martial. A gloomy outlook for an ordinarily well-behaved soldier.

Eventually a British escort conveyed me to Kasr el-Nil Barracks, where in an army prison without food or bed, I spent the remainder of the night. A guard from my own battalion escorted me back to my unit, and the following day I stood before my colonel telling him the whole story, which, fortunately, he believed. I was exonerated from the charge of 'creating a disturbance' brought against me by the Wassa chief of police.

But the matter was by no means allowed to stop there. The groundless charge by the police and their trickery had the troops puzzled and irritated, especially with the knowledge that many of their mates were in hospital with wounds and other injuries. Deputations were sent to the military heads, and an enquiry was set in motion. It revealed that the Wassa chief of police was working for the Turkish government and was creating trouble with the British troops by frequent unnecessary imprisonments. Moreover, it gave a line on the mysterious disappearance of various members of the units. There was no doubt that he was a dangerous man, and an enemy to the Empire. He was dismissed from the service, while a number of his men were imprisoned on charges of rebellion and inflicting bodily harm.

The Queensland Digger, April 1939

Frederick Edmund Trotter sailed on the Hororata *in the fleet that left Albany on 1 November 1914. He was then a 26-year-old salesman living at Pleasant Hill in central NSW. He enlisted as a private but was promoted to lieutenant and in October 1917 was awarded the Military Medal for devotion to duty and assisting the wounded at the Battle of Broodseinde Ridge, east of Ypres.*

Battle of the Wazza

By Major Dick Radclyffe

One evening, I was walking past Shepheard's Hotel in Cairo with an Australian officer, when I saw a huge crowd in the distance. Investigating, we found a large number of troops assembled in the Wasser. Some men had set fire to a brothel, and the crowd was enjoying the sight. We hurried back to Shepheard's and reported the incident to a British staff officer, but, as he received the news very casually, we went back to the scene and joined the spectators.

The brothel had been fired on the ground floor. While the bottom of the house was burning, some of the troops went to the upper storeys and threw the furniture into the street below. Down below there were willing hands to help in building a pile for a bonfire. Soon came the Gyppo fire brigade, which got its engine to work and its hose out in record time, gleefully assisted by the troops.

When all was ready, the leaders lifted the nozzle of the hose, and stood poised, waiting for the water to come. Nothing happened. The Diggers had cut the hose in a dozen places and the precious water was flowing down the gutters. The fire brigade retired sheepishly. They had come at a trot ready to show the Australians and New Zealanders how fires were handled in Cairo. It was a pity to have disappointed them.

An Australian picket arrived. The officer halted his men in the middle of the road and walked over to the burning building, but the crowd immediately jostled him. We went over and suggested that he could do nothing single-handed against so many. We had, we told him, reported the occurrence to headquarters staff, so that the best thing to do was to stand by until reinforcements came. Like a sensible man he accepted the advice and became an onlooker, with his men.

The fire blazed away merrily. As soon as the fire got too hot in one house for the furniture throwers, they would proceed to the next, mostly by way of the roof. Altogether, about six brothels were burnt in this way. The crowd below continued to swell, and the raiders were given increasing encouragement.

After the orgy of destruction had been going on for about an hour, General Maxwell, GOC [General Officer Commanding] Egypt, arrived and took charge. All officers in the vicinity were called upon to serve and asked to form a line in front of the burning building to keep the crowd back. The fire brigade returned, and, with new hoses, protected by the line of officers, put out the flames.

Orders were then issued to clear everybody out of the surrounding buildings. The owners of the houses and rooms did not relish this intrusion. Many of the rooms were locked, and the doors had to be battered in. On one floor, some troops were found locked in – in a building next to the fire. The Battle of the Wazza might have been their one and only battle, had the fire not been put out when it was.

After the hubbub had quietened down, and most of the crowd had been dispersed, a troop of yeomanry commenced to clear the street. Another troop advanced from the other direction. In the middle of the street, riding a donkey, was a Digger. Realising that there was no escape, this Digger waited until the yeomanry troop reached him, and then he placed himself at their head and gave the order to charge! Even the generals could not help joining in the laughter.

Hardly anybody regretted the destruction of a few houses in the Wasser. The authorities had reason to be grateful to the Australians for helping towards clearing an area which was as much a disgrace to the army as it was to the civil authorities.

Mufti, November 1940

Major Dick Radclyffe (1881–1950) was an officer with the NZ Army Service Corps when the above took place. English-born, he had served with the South African Constabulary in 1906, arrived in Victoria in 1908 and married. He was in Auckland when he enlisted for WWI and sailed from Wellington in April 1915, serving on the Western Front, and landing back in Melbourne in May 1919. He served as president of the Merbein RSL sub-branch.

The Story of a Patrol

By Brigadier General L.C. Wilson, CMG, DSO

The period was the end of July 1917, the scene the neighbourhood of the River Gaza, in southern Palestine. In the previous March and April had occurred the two attacks on Gaza which had resulted in the repulse of Murray's army, followed by the appointment of Lord Allenby to supreme command.

Then followed a period of reorganisation and reinforcement prior to the breaking of the Turkish line in October 1917. During this period of comparative inactivity, the opposing armies took up fortified lines facing one another. The lines on the sea coast at Gaza were only a few hundred yards apart, but as they stretched out for some thirty miles to the south-west, towards Beersheba, they widened out to about fifteen miles apart.

This no-man's-land between the two lines was open, treeless, undulating country, with practically no obstructions – ideal country for mounted troops. A mounted division was always stationed on our extreme right and supplied patrols to watch and reconnoitre this unoccupied land, to give notice of any threatened advances and to ascertain any retirements of the enemy. These reconnaissances were done by varying bodies of mounted men – sometimes a troop, sometimes a squadron, sometimes a regiment, and sometimes a brigade. The parties went out by day and night and many were the clashes which took place between the opposing cavalry. I must say that we usually had the better of these conflicts.

On the night of 30 July 1917, the Anzac Mounted Division was holding the right flank, and to the 2nd Light Horse Brigade fell the duty of sending out parties to Gaza and Beersheba. The 6th's job was to scour the intervening country, ride off any Turkish patrols, and see that the Turkish posts were still occupied and note any movement of large bodies of troops.

Shortly before 11 p.m. that night news was received by brigade headquarters from the British posts in the neighbourhood of Gaza that a Turkish infantry division had that night been observed marching south-east along the Wadi Imleh towards Beersheba. This would mean that that division would in ordinary course march between the 6th Regiment and that regiment's bivouac, and possibly cut them off. In view of the fact that the Turkish line was well supplied with artillery, and the 6th Regiment would in its present position be within easy range of the Turkish batteries, it was most important that that regiment should get back before daylight, as if it were caught in daylight between the Turkish division and the Turkish line of posts, that would have been the end of it.

It therefore became necessary that the 6th Regiment should be warned as soon as possible of the dangerous position in which it was now, so that it could lie quiet until the Turkish division had passed, and then return safely to its lines before dawn.

Instructions were sent to the 5th Regiment to send out a patrol at once to warn the 6th. As commanding officer of the 5th Regiment, I instructed Lieutenant David Broughton to take his troop and carry out the required duty. In a job of this kind one can only give general instructions, and the officer in charge of the party must be left to act according to circumstances. Broughton left camp at 11.10 p.m. with his troop to find the 6th Regiment.

The night was clear and the moon was four days to the full. When Broughton had proceeded some miles in the direction of the 6th Regiment, the Turkish division was seen a half-mile ahead, as a long dark ribbon stretching away to the right and left until both ends became lost in the moonlight. This division consisted of some 8000 to 10,000 men marching in columns of fours, with varying distances between the battalions – anything from 100 to 200 or 400 yards apart. The Turks had a few small cavalry patrols on the right flank, that is, on the side Broughton was coming.

Broughton now had to make a decision. He could have adopted the attitude that he was too late, as the Turks had got between him and his objective, and he would have been justified in standing fast. The alternative was to try to ride through the Turkish column. It would have been no good galloping through a gap, for the unusual movement would have immediately attracted the attention of the Turks and would probably have resulted in the destruction of his patrol and of the 6th Regiment.

The only course was to try to slip quietly through one of the gaps in the column as if his party were one of the Turkish cavalry patrols changing from their right to their left flank. This he decided to do, and after riding for some time along the flank of the Turkish column until two battalions had a gap of some 300 or 400 yards between them, he quietly worked in and went through the gap at a walk.

The Turks, as hoped, apparently thought he was one of their own patrols changing flank. After passing through, he gradually moved out towards the left and carried on until he found the 6th Regiment. He gave the necessary warning and that regiment stopped all movement, kept quiet and out of sight of the Turks until the Turkish division had completely passed.

When they had done so, the 6th Regiment, accompanied by Broughton, came back to their lines across to Wadi Ghuzzi without its presence having been suspected by the Turkish division.

I consider this the finest example of light-horse patrol work that came to my knowledge during the war.

The Queensland Digger, April 1938

Lachlan Chisholm Wilson was a 43-year-old solicitor from Albion in Brisbane. A Boer War veteran, he embarked with the 5th Light Horse in December 1914 with the rank of major. He served with distinction at Gallipoli, where he led troops in seizing a position known subsequently as Wilson's Lookout. In the Middle East he took part in almost all the major engagements between the Battle of Romani (4–5 August 1916) and the capture of Damascus (October 1918). On the eve of the 3rd Battle of Gaza (30 October 1917), Wilson was given command of the 3rd Light Horse Brigade as colonel and temporary brigadier general. In the 2nd Battle of the Jordan (30 April to 4 May 1918) he seized Es Salt. Forty miles behind the Turkish lines after the breakthrough at Megiddo (20 September), Wilson's brigade advanced on Jenin, capturing three or four times their own number. On 1 October Wilson changed the course of the Battle for Damascus by directing his brigade through the city at dawn, leaving thousands of Turks cut off while his regiments pressed up the road to Homs. He called off the pursuit on 2 October after taking another 2000 Turks; in a fortnight the 3rd Brigade had captured over 11,000 prisoners. After WWI Wilson returned to his law practice and became a director of the AMP Society.

The Camel in Warfare

By 'Billzac'

To the average Australian landing in Egypt with the AIF, the camel was rather a smellful novelty. My initial experience with these splay-footed, humped backed, ungainly looking animals was at Zeitoun, near Cairo. Hearing myself hailed, I saw an Imperial officer with a very worried expression on his face, holding a rope to which a camel was affixed.

'Do you know anything about camels?' he queried. 'If you do, would you mind folding this bally thing up for me so that I can mount it?'

I did not know anything about camels, but I recollected that in the early days of the goldfields of Western Australia, where camels were extensively used for the transport of goods, the Afghans used to induce the animals to kneel by the use of the word '*Hooshta*'.

The species of camel utilised in Egypt, I discovered later, did not understand the language. The Gyppo, when he wanted the camel to 'fold itself up', or what is known in Egypt as '*barak*', made a gurgling sound and sometimes used a little persuasion by tapping the back of the camel's forelegs. The more we tugged at the camel's head and the more we tried to relax its forefeet, the more obstinate it became. The head lifted disdainfully higher and the feet became more firmly implanted in the sand. After the use of much language, and the shedding of much perspiration on our part, the camel eventually condescended to *barak*.

Later on, I had a good deal of experience with camels. Closer acquaintance altered my opinion. The camel, I found, though not a thing of beauty, was a great asset in surmounting the difficulties of transport encountered over the sandy waterless wastes of Egypt and the Sinai Desert. Indeed, without the camel the desert would never have been conquered. These beasts often carried their riders for nine days without a drink over dry sand, with the glass registering 120 in the shade, carrying his own and the rider's provisions.

The camel was utilised for the conveyance of both fighting men and supplies. Hundreds of Australians who had embarked for Egypt as infantry or light-horsemen were included in a fighting unit mounted on camels and unofficially designated 'the Cameleers'. They were first utilised in squelching the troublesome Senussi. Then they participated in the Sinai Peninsula campaign right into Palestine.

After reaching the hills, and the sometimes slippery ground, of Palestine, the camel's usefulness was not so manifest. They were not so sure-footed as horses over such country, and too slow compared with horse-drawn and motor transport, which the harder nature of the Palestine country made possible and which was an impossibility through the Sinai.

Before the last big dash in 1918, which culminated in the complete overthrow of the Turks and the capture of Damascus and other important centres, the camels were replaced with horses and 'the Cameleers' became light horse. They were a cosmopolitan crowd – fair-skinned and helmeted British 'Tommies'; brown, grave-faced turbaned Sikhs of the Hong Kong and Singapore battery; carefree, irreverent, felt-hatted New Zealanders and Australians.

'The Cameleers' did wonderful work. Everything necessary for the sustenance of man and beast until Palestine was penetrated was carried by camels, of which tens of thousands were used. A Camel Transport Company was controlled by an officer and a non-commissioned officer, either British or Australian. One native was set for three camels, which were led in Indian file. Loads of 200 to 300 pounds were carried, and anything from five to thirty miles were walked in a day.

Each convoy was accompanied by members of the particular army service corps by whom rations were being supplied to units in the field. With the natives chanting that well-remembered dirge of 'Carm Leeilo, carm youm', the ships of the desert meandered slowly over the landscape. It was slow and tedious travelling but the escort of horsemen had to keep awake – particularly in the vicinity of the grocery section.

Gyppo camel men were natural thieves. The ingenuity of the thieving, too, was remarkable. Garbed in a shirt-like dress reaching to the ankles and termed a *'galabeer'*, they were never lost for a hiding place for stolen tins of food. A popular method was to tie the tins about the thighs, and with the *galabeer* as a covering, detection was possible only when a native, through the stolen article slipping its mooring, walked awkwardly.

Possession was sufficient evidence of guilt and the thieves were promptly ordered to lie face downwards while a flogging was administered by a native 'Bas-Ryce' (the equivalent of a sergeant major). The punishment might seem severe but it was the only deterrent. Thieving was second nature with most of the Gyppos. For their five piasters a day (the equivalent of an English shilling) they regarded the job as a most lucrative one. He got many kicks and rebuffs, yet the Gyppo did his part towards winning the war.

The WA Digger Book, 1929

Blue

By 'Camelo'

The Imperial Camel Corps, together with a section of the Light Horse, English Yeomanry, Indian Mounted Battery and minor units, had ridden through the night and succeeded in surrounding the strong enemy positions at Rafa by daybreak.

We had dismounted from our smellful beasts and were preparing to advance when I heard our company commander talking angrily to 'Blue', his diminutive ginger batman.

I heard Blue say, 'You always keep me out of action, sir; and if the war should finish early I should be ashamed to go home without having been in at least one scrap.'

The captain eventually surrendered, saying, 'I promised your mother back in the West to look after you, and look after you I will, and if I let you go today it will be the last time; do you hear?'

I was then called over and the captain remarked: 'Sergeant Major, I am leaving now with the first line. You come up with the second, and keep this young fool near you. Detail someone to stay behind to look after HQ's camels.'

Blue was obviously excited and was jumping with delight. He was a lovable little kid and looked and acted like a schoolboy leaving on a vacation.

We were soon off to the attack, and at about 1500 yards from the enemy's position, stray bullets were flying past and we deployed from echelon to extended order. Blue was chatting merrily to me about four feet on my right, when I saw him lurch forward. I rushed to the kid's assistance and called for stretcher-bearers.

I soon saw that the boy was mortally wounded and before the stretcher-bearers arrived he opened his eyes, and, smiling sweetly at me, said, 'I didn't get far, did I, Sergeant Major?' and fell back lifeless into my arms.

God rest the dear kid's soul. Death was no stranger to me, but his passing affected me queerly.

The Listening Post, January 1925

Es Salt and the Jordan Valley

By S.J. Barrow

Es Salt is a small town about halfway between Amman and the River Jordan. It sits on a plateau which General Allenby considered ideal as a launching point for an attack on the major railway junction at Deraa. A combined British, Australian and New Zealand force took the town in March 1918, but an attempt to capture Amman failed in the face of heavy Turkish and German opposition, and they were forced to retreat back across the river. This article describes the second assault on Es Salt, which took place in late April 1918.

The Valley of the Jordan lies between the hills of Judea and the mountains of Moab. There is little or no vegetation. At the lower end is Jericho, which we found to be a squalid village and very malarial. Snakes, scorpions and insects abound. During the day we were pestered with sand flies, and at night by myriads of mosquitoes.

The River Jordan is very rapid and runs for the greater part of its course between high banks, which are covered with vegetation. The Dead Sea lay to the south-east, about ten miles from our camp, but so flat is the country that it looked about three miles away.

A few days after arriving in the valley, in April 1918, our brigade (the 4th) crossed the Jordan to take part in the second Es Salt stunt. We moved off just after dusk, leaving our fires burning to deceive the enemy. We rode on for about four hours, rested a while, and then moved on again.

Just on daylight Jacko discovered us and started to shell us from the opposite side. We were now around his flank and so between his force at Es Salt and the main body. The shelling continued and we were compelled to trot, and so this part of the Jordan Valley became known to us as 'Iggri Flat' – Iggri being the Arabic word for 'hurry up'. Finally we reached our destination and camped, the 3rd Brigade going on up the mountain to attack Es Salt.

The Hong Kong and Singapore Mountain Battery (a camel corps battery), better known as the 'Bing Boys', now came on the scene, and Jacko started shelling again. The shells landed very close, so we moved out of range. Our 'B' Squadron and the 11th Regiment were at this time holding the ford and all the time were sustaining casualties through shell fire.

We watered our horses at a stream running through a Bedouin encampment, and on our way back made a detour to avoid the shelling. The same night we took over an outpost line, and anxiously watched the ford whence the Turkish attack was expected.

The night passed uneventfully, but next morning we received orders to saddle up, and to go out and meet the enemy. 'C' Squadron leading, we galloped away to get into position to cover the retirement of the 4th and 11th Regiments. We immediately came under a hot fire. Jack Halpin, Grewcock, Dobson, Steele and several horses went down, but the rest of us got to cover. Captain Robey received a bullet in the leg and had to go back to the ambulance.

We now found we were in the wrong position and the brigadier ordered us to a new position. It was necessary to gallop across Jacko's line and he gave us a hot reception, but only a few horses were hit; all the men escaping. The Turks were about 5000 strong and were advancing in good order. Our strength was only about 900 for the whole brigade.

Bill Varney stopped a bullet in the leg. I carried him out of the line, but as the Turks were so near and our stretchers were lost, he was compelled to ride out. Retiring slowly, one regiment covering the other, we managed to get out all right, but were compelled to abandon nine guns, and a part of our field ambulance was captured.

The position was now critical in the extreme. The 3rd Brigade and Anzac Mounted Division were up at Es Salt, and it meant if we lost the road, they would be cut off.

That night we took up a new position. The 11th Regiment was on Saddle Back, the 4th Regiment on Black Top, and the 12th on the flat, our left flank being in the air. We made ourselves comfortable for the time being; two hours on, two hours off.

When day broke, Jacko immediately started shelling and got right onto us first shot. Quinnel, of 2nd troop, received a shrapnel bullet through his steel helmet, the bullet penetrating his head. No one else was hit.

The sun was very hot and our steel helmets were like ovens. Several of our men went down with 'pyrexia' and had to be evacuated. About 4 p.m. the Turks again attacked, and after a great fight against superior numbers, the 4th Regiment retired from its position. The loss of Saddle Back Ridge caused the 12th to be enfiladed so we retired right back to the wadi [a valley or dry riverbed]. All hands were tired out, but we worked all night building sangars [small temporary fortified positions of stone or sandbags]. Both sides slammed over shells for about ten minutes and all was quiet once more.

The next day we were reinforced by the Canterbury Mounted Rifles and the Middlesex Yeomanry, and the following day we evacuated our position. When we had marched some distance our horses were brought to us and after a long ride we re-crossed the Jordan River. By the time we reached Jericho most of us were asleep on our horses. We arrived at our camping ground about 3 a.m., off-saddled, and turned in.

During this stunt our horses were for one period without water for sixty-three hours. It says volumes for the staying power of the good old Waler that in this engagement we did not lose a single horse, except by enemy action. Besides being without water, our horses were compelled to stand with the saddles on, linked up in the blazing hot sun, tormented by the flies, and had very little to eat except barley.

The next day we spent fixing up our camp and finding the gear we had left behind. The night passed uneventfully, but the following morning I was awakened by the stable picquet calling out, 'Taubes over, get to your dugouts!' I think there is nothing more awe-inspiring than a bombing raid. There were fourteen planes over, all dropping bombs.

One bomb fell into the bivouac area of 'B' squadron of the 11th, killing and maiming thirteen men and several horses. Another fell into the Jericho dump, killing a number of Gyppos. Another got our unlucky 4th Field Ambulance, and yet another fell into the lines of the 7th Regiment. Altogether our troops sustained nearly 100 casualties in the Jordan Valley that morning.

Reveille, January 1936

Private Sydney John Barrow, of the 12th Light Horse Reinforcements, was listed as being a 23-year-old stock salesman, his next of kin being a brother in Ontario, Canada.

General Overboard

By General Sir Harry Chauvel, GCMG, KCB

Christmas Day 1917, I spent in a Jewish village called Rehoboth (we called it Deiran) on the Philistine Plain. It was teeming with rain, and we had to get some of our troops back closer to the railhead on account of supply difficulties, so I spent most of the day riding about with my quartermaster-general, seeing that those troops who were 'for it' got across the Nahr Rubin before it became uncrossable.

In the course of our peregrinations, we had come across a dispatch rider of the Desert Corps Signals in difficulties on the new railway bridge over the Nahr. The deck of this bridge consisted only of sleepers. Anyone who has crossed one of these bridges knows how awkward it is without a handrail of any sort.

This dispatch rider had tried to ride his horse across it, and the inevitable had happened. The horse was down, with both legs on one side between the sleepers, and the rider had been in the water. General Trew and I went to help.

There is only one method of rescuing a horse in such circumstances, and it is only feasible when there is plenty of water under the bridge. You unsaddle your horse and unbuckle the reins on one side; then you push him on to his side with his back as near to the edge of the bridge as you can; then you get his two legs out simultaneously, and, using them, tip him quickly over backwards into the water.

This worked out all right on this occasion but, later on after I had left him, General Trew, when returning by the same route, found another horse and man in the same predicament, with some two or three other fellows standing about at a loss how to help. Full of confidence, Trew went to show them how, but, in his enthusiasm to see that it was done properly, did not get out of the way in time, and the horse, in going over, kicked him in the stomach with both hind feet, and put him overboard too. Both were got out satisfactorily, but it was a muddy business.

Reveille, December 1935

General Sir Harry Chauvel was born in Tabulam, NSW, in 1865, his family later moving to Toowoomba. He saw action in the Boer War as a captain, commanding the 'A' Squadron of the Queensland Mounted Infantry. In 1914, as a full colonel, he became Australia's representative on the Imperial General Staff in London.

Chauvel served on Gallipoli as commander of the 1st Light Horse Brigade. Arriving on 12 May, he took command of a sector that included Quinn's Post, Courtney's Post and Steele's Post. Illness forced his evacuation but he returned to take command of the NZ and Australian Division. In November he was given command of the 1st Australian Division and was promoted to major general. Given his choice of commands in Egypt after the Evacuation, Chauvel took charge of the Australian and NZ Mounted Division, then became general officer commanding, AIF in Egypt. Chauvel won the first decisive British victory of the war when he defeated the Turks at Romani.

In August 1917 Chauvel became the first Australian to permanently command a corps – the Desert Mounted Corps – and the capture of Beersheba by the 4th Light Horse Brigade followed. He retired from the army in 1930, having become the first Australian to reach the rank of general.

The Holy City

By Colonel A.C. Olden, DSO

It was at Soba, about six miles from Jerusalem as the crow flies, but considerably further than that in actual distance to be traversed, that we were afforded a first distant view of the Holy City.

The Sheikh – or headman – of Soba approached our troops and, with a profound Arabic salutation, indicated a desire to be on friendly terms with the 'Ingleesi'. Beckoning our men to follow, the Sheikh led the way to the summit of the hill on which the village stands, and, pointing eastward, exclaimed ecstatically, '*Shouf. El Kuds.*' (Look! Jerusalem!).

There, over line after line of terraced hills covered with olive trees and vines, with the limestone road winding its way in and out of them like a tiny white thread, could be seen the glistening domes and spires of the 'City of our Dreams'.

Accustomed as we were by this time to traverse country rich in historical significance, the imagination nevertheless was deeply stirred at the thought that at last, we, the latest of the Crusaders, were within sight of Jerusalem, the Golden.

But there was little time for reflection just then. Away to the north the roar of guns and crackle of musketry told us that the battle was not over yet. Jerusalem itself was not to be harmed, and doubtless the Turks knew it. Also did they know that, could their bastions of Nebi Samwil (Mizpah) and El Job (Gibeon) but hold out, the city might yet be saved from falling into our hands.

Reports were circulated that they had decided to evacuate, but later these reports were contradicted by others to the effect that Jerusalem was to be held at all costs.

The 75th Division had made several desperate attempts to storm Nebi Samwil and El Job, but this splendid division, composed of British and Indian troops, including several battalions of Gurkhas, the division which in reality broke the back of the Turkish resistance at these two all-important points, had lost two-thirds of its strength before it was relieved by the 60th Division, under General Shea, whose right flank it became the duty of the 10th Light Horse Regiment to protect and whose destiny it was to deliver the final knock-down blow which gave us possession of the Holy City.

The city presented a most gloomy appearance on our entry. The inhabitants made an effort to express their pleasure at the arrival of the British, but they had not yet the full confidence in our arms to thoroughly believe that we were 'there to stay', and their reception of our troops was something of a half-timid, half-wistful nature.

The streets of the outer city, though containing many fine buildings of the more modern class, were in a state of indescribable filth and squalor. Hardly a light showed in the houses – the inhabitants having long since burnt their last drop of oil or bit of tallow – and the people, for the most part, were in a pitiful physical condition from want of food. Apparently they had suffered greatly. Certainly, 'Jerusalem the Golden' was not at that time 'blessed with milk and honey'.

Wealthy people had, during the previous two years of war, been reduced to penury in their efforts to obtain food. Their costly apparel, furnishings and other effects had been sold to purchase the necessary bread and meat. In many cases their beautiful houses were bare and destitute within. Most harrowing were some of the stories they told. And yet, such were the natural instincts for trade and the desire for money, many inhabitants of the poorer classes had hoarded small supplies of grain in order that they might sell bread to the British when they arrived.

Even while our guns were thundering from the outskirts of the city at the enemy positions – a bare three miles away – our billets were besieged by hordes of these people, each one with bread and cakes to sell, whilst with our own eyes we saw, in these self-same streets, people, beyond the power of human aid, collapse and die of starvation.

The only sentiment universally expressed by the populace generally was that the 'good English' had come and soon everything would be put right. It was an old cry, and many a time and oft during our sojourn in that war-stricken country was that cry heard from the natives.

That Australia may never see the like within our own shores is the prayer of every ex-service man who witnessed this pitiable picture.

The Listening Post, April 1932

Colonel Arthur Charles Niquet Olden was born at Ballarat, Victoria, in July 1881 and after studying dentistry, set up practice at Narrogin, WA. He joined the Western Australian Mounted Infantry as a 2nd lieutenant in January 1913. In February 1915 he embarked for Egypt with 'C' Squadron, 10th Light Horse Regiment. He landed at Anzac on 20 May and was twice wounded. Promoted to captain and major early in 1916, he returned to the 10th LHR for the Gaza–Beersheba operations of 1917. Olden was in command in September 1918 when the 10th LHR led the Australian Mounted Division in 'The Great Ride' to encircle Turkish armies in Sharon and Samaria. He took the town of Jenin with a charge by a single squadron and captured 8107 prisoners and five field guns in two days. He was awarded the DSO.

On 1 October Olden led a 3rd Light Horse Brigade vanguard through the outskirts of Damascus in pursuit of retreating Turks. He formally accepted the surrender of the city, receiving a remarkable document which hailed him as 'the first British officer to enter Damascus, in the bravest manner known of the Saxon race'. He left the city two hours before the triumphant arrival of Lawrence of Arabia. In retirement Olden served on the executive of the WA branch of the RSL. He died in 1949, survived by his wife, two sons and two daughters.

Ali's Avarice: A Damascus War Story

By 'Camelo'

Turkey's administration of Palestine and Syria prior to and during the war was stagnant with bribery and all forms of corruption. If a servant of the Sultan holding office in those parts for a few years did not accumulate sufficient wealth to retire into affluence with a large harem for the remainder of his days, he was considered to be a stupid unworthy person.

When the Light Horse Regiments were encircling Damascus on 30 September 1918, a party from the 5th and 3rd Brigades captured a train which was trying to escape towards Beirut, through the Abana Gorge. This train consisted mostly of vans filled with valuable goods belonging to high Turkish officials, and in one van was discovered a box containing hundreds of golden Turkish sovereigns.

The lucky men nearest at hand soon relieved headquarters of the responsibility of protecting this wealth, by posting special guards etc., by quickly helping themselves. The difficulty of how to transport the sovereigns appeared, and I know of one man who, after carrying his nose bag full for days, gradually changed them with his mates for the lighter paper notes.

Most light-horsemen heard of this lucky find, but I was fortunate enough to learn the story of the source of the wealth, and the tragedy connected with it.

Two days after Damascus was captured my mate and I were eating in a café in the city when an intelligent-looking Arab seated nearby spoke to us in English. We eventually drew him into conversation, and after relating some of his experiences in Damascus during the war, [he] told us the story, which I will relate, which, by his manner and the earnestness of his tone, we believed to be true.

When war was declared by Turkey every able-bodied man was ordered to report for service. Turkish enlisting officers were appointed in all centres of population to ensure that the unwilling should not evade their responsibilities. At Damascus a particularly corrupt ruthless tyrant named Ali (I forget his name but this will do) was appointed. Ali and his staff combed the city and soon discovered an army of men who had ignored the summons.

Ali was essentially an opportunist, and here was unprecedented opportunity. For two golden sovereigns he gave his captives freedom with the promise that they would not be further troubled by him.

He soon accumulated fabulous wealth, which he managed to transport to his home near Constantinople, but as time progressed his captives became fewer and his income from this source became a diminishing quantity. He broke his promises regarding exemptions and used his squad of slackers as his reserve fund, and if the gold was not forthcoming on every occasion demanded, into the army went his victims. His exemption fee also increased according to his victims' capacity to pay. Ali naturally became the best hated man in the city, and the populace feared even the mention of his name.

When the Aussie troops were approaching the city, Ali tried to escape, but he made a fatal mistake when he advertised his intention by having his belongings, including the box of gold which later pleased a few dead-broke Aussies, removed to the train.

A number of Ali's victims, hearing of his attempted flight and knowing that the city must soon fall to the British, dragged him from the moving train, and next day, just after Colonel Olden and his 10th Light Horse Regiment entered the city, they strung the unfortunate kicking Ali up by the two legs and cruelly finished him off by quartering him.

The Listening Post, September 1923

Armistice Days in Syria

By Sergeant David Woodward Harris

When the Turks finally surrendered on 31 October 1918, the Australian Mounted Division was in the vicinity of Homs, advancing towards Aleppo. The news of the Armistice was received without enthusiasm, for we were utterly weary. Casualties, malaria and all the Biblical plagues had reduced us to a deadly apathy.

The following morning, 1 November, a general was breaking the glad news to the brigade when he caught sight of a trooper wearing an outsized emu plume which had moulted badly – the climate probably, as the Syrian hens have a minimum of meat and feathers. The plume had been issued to the trooper, and though the bare ribbing was incongruous it couldn't have looked more gaunt than its wearer at the time. However, the general considered it was the greatest insult the NSW Lancers had ever received. But the fact that we had offended a general, busted a tradition started by the NSW Lancers and won a war, didn't matter a hoot to us. Nothing short of embarkation on a troopship bound for Australia could have stirred us.

However, we automatically saddled up once more and headed south-west for Tripoli, passing through Homs. In contrast to the majority of Syrian towns, which mostly cling precariously on the sides of steep hills, Homs was built on a large plain. The unusual flatness, and domination by the single mosque and minaret, made a very effective picture, combined with a background of great towering ranges.

Skirting the town, we passed a large cemetery, in which parties of wailing women were trying to out-shriek each other. These marathon mourning contests are part and parcel of the East, but in between rounds the ladies are fanned by their retainers with the most spicy gossip from the four corners.

Our destination was a camp some miles north of Tripoli and our arrival coincided with the commencement of the rainy season. Some Syrians were engaged to make a road along a steep siding. Their ganger told off three men to each shovel, a rope about eight feet long making the dilution of manpower possible. A half-hitch was made in the centre of the rope around the base of the handle. One man dug the shovel into the ground while the other two, with their backs to him, strained at a 45-degree angle in front, on either side. And didn't the two gents on the tow-rope roar if gent No. 1 dug too big a shovelful.

How it rained, never letting up for a minute except on Christmas Day, when by some chronological miracle it ceased for a few hours. In desperation we consulted the oldest inhabitant as to when it would ease up, and he remarked that it never stopped before the end of February. The Lebanon is a narrow fertile strip of volcanic formation between great ranges rising up to 10,000 feet. As in Palestine, all the rain falls in winter. Palestine receives about twenty inches and the Lebanon forty inches.

We had no tents, only a small 'bivvy' sheet, not waterproof like our ground sheet. About 25 per cent of the men were off duty owing to shortage of boots; rations were even lighter now than during fighting, when we thought they reached the indivisible stage.

The horses were in a pitiable condition with the continuous cold and rain and light rations. Those of ten years and older were mercifully shot. My troop horse, a well-bred chestnut from the Charleville district in Queensland, that had carried me right through from the Canal, passed out that way with full honours. But many horses, as game as the best of their riders, were afterwards sold into slavery. In the East animals are treated brutally, and troop horses, above all others, should never have been sold to brutal owners.

Sergeant David Woodward Harris had embarked as a 24-year-old private with the machine-gun section of the 12th Light Horse Regiment in June 1915. His occupation was given as station overseer and his next of kin as his sister, living in Turramurra on Sydney's North Shore. He returned to Australia in July 1919 and recorded, in a handwritten manuscript, 'The 4th Brigade Trek from the Canal to Khan Yunis and the 2nd Gaza Battle'.

For Old Times' Sake

By G.L. Gardiner

Among your old light-horsemen in town and country are there not many who would like to share once more the hardships and dangers of that old time companionship? If so, ride with me once more to Rafa, and as you ride, think of those with whom you rode and fought during those hard adventurous years.

All the morning our lines have been full of that ordered bustle which precedes a stunt. Extra rations have been drawn for man and horse, extra ammunition served out. Now all is ready.

At last the order comes 'Saddle up everywhere!' to be followed in a remarkably short time, for training has made us a very efficient regiment, with 'Lead Out!' We fall in squadron column. Our colonel canters up. There is no fuss. 'Prepare to mount! Mount! The regiment will advance in column of sections! Walk March!'

Gradually the column lengthens as each section swings into place. Now at least we feel that we are off. We march at ease, pipes are lit, and we settle down to the rhythm of our horses.

About dusk we rendezvous with the rest of the attacking division. We halt for some time and make as good a meal as we can, not knowing when our next will be. 'Stand to your horses!' 'Mount!' and we are off on our long night's march. Soon weariness tugs at our bodies. Our rifles grow heavy, and each separate part of our equipment seems weighted with lead. At the end of each hour we halt for ten minutes and perhaps snatch a few seconds sleep.

Dawn comes. We shake off our weariness and look round. We can scarcely believe our eyes. Gone is the desert and in its place we actually see grass. A cock crows and a spontaneous cheer rises from the brigade. We halt while the centre regiments swing into position. The Colonel gives his final orders. 'We will gallop as close as possible; the horse holders will take the horses out of action, and we will continue the advance on foot.'

We are off. Galloping horses everywhere. Soon the airy puff of smoke as the first shrapnel bursts overhead. We see the bullets pecking up the dust ahead. Soon we hear the hum as the long-range ones pass. The fire gets sharper, here a man falls, there a horse. 'Halt!' 'Dismount!'

A flurry of hooves as the horses are galloped under cover. We feel small and insignificant as we continue the advance on foot. Short rush follows short rush; we are getting close up now. Casualties are mounting. The fire grows hotter as we settle down to fight in earnest. The Turks are strongly entrenched. We slowly advance. The day is drawing to a close; our ammunition is nearly spent. Can we do it? German planes are everywhere. They bomb and machine-gun us at will.

Suddenly just behind the redoubt we see the advancing figures of men. They are the fighting New Zealanders coming in with the bayonet. Jack Royston, our brigadier, dashes forward. 'Come on, boys, we've got them!' The whole line surges forward. A short, sharp fight and the redoubt is ours.

The Listening Post, May 1935

Private Geoffrey Gardiner joined the 10th Light Horse Regiment, 4th Reinforcements, as a 22-year-old farmer from Applecross, WA. He sailed on the Argyllshire *in April 1915 and returned to Australia in March 1919.*

Masters of the Air: Palestine

By H. Bowden Fletcher

The Battle of Megiddo – described here by Flying Officer Bowden Fletcher – was fought between 19 and 25 September 1918 on the Plain of Sharon, which was then part of the Turkish Ottoman Empire and today forms parts of Israel, Syria and Jordan. Deceiving the Turkish high command that his next offensive would be launched across the Jordan River, General Sir Edmund Allenby secretly concentrated his forces on the coastal plain. His offensive began with a massed infantry assault that tore a hole in the Turkish line and allowed the mounted forces to be unleashed into the Turkish rear to sever the routes vital for supply and reinforcement. Within twenty-four hours the mounted troops had advanced over fifty kilometres into the Turkish rear areas. The Battle of Megiddo brought about a rapid Turkish collapse, facilitating a swift advance on Damascus by the Allied mounted troops.

For a fortnight preceding the offensive, only one machine succeeded in crossing our lines, and returning in safety, and within seven days the Australian squadron destroyed four two-seaters and eight scouts – a feat that evidently so impressed the enemy with our superiority that thereafter he failed to put in an appearance.

It was during that period that two of our machines encountered the famous 'circus', which, using a two-seater as a decoy, made a bold but unsuccessful bid for aerial supremacy. With the odds seven to two in his favour, the enemy anticipated an easy victory, but in a fast and furious battle he was outmanoeuvred and outfought, losing five of his machines with their occupants, while the remaining brace were sent helter-skelter homewards to tell the tale of their disgrace.

A bullet hole through the tail plane of one of our machines was the total damage inflicted upon us. Two days later a brace of two-seaters attempted a reconnaissance, but were promptly engaged by two of our machines and destroyed.

Afterwards, though we hunted for him day after day, even over his own aerodromes at 1000 feet, not an enemy could be induced to do battle. Having been driven to earth like rabbits in a warren, they refused to come up. As a result of our activities during the early days of the offensive, not a Taube was seen in the sky, and though we bombed and machine-gunned 'Jacko' to our heart's content, our own infantry and mounted troops were left unmolested.

During the battle our work consisted of strategic reconnaissance and bombing, starting with the first grey streaks of dawn, and finishing with the dusk of evening, so that, in many instances, machines made night landings with the aid of flares. As soon as the Turkish retreat commenced on the morning of 19 September 1918, Bristols, 'loaded to the eyes' with bombs and ammunition, started the exciting game of strafing, and kept it up incessantly. Jagged, wicked-looking clouds were plentiful at about 2500 feet, and consequently we flew backwards and forwards just underneath, being bumped and buffeted about by a never-ending series of air pockets. Once over the fleeing Turks we glided down to about 1000 feet, loosed off our bombs, and then, with machine-guns rattling, sprayed the hapless enemy with streams of lead.

While hanging over the side of the fuselage to watch the bombs hurtling earthwards, thoughts went back to the second Gaza stunt, when, in the light horse, we were treated to a plurality of bombs by Fritz, who was then very much cock of the air. After dropping all our bombs and expending all the ammunition, we returned to the aerodrome for a fresh load, glowing with the satisfaction of a job well done and a blow repaid.

While escorting a formation of our big bombers to Afuleh, one of our pilots (Lieutenant Harold Maughan) noticed a machine low down, and taking it for hostile, he immediately dived on it, only to discover, on closer inspection, that it was a bomber landing in enemy country owing to engine trouble. As the ground appeared suitable the Australian landed, just as the first machine went up in flames. Promptly picking up the stranded pilot and observer, he coolly took off in face of a strong body of hostile Turks and Bedouins, armed to the teeth.

During the afternoon of 19 September, congestion of traffic on the Tulkarem–Anebta Road reminded us of a busy city street, and naturally, flying low over such a target, we scattered death and destruction. Like huge vultures we swooped until the Turks became a demoralised rabble, cringing in terror beneath a hail of bombs and lead, and crying to Allah for deliverance. When the light-horse arrived shortly afterwards the Turks surrendered in thousands without firing a shot, and even after capture, persisted in waving white flags whenever one of our 'Tiaras', as they term an aeroplane, flew overhead.

On 20 September, finding that a column of transport we were detailed to bomb had been deserted, the formation split up to hunt for suitable targets. Flying over the hills at a couple of hundred feet, we chased small parties of Turks with bombs and machine-gun fire. The mechanics of the squadron, keen to have their share in putting the wind up Jacko, on this occasion fastened empty cartridge cases to the bomb fins, so that in their mad race earthwards, the ordinary whirr became a terrifying scream.

For the Flying Corps, 21 September was the day of days, and the Australians thoroughly in their element, played an important part. Infantry operations started a hurried retirement of the Turks northwards, along the Nablus–Beisan Road, but just as the huge column of transport and guns entered the narrow pass at Kurbert el Furweh, a formation of machines arrived overhead, swooped down to a few hundred feet, and very quickly had completely blocked the pass with a hideous shambles of dead horses, mules and oxen, smashed transport, wagons and guns, making escape for the terrified Turks by this road absolutely impossible. The accuracy of the bombing and machine-gun fire on this occasion resulted in the whole column, consisting of ninety-seven guns and about 1000 transport wagons (both horse and mechanical) falling into the hands of the victorious troops without a shot being fired – a feat probably without precedent in the brilliant history of the air forces.

One of our machines, which had been attached to the Arab forces under Colonel Lawrence, operating east of the Mecca railway, whilst returning from a reconnaissance, encountered an enemy formation of nine, and, after a running fight of considerable duration, succeeded in landing safely. On receipt of this information, four of our machines were dispatched as reinforcements, and in a couple of days we again decisively drove the enemy out of the air. The Arab outposts were in such a position as to be able to hear the enemy pilots running up their engines, and promptly advised us.

Thus, on many occasions, the rival machines left their respective aerodromes simultaneously, and the subsequent fights were waged at low altitudes in full sight of the Sheriff's army, and as in every case they resulted in the dispatch of a Fritz, the Arabs went mad with delight, capering about like a crowd of children, firing rifles and revolvers promiscuously in sheer exuberance of spirit. When the buses landed they gathered round in open-mouthed admiration of the 'Tiaras' and their occupants, whom they regarded as super men, while the spectacular defeat under their immediate observation of the Fritz airmen brought thousands of recruits to the army of King Hussein.

The capture of the Turkish armies west of the River Jordan caused the troops in the Amman–Es-Salt area (when they heard the news) to mind their Ps and Qs, and as soon as the retirement north along the railway commenced we once more carried out a series of bomb raids day after day. At Mafraq, where the line had been blown up, the trains were disgorging their human freight, and we literally gave them Hell, turning what in the beginning had been an organised army into a demoralised rabble. After the first couple of raids, the roar of an aerial engine was sufficient to send troops and transport off in a mad stampede for safety, over railway wadis and hills in a wild and useless endeavour to escape; thousands falling easy prisoner to our friends the Arabs.

The prisoners, after capture, could talk of nothing else but 'Tiaras' and bombs. German, Turk and Austrian with singular unanimity paid an unwilling tribute to the Flying Corps, by stating that they could stand everything but the everlasting bombing and machine-gunning from the air, which shattered their nerves and brought about utter demoralisation. For weeks before this stunt the squadron had worked early and late on reconnaissance, photography, fighting, patrol and escort duties, so that pilots and observers had piled up big totals of flying hours that would hardly be credited on other fronts.

The close of the offensive, commonly known as the Battle of Armageddon, which resulted in one of the most complete and brilliant victories in the history of British arms, and in which our squadron took a formidable part, found us weary but happy, and distinctly proud of our unique distinction of having won twenty Distinguished Flying Crosses in about six weeks.

Reveille, August 1930

Flying Officer Howard Bowden Fletcher was a 24-year-old auctioneer from Mosman, Sydney, who embarked with the 12th Light Horse Regiment in January 1915 as squadron sergeant major. His DFC was awarded for outstanding service in aerial photography and intelligence gathering, and for the action he described above; he was the observer in one of the two aircraft that engaged seven enemy machines on 24 August. He returned to Australia in December 1918.

Harold Stanley Ryott Maughan, a 21-year-old printer at the time of enlisting as an air mechanic, was the son of Senator William Maughan, of Ipswich, Queensland. Commissioned as a lieutenant with the Australian Flying Corps, he was awarded the DFC for the incident mentioned above, rescuing the pilot and observer of another aircraft, 'displaying cool courage and presence of mind, deserving of high praise'. He returned to Australia in May 1919.

The Sack of Surafend

By H.S. Gullett

An unfortunate incident was destined to throw a shadow over the last days in Palestine of the Anzac Mounted Division. Close to the camps of the three brigades in December 1918 was the native village of Surafend. All the Arabs of Western Palestine were thieves by instinct, and those who dwelt close to the Jewish settlements were especially practised and daring.

Throughout the campaign the British policy was to treat these debased people west of the Jordan as devout Moslems, kin not only to the Arabs of the Hedjaz but to the Mohammedans of India. And the Arabs, a crafty race, quick to discern British unwillingness to punish their misdeeds, exploited their licence to extreme limits.

They learned, also, that there was a disposition in the British Army to assume without justification that any looting and other similar offences practised by the troops against the natives had been committed by Australians. Consequently, if the Arabs missed a sheep from their flocks, they were emphatic that a soldier in a big hat had been seen prowling in the neighbourhood. Seldom punished, they became very impudent in their thefts from all British camps, and at times ventured to murder.

All troops may have suffered equally; but, while the British endured the outrages without active resentment, the Australians and New Zealanders burned with indignation, and again and again asked for retaliation, but without obtaining redress. After the Armistice a few men of the Anzac Mounted Division were shot by Arabs, and the resentment in Chayter's division became dangerously bitter.

The natives of Surafend were notorious for their petty thieving. Prompted, perhaps, by the knowledge that the Anzac camps would soon pass forever from their midst, and emboldened by the immunity they enjoyed, they grew audacious in their pilfering. They were reinforced, too, by a body of nomad Bedouins camped close to their village. The Australians and New Zealanders, sleeping soundly, were a simple prey to the cunning, barefooted robbers, and night after night men lost property from their tents.

One night a New Zealander of the machine-gun squadron was disturbed by an Arab pulling at a bag which served him as a pillow. Springing up in his shirt, he chased the native through the camp and out on to the sandhills, shouting to the picquets on the horse lines as he ran. As he overtook the native, the man turned, shot him with a revolver through the body, and escaped. The New Zealander died as the picquets reached him.

The camp was immediately aroused, and the New Zealanders, working with ominous deliberation, followed the footsteps of the Arab over the loose sand to Surafend. They then threw a strong cordon round the village and waited for morning, when the headmen were summoned and ordered to surrender the murderer. The sheikhs were evasive, and pleaded ignorance. During the day the matter was taken up by the staff of the division, but at nightfall the demand of the men for justice was still unsatisfied.

Meanwhile they had resolutely maintained their guard about the village, and no Arab was allowed to leave. That which followed cannot be justified; but in fairness to the New Zealanders, who were the chief actors, and to the Australians who gave them hearty support, the spirit of the men at that time must be considered. They were the pioneers and the leaders in a long campaign. Theirs had been the heaviest sacrifice.

The three brigades of Anzac Mounted Division had been for almost three years comrades-in-arms, and rarely had a body of men been bound together by such ties of common heroic endeavour and affection. From the Canal onward men had again and again proudly thrown away their lives to save their wounded from the enemy. Not once in the long advance had a hard-pressed, isolated body ever signalled in vain for support. The war task was now completed and they, a band of sworn brothers, tested in a hundred fights, were going home. To them the loss of a veteran comrade by foul murder, at the hands of a race they despised, was a crime which called for instant justice. They were in no mood for delay.

In their movement against Surafend, therefore, they felt that, while wreaking vengeance on the Arabs, they would at the same time work off their old feeling against the bias of the disciplinary branch of General Headquarters, and its studied omission to punish Arabs for crime. They were angry and bitter beyond sound reasoning.

All day the New Zealanders quietly organised for their work in Surafend, and early in the night marched out many hundreds strong and surrounded the village. In close support and full sympathy were large bodies of Australians. Good or bad, the cause of the New Zealanders was theirs.

Entering the village, the New Zealanders grimly passed out all the women and children, and then, armed chiefly with heavy sticks, fell upon the men and at the same time fired the houses. Many Arabs were killed, few escaped without injury; the village was demolished. The flames from the wretched houses lit up the countryside, and Allenby and his staff could not fail to see the conflagration and hear the shouts of the troops and the cries of their victims.

The Anzacs, having finished with Surafend, raided and burned the neighbouring nomad camp, and then went quietly back to their lines. In the morning all the disciplinary machinery of the army was active as hitherto it had been tardy. General Headquarters demanded the men who had led the attack and had been guilty of the killing. The Anzacs stood firm; not a single individual could definitely be charged.

The Queensland Digger, December 1929

Sir Henry Somer Gullett *(1878–1940) was a Victorian-born journalist based in London when WWI began. In 1915 he was appointed official Australian correspondent with the British and French armies on the Western Front. Charles Bean asked him to contribute the official war records for the Sinai, Palestine and Syria campaigns. The extract above (reprinted here by permission of the Australian War Memorial) was taken from his Volume VII of* The Official History of Australia in the War of 1914–18, *published in 1923. Gullett was briefly the initial director of the AWM. He later became Nationalist MP for Henty and a cabinet minister. Sir Henry was killed in the crash of an RAAF aircraft near Canberra on 13 August 1940. Among those killed with him were General Sir Brudenell White, Chief of the General Staff, G.A. Street, Minister for the Army and J.V. Fairbairn, Minister for Air.*

The Western Front

'We lay close to the ground in the snow for a while and listened to a noise like thousands of bees passing overhead. I saw a tank smothered with little sparks where the bullets were striking. Various coloured star shells, flashes in the rear, and overhead, where their shells were bursting, lighted up the snow-covered ground, which was dotted with dead and wounded.'

— Lance Corporal Bert Knowles

Early Raids in France: 9th Battalion's Coup at Fleurbaix

By Sergeant Harold 'Squatter' Preston

Soon after the Australians' arrival in France orders were issued for the capture of German prisoners, and, despite numerous tries, it was not until the end of May 1916 that a prisoner was taken. After this several strong patrols and raids were organised to capture prisoners and inflict loss on the enemy.

Probably the most brilliant of these raids was one conducted by Captain Wilder-Neligan of the 9th Battalion, at Fleurbaix, on 1 July 1916. This officer had already distinguished himself as a sergeant at Anzac, and had the confidence of all who were attached to him.

As one who took part in the preparations and in the actual raid, I would like to recount my experience.

The raid was a 'silent one', without preliminary bombardment. The raiding party consisted of Captain Benson, Lieutenants Young and Ramkema, and 150 other ranks. For days previous the enemy barbed wire was cut by our trench mortars. I well remember one day during one of these bombardments, where the trenches were separated by 350 yards, seeing the butt of a German rifle flung 100 yards behind our lines. What happened to the poor devil who was holding it, I wondered.

Preparatory to the actual raid, no-man's-land was well patrolled. I took part in all these patrols, which were not without excitement and anxiety. During the reconnoitring of the enemy wire on the night of 18 June, Captain Warren was killed. I was one of his patrol, and we were right on the German barbed wire, when suddenly there was excitement in the enemy lines. Evidently we were spotted. There was a lull; then a flash, a bang, and Captain Warren was dead. I will never forget that night, and the trouble we had in getting his body back to our lines.

The raiders, who were volunteers, were trained behind the lines, in the vicinity of Steenwerck. We were kept in ignorance of the date of the raid until the night of 1 July, when we were moved to the final rehearsal point – an old farmhouse just behind the lines.

Our hands and faces were blackened, and we were given chewing gum to prevent us from coughing. My wristlet watch with an illuminated dial was taken from me, and this was my first intimation that the actual raid was about to take place. I was allotted to Lieutenant Ramkema's party, which was in the centre. After taking up our position about 12.30 in no-man's-land, fifty yards from the enemy, word was sent to the artillery and machine-guns.

The artillery laid down a barrage beyond the objective, while the machine-guns swept the flanks. I will never forget that mad rush to the enemy lines, men falling on both sides of me. My gas helmet was torn from me by barbed wire, and I fell into a deep shell hole and lost my rifle, but soon recovered it. Shells were screeching overhead and bursting behind the enemy front line. The wall of flame resembled a bushfire. I could see quite clearly the heads and shoulders of Germans above the parapet – the enemy shooting at us from only a few yards distant.

Just as I reached the parapet somebody alongside of me – I think it was Sergeant Barry – was shot, and fell into the trench. I next heard someone call out, 'Gas!' I reached for my helmet but it was gone.

When I jumped into the trench, which was about eight feet deep, I was confronted by a number of Fritzies in an overhead covered communication trench. I had a good mate in Tom Horsington. He had a good supply of bombs so we soon disposed of the Fritzies and cleared the trench.

Turning into the next bay I saw a dark object. Flashing my torch onto it (the torch was attached to my rifle), I noticed a big Fritz. All he had to defend himself with was a dagger. This Fritz was taken prisoner. I still have the dagger as a souvenir.

Further down the trench an enemy machine-gun was collared. Dan Mahoney did good work here, and was rewarded with the Military Medal. Then came the word 'Imshee' – the signal for all to leave the trench. As I ran along to find a way out I came across Lieutenant Meyers wounded in the neck. I helped him out over the top and then turned in the direction where a lot of fuss was going on.

Lieutenant Ramkema had discovered a dugout with about twenty Germans in it. He emptied his revolver into them and ordered the survivors (about twelve) to come out. Sergeant Kenyon and myself drove them towards our lines.

By this time no-man's-land was being swept by machine-gun and artillery fire. Well on our way our prisoners, terrified by the bombardment, started to give trouble. Some were shot, and the remainder came in without further resistance.

During the stay in the enemy lines all parties had heavy fighting. Captain Wilder-Neligan found an outpost with three men in it. He shot two, the third threw a bomb and Neligan was wounded in the head, but he carried on in command. All parties returned and the artillery ceased firing. Sergeant Lucas and myself returned to no-man's-land and recovered a lost telephone.

The prisoners, about thirty, were blindfolded and taken behind the lines. The raiders – those who were left – were taken back by motor lorries, given a bath and an issue of coffee and rum, and allowed to sleep all next day. The casualties which the raiders estimated they inflicted on the enemy were fifty killed and thirty captured. Our casualties were about seven killed and twenty wounded.

Each raider who survived was promised a holiday in Blighty, but instead had a three days' route march to the Somme and put into Pozières.

Reveille, January 1935

Harold Preston, a nineteen-year-old farmer from Ulmarra, NSW, enlisted in June 1915 and embarked three months later as a private with the 9th Battalion, 9th Reinforcements. He returned to Australia as a sergeant in May 1919.

Two Errors with Neutralising Consequences

By 'Alice', 6th Battalion

It was during the first large raid by the 1st Division in France, carried out by the 6th Battalion at Fleurbaix in 1916. The raiding party of about fifty was divided into four groups, the first under Jack Rogers was the Mat and Wire party, the second under myself was the Left Trench party, and the third, under Alby Hyde, the Right Trench party. Alby – gallant lad – was later killed, I think, at Factory Corner. The covering party, which was to lie under the enemy parapet while we were in his trench, was in charge of Percy Moncur, who was Officer Commanding of the whole raid.

The plan, briefly, was to file out into no-man's-land at 12.30 a.m., lie halfway out there, until at 12.50 a.m. a heavy barrage was to be placed on the enemy trenches and communications. At 12.59 a.m. we were to dash forward from the middle of no-man's-land, and at 1 a.m. precisely, the barrage was to lift from the front trench we were to raid, leaving a box barrage playing on communications and flanks for our protection.

The first error which might have proved disastrous was one of synchronisation. As the party was crawling out through a sally-port, and actually when about half of us were out in no-man's-land, word came to Major Daly (later killed in 1918 when commanding officer of the 6th) standing at the sally-port, that all times had been put back two minutes.

This information was given to Alby Hyde as he was going out, on the understanding that it would be passed on to the rest of us lying out in no-man's-land. Alby, however, apparently assumed that the information had already been passed on and that he was receiving it in his turn – and consequently did not pass it on to us in front.

The barrage started two minutes later, but while we noticed it was a bit slow in starting, we were too strung up to attach any significance to it.

At 12.59 a.m. we dashed forward and began ploughing through the wire in good time to reach the parapet at 1 a.m., when the barrage was to lift – as we thought. But it actually had another two minutes to go!

And then occurred the consequences of the second error, which fortunately neutralised the consequences of the first. I had been patrolling the enemy wire during the previous nights and had got, as events proved, a pretty accurate idea of the strength of the wire defences – but I had completely missed a ditch about ten or twelve feet wide, just under the enemy parapet, and filled choc-a-bloc with barbed wire.

With, as we thought, only a few seconds before the barrage lifted – but in fact with over two minutes to go – we tumbled head over heels into this wired ditch and our parties were completely disorganised. It took us exactly two minutes to plough through that wire and reorganise – and we leapt into the enemy trench just after the last shell of our accurately placed barrage burst. So close were we, in fact, that we got to a machine-gun, enfilading the very spot where we had been struggling, before its crew were out of their funk holes.

We brought back six prisoners and estimated that we killed twelve (later, a report of the 50th Prussian Reserve Division gave its losses in this stunt as killed eleven, wounded twelve and six missing, so our estimate was not far out). We captured a machine-gun and trench mortar also. We had only four wounded, of whom McKenzie died later back in Caulfield Hospital.

And that is how two errors, either of which alone would have had disastrous results, actually resulted in self-neutralising consequences which made possible a raid quoted for many a long day as the most successful of its kind undertaken in France.

Mufti, February 1935

Cookers in the Front Line

By H.J. Maynard, 'C' Company, 55th Battalion

Looking back from the mud holes of the Somme one soon realised that the land of the Pharaohs wasn't too bad after all. But our turn was to come and the late spring of 1916 found us across France. Our line of approach was via Hazebrouck, and eventually we fetched up at a village called Bac Saint Maur, a few miles behind the lines.

The village of Fleurbaix was a couple of kilometres further forward – roughly a mile behind the front line. So peaceful was this village in the ordinary way that the inhabitants continued in residence, and indeed did a very thriving trade, especially the several estaminets. One in particular possessed a gramophone, which I can almost hear now playing 'I'm On My Way to Dear Old Dublin Bay'.

Many of the boys used to carry a bottle of vin blanc up the line with them, and of course, sling the bottle away after finishing it. I can remember one occasion, in company with Frank Tate, Small and 'Puddin' Nelson, when we were on the rocks. We got a bag and made a 'baksheesh' trip up the line and collected fifty or sixty bottles, on which Madame allowed 3d [threepence] each.

Our first trip into the front line was accomplished and great was the surprise of the mob when they found no trenches – only built-up sandbags on the surface. This part of the front was reckoned a real 'rest home' – and so it was, until our stunt at Fromelles on 19 July altered it all.

Our cookers were only just behind the actual front line, and across the way, Fritz's could be seen stoking up after stand-down in the morning. Rations and rum were obtainable without any difficulty, and were plentiful. Those were the days of 'two to a loaf'. Hidden in the mists of the future was the time when it was 'ten to a loaf' and lucky to get that.

A few miles away the sky was lit up every night, and the roar of the guns was unceasing – that was Ypres, they told us. Our days were spent mostly in sleeping, with an occasional sentry posted here and there with a periscope. The heavy fatigues that were such a feature of the days at Gallipoli were absent here. Looking back, it seems that Fleurbaix served the purpose of a kind of short apprenticeship for the more deadly parts of the front we were presently to visit.

Colonel 'Dave' McConaghy was the Commanding Officer of the 55th at this time – a splendid gentleman and a gallant soldier, whom we were to lose in April 1918. Major Cowey was second-in-command and Captain Woods the adjutant. I find my memory failing a bit but I think Captain Holland was in charge of 'C' Company, and big Jim Fraser was quartermaster-sergeant. I have heard it suggested that all the rum issued didn't find its way to the troops – but I'm not expressing an opinion about that. Mick Cantwell, of Singleton, was C.S.M. – he 'went west' at Bellicourt on 30 September 1918.

Pay-Corporal Hancock was another old original. I waited for Blighty leave with him later during the winter on the Somme, but I don't know if he survived the war. Sergeant Jim Doig was wounded in the small attack at Doignies and did not return to the battalion. Jim went with us to the Somme and was with the company in Needle Trench in the early spring of 1917 when we had word that the Germans had gone back. Following up, we came to a halt in a sunken road by the town of Villers-au-Flos. Hereabouts an Aussie, in a very dirty, muddy overcoat, stopped Jim and asked if he knew where to find the 53rd Battalion. Jim, who had an extra drop of rum inside him, said, '—— the 53rd. I don't know anything about them.' The other at once slipped off the overcoat and invited Jim to 'Hop out, you ——' We saw then that he had two stars on his tunic. However, no blood was shed after all.

So things went along quietly enough at Fleurbaix until 19 July. The *Official History* has showed us what a ghastly mistake and tragedy it all was. My own impressions of it were the ridiculous ease with which the first objective was taken and the hopeless 'left in the air' feeling when we were finally withdrawn to our own old line, leaving so many good cobbers behind. A company of the 56th was occupying the old line, and I heard an officer (who seemed boiling over with rage) say that he had a fresh company of men and they wouldn't let him counterattack.

Reveille, February 1936

4th Divvy's First Raid: The OC's Story

By Captain Harold Boyd Wanliss, DSO

The following is an account written to a friend of experiences in the first trench raid made by the 4th Division in France, carried out by 'A' Company of the 14th Battalion on the night of 2 July 1916. The assault party consisted of four officers and fifty-four other ranks, three-fourths of whom had never been in action before. All the officers were serious casualties and forty-one of the fifty-four other ranks were killed or wounded. The writer, Captain (then Lieutenant) Wanliss, was the Officer Commanding assault and the first man to reach the German parapet. He won the first Distinguished Service Order awarded to a subaltern in the AIF.

When we went into the front line we were put in what was known as the 'Nursery'. Hun and Tommy used to fraternise in no-man's-land, send messages across, come out and put up their wire by day, but we (the AIF) changed that. Now it is a veritable Hades, strafes [machine-gun attacks by aircraft] every night, and never the sight of a Hun, though prisoners say they dare not sleep at night for fear of raids, bombs etc.

I got one in the neck just as I rushed up the German parapet, which made me feel silly, but I got our bombers in and scouts along. We blew out the listening posts and cleared the back track; then I had to wait there and see everyone out. Well, I won't mind Hell after that.

There was a lurid glare caused by the bursting shells and flares, a deafening din, and one could hardly stand up for the concussion. Bomb mortars seemed to be bursting everywhere. Under your eyes great masses of trench would float up and disappear; machine-guns and shrapnel were going like Hell.

I was damned annoyed about the wire not being cut and bleeding profusely. Everyone was cursing, though of course you could not hear them. Anyhow, after a few minutes I got the boys out and we struggled back. I got stung then again, shrapnel this time. One officer – Julian from Geelong – was flattened. I lifted him by his vest, but he got caught in the wire and I was too weak from shock to move him. He was dead.

Another fine chap, from Avoca – Sergeant Croft – also went down and we had to leave him, after an effort to bring him back. He too got caught in the wire.

After that I don't remember much until I fell into the stream. That cooled me down and bucked me somewhat, so I crawled and got into a drain, where I waited until Fritz quietened and some stretchers came out. It was awfully cold there. I did not seem to get warm for days.

It seemed to me that we had not done too well, but old General Cox – the general of the division – visited me in hospital and was awfully pleased, and let off the usual talk about 'Anzac spirit' etc. He said we had two killed and twenty-four wounded, and the Huns had fifty outed (no wounded or prisoners) and that included at least two officers of theirs, so that it was not a bad speck really.

I got a No. 9 bullet in the neck under the left ear; it went up through the side of the tongue, smashed through some molars on upper right jaw, and out through the right cheek. The second went in under my right arm and is now visible in the front of the chest. The third just took a nick out of my left side. I put in a day or two in field hospital, and am now in the No. 3 General Hospital, Wandsworth.

Reveille, July 1936

Harold Boyd Wanliss was born in December 1891 at Ballarat, and educated at Ballarat College and Hawkesbury Agricultural College, NSW, before becoming an orchardist near Lorne, Victoria. After enlisting on 28 April 1915, he was selected for officer training at Broadmeadows and embarked with the 2nd Reinforcements of the 29th Battalion on 29 December. Having recovered from the wounds described above, Wanliss became battalion adjutant in January 1917 and a captain in March. His work was marked by attention to detail and concern for his men, notably during the 1st Battle of Bullecourt in April. He began a range of recreational activities for troops out of the line, including a series of lectures and debates on post-war Australia and the Empire. In mid-1917 he requested transfer to a fighting company and was made commanding officer of 'A' Company on 13 August. On 26 September he led it into the Battle of Polygon Wood. Just as he reached his battalion's objective a German machine-gunner shot him through the heart, throat and side. He died instantly, and was buried where he fell.

Memories of Fromelles: 19 July 1916

By Captain A.D. Ellis, MC

At Fromelles all the advantages lay with the Germans, who occupied the higher ground and had been building their defences for eighteen months. The 61st British Division and the 5th Australian Division attacked on a narrow front across waterlogged ground after their artillery bombardment had proved ineffective in cutting the German wire defences. The British troops failed to capture the main German position, a higher point known as the Sugar Loaf, with raised earth and reinforced concrete; as a result German machine-guns had easy targets in the Australian troops on their flank. Fromelles was an Allied disaster, botched by poor planning, decisions and communications. It remains Australia's worst loss of life: 5533 casualties in the one night. The British 61st Division lost 1547 men. The Germans had between 1500 and 2000 killed. Adding to the tragedy was the subsequent knowledge that the British commanders, General Sir Douglas Haig and Lieutenant General Sir Richard Haking, had planned the battle only as a diversion to stop the Germans moving troops further south.

We will never forget the dawn with its beautiful clinging French mists and the promise of a cloudless sky and a bright sun later. We will never forget the conviction so irresistibly borne upon us before the battle opened, that this was to be in truth an ordeal; but that it would prove to be so great an ordeal as it in fact became, nobody, I think, even remotely conjectured. It was the division's first battle, and for that reason it has a significance that no other engagement could achieve.

The total front of attack was to be 4000 yards, the right half of which the 61st British Division occupied, while the left half was committed to the 5th Australian Division. Sir Richard Haking, Commander of the 11th British Corps, was in charge of the operations.

We know now why the operation was determined upon, and we know also why the preparations were expedited to such a degree that they were necessarily incomplete. Sir Douglas Haig, then engaged in the terrible Somme struggle, was repeatedly securing German identifications which showed that the enemy was withdrawing troops from the Fromelles sectors to support the battered German divisions on the Somme. Sir Douglas desired those northern reserves to be kept pinned in the north, and the Fromelles attack was hurriedly conceived and still more hurriedly executed in an attempt to teach the enemy that he could not deplete his northern sectors with impunity.

We all know now that the artillery preparation was inadequate – inadequate, not from any shortcoming of the units concerned, but simply because the guns in the sector were insufficient both in numbers and in weight, and also because the artillery ammunition was all too little. We learned a bitter lesson at Fromelles – that infantry cannot attack prepared positions with any hope of success without a tremendous volume of artillery support.

That curious feature in the German front line, which we called the Sugar Loaf, perhaps did more than anything else to determine the issue of the conflict. It was on the left front of the 61st Division, but so near to the 5th Division's right brigade (15th) that it readily commanded the wide stretch of no-man's-land which General Elliott's troops had to cross to reach the enemy front line.

With an effective artillery bombardment, it is probable that the Sugar Loaf defences would have been shattered. As it turned out they were not shattered, and an ominous rattle of machine-gun fire broke from it as the assault opened at 5.45 p.m. on 19 July 1916. The onus of taking the Sugar Loaf lay on the 61st Division because it was in that division's sector of attack. The division failed to take it, and it enfiladed General Elliott's gallant battalions as they strove to cross 400 yards of no-man's-land. A few of them almost reached the enemy wire, but the rest were all killed or wounded within a few minutes of the opening of the attack. The survivors dug in and fought on. They did everything but retreat.

Sir Richard Haking heard of the hold-up occasioned by the Sugar Loaf, and proceedings were set in train for a special assault upon it to be conducted by two companies from each of the two divisions. Later information showed General Haking that this project was impracticable. He countermanded the order for the special attack on the Sugar Loaf; the countermanding order reached the 61st Division's troops in time, but failed to reach the Australian battalions before Major Hutchinson and the gallant officers and men of two companies of the 58th Battalion had perished gloriously in a hopeless assault on the Sugar Loaf.

We all know how the 8th and 14th Brigades reached their objectives. They crossed no-man's-land, which was much narrower on their fronts. And stormed the enemy front line and beyond it. We know how all through the night they strove to organise a line of defence some hundreds of yards behind the enemy front line so as to be able to withstand counterattacks in the morning. We know how grimly they strove on through the night, losing officers and men steadily as the hours passed. We know how frantically the engineers worked to get communication trenches across no-man's-land to our men in the enemy trenches.

As dawn of the 20th became manifest, comparatively few survivors of the 8th and 14th Brigades were left. These were holding positions devoid of natural advantages and wholly inadequately prepared to sustain determined counterattacks. The pressure on General Tivey's left front became irresistible. Fighting to the last, the wearied men were forced inexorably back. It was obvious that it was impossible to retain the position, and the survivors made the best of their way back to their own front line.

The 14th Brigade held on a little longer. The 8th Brigade had, in a measure, protected its left flank, but when that protection was withdrawn the same relentless pressure compelled their withdrawal.

The 61st Division did not attain even the measure of success that the Australians achieved. On the extreme right, a few Warwicks did penetrate the German positions and take a few prisoners, but they appeared to have left almost immediately, and the attack in the centre and on the left, again largely by reason of the Sugar Loaf, failed to reach the enemy front line at all.

The attack was launched at 5.45 p.m. on the 19th; by 9 p.m. that night all of the 61st Division troops who survived were back in their own front line. The remnants of the 15th Brigade battalions, which had dug in near the German wire, gradually drifted back to their own front line as the impossibility of achieving anything became obvious. The 8th Brigade survivors reached their front line shortly after dawn on the 20th, and the 14th Brigade elements were all back within an hour or two later.

For a time the enemy troops were heavily massing for counterattack, and it appeared extremely probable that they would make some attempt to assault our front line. Apparently, however, they thought better of it, for no attack eventuated.

The total casualties of the 61st Division were 1547. The Australian casualties in the twenty-four hours amounted to over 5000, distributed amongst the infantry brigades as follows: 8th Infantry Brigade, 1900; 15th Infantry Brigade, 1776; 14th Infantry Brigade, 1717. The Divisional Engineers lost three officers and eighty-five other ranks, and doubtless other units had casualties.

One cannot help wondering if the 5th Australian Division as it existed in 1918, with all its ripe experience, would have succeeded in the Fromelles attack where, as an inexperienced formation in 1916, it failed. For us it is enough to reflect that the division in its first terrible ordeal did all that could be done; that whatever fortitude and courage and the highest devotion to duty could accomplish, it accomplished. In all the magnificent annals of the British armies there is not a page where the virtues of heroism and sacrifice are more magnificently recorded.

Mufti, August 1936

Alexander Donald Ellis was a thirty-year-old student from Canterbury in Melbourne who was assigned initially to the 31st Battalion as a 2nd lieutenant. Part of the 5th Division, the 31st Battalion plunged into the Battle of Fromelles within days of arriving at the front. Ellis was to reach the rank of captain and win the Military Cross before his return to Australia as part of the 29th Battalion in September 1919. He became the 5th Division's historian.

A Sapper's Diary: The Battle of Fromelles

By Sapper W. Smith

Fromelles – the 5th Division was on the brink of its baptism of fire. The party of myself and Sapper Carl Smith, an old friend of Gallipoli days, was to accompany Major Bachtold on special and emergency duty. He was an efficient and gallant officer of exceptional courage, and a born leader.

We reached the firing line behind the big breastwork at 9 a.m. All the troops were in position and everything appeared to be ready for the attack, which was timed for the evening of 19 July 1916. The general bombardment opened at 11 a.m., developing into a regular inferno. From 4 p.m. until 6 p.m., the artillery duel was at its worst, and practically every gun on both sides was brought into action.

Our breastwork, which was a wonderful target, was blown to pieces in places; dugouts were destroyed; and timber was sent skywards. Large enemy guns gave us a bad time with enfilade fire. Every gun had been previously registered, and had our position accurately.

One could not imagine a more nerve-wracking ordeal. There were no deep dugouts, the ground being waterlogged – and yet the Diggers – most of them raw troops – faced this fierce bombardment; crouched against the breastwork watching their comrades being killed or wounded beside them; grimly waiting for the time to 'hop the bags'.

At 5.30 p.m., a large dump of ammunition and bombs of the 8th Brigade went off with a terrific explosion, and sent up a large column of gaseous smoke – evidently a direct hit from a shell of a 'Minnie' [a German trench mortar called a Minenwerfer, nicknamed 'moaning Minnie']. This was a serious loss, as the ammunition had taken three days to carry to the line and it could not be replaced. All along the line the stretcher-bearers were busy picking up the wounded. Their numbers were hopelessly inadequate to cope with the casualties, but their spirit was fine, and they did magnificent work.

'Five minutes to go!' Those five minutes were the longest of my experience, but at last they were up, and a mixture of yell and cheer went up from the line. Time, 5.50 p.m.

An officer near to me, of the 53rd Battalion, mounted the parapet, shouting, 'Come on, lads!' and away they went, up the ladders, over the top, and away across no-man's-land – a stretch of 300 yards at this point. As they mounted the parapets Fritz opened up with machine-guns and rifles, but on they went, undaunted, crossed his wire entanglements, vaulted his parapets, and got busy with bombs and cold steel.

They were up against some of the Kaiser's best troops, and these – good soldiers that they were – threw their hand grenades and stuck to their machine-guns as though nothing but death would stop them. But our boys rooted them out with the bayonet, and in less than half an hour after leaving our breastwork, some of them were back with prisoners.

The chief work which was allotted to the field engineers was the cutting of communication trenches from our line across what had recently been no-man's-land. Each company of engineers had to cut a communication trench for its own brigade, and so, about 9 p.m., we of the 14th Field Company took over about 100 men of the 55th and 56th Battalions, divided the 300 yards distance into sections, and started digging in earnest.

The passing of stores, ammunition and rations to the 14th Brigade's sector of the new front line depended upon this trench being completed by 3 a.m. The section allotted to my squad was immediately in front of our old parapet, and we also had to cut through the breastwork. This was probably the worst section of the trench, for we were just at the range where the majority of the German shells were bursting. From all directions one frequently heard the call of wounded asking for water or calling for stretcher-bearers. The cries of the wounded are the hardest of all to hear.

Just before daybreak, Colonel H. Pope (14th Brigade) and Lieutenant Colonel Cass (54th Battalion) came along the new trench and through our cutting in the breastwork. Both of these officers had been across to the enemy lines. Colonel Cass was obviously overwrought and distressed. He and Pope were having a heated argument about the attack, and Colonel Cass unburdened his mind.

'I tell you that it was wholesale murder, they have murdered my boys.'

'Oh pull yourself together man, this is war!'

'This is not war. They have murdered my boys.'

I had served under Colonel Cass in the 2nd Battalion for three months on Gallipoli and my full sympathy went out to him. I did not then realise that Pope and Cass had fought their last battle. They were both heroes of Gallipoli and very efficient commanders. The AIF was the poorer for their departure from the fighting zone.

I looked round for the men of my own company, but could not find an engineer anywhere, and so I stuck my bayonet on my rifle, picked up a couple of bandoliers of ammunition, and mounted the firing step with the infantry, and waited for the expected attack by the Germans. However, the enemy proved to be by no means anxious to try his luck, and so, after waiting for about half an hour, I dropped down.

Our engineer dumps and tramway were knocked all to pieces, and as I took stock of the wreckage, a battery of German howitzers suddenly sent over about twenty shells into the dump of hurdles, duckboards, picks and shovels, wire, timber, etc. I got a nasty smack on the chin with a fragment of shell. This was the only piece I had stopped during the whole engagement. I had been lucky.

The casualties of our small field company of engineers were seven killed and twenty wounded. Heavy artillery fire was still being exchanged. The wounded were receiving attention. The doctors and stretcher-bearers were working hard. The dead were lying all around. They would receive attention later.

Reveille, July 1936

The Aussies Stage a 'Melbourne Cup'

By 'The Man in the Green Felt Hat'

Even mucking about knee-deep in mud and blood south of the La Bassee Canal none of our bunch forgot the Melbourne Cup.

We hardly knew the horses nominated for the Cup of 1916, but round about the first Tuesday in November there was more talk about Cup horses and what it was like in old Brisbane and Sydney and Melbourne than about the wounded being brought in – anyway, even when we had to eat and sleep next to the horror we tried to forget it.

'Chipper' Andrews had been a bookmaker's clerk, Bluey W. had owned a stud, Bing Ralston's father had been a 'stipe', 'Soda' had been a bookmaker, 'Nig' Wallace had been a lucky punter; even the ex–civil servants, the schoolteacher and the rag-store floor walker had been used to having their bit on for the Cup, and a Digger would bet on anything.

It was Bluey who saw possibilities for a race in the 'chats' [lice]. He noticed that when he struck a match in the filthy black of dawn to locate the concentrated army of chats on his flannel shirt that one of the blighters would move up a bit.

As every Digger knows there were four distinct varieties of chat. There was the big loose-looking blackie we christened Fritz; then there was the smaller brown, nimble and with a poignant nip, he was Froggie; there was the rather genteel-looking grey with a longer body and we christened him the Old Contemptible; and there was the dirty white bloke we called Aussie.

We got to training them to run straight, and fixed up a race course, rather snappy I think it was – one of the flannel shirts, though the poor cow who was unlucky in the cut of the cards and had to hand it over did a perish while the training and the races were on! The seam of the yoke was the winning post, and the extreme tail was the starting point. To keep the 'horses on the course' the Diggers used to look after their own horses with a lighted match, and after a few days' training they kept to the centre of the shirt all right.

Betting went up to 25 francs on their fancies, and I tell you that on Cup day there was as much excitement over our 'chat cup' as the punters and odds layers back home got out of their big Cup.

The favourite for the race was Fritz. He was longer than the others and had a habit of rolling in his crawl. However he kept to the course and didn't attempt to run wide. The Aussie chat was unreliable. He would get a move on and look like the winner and then he'd sidetrack and double back. The big grey used to dig into the flannel too much, and the Froggie would go round in a circle.

However, with all money up and Bluey with his on the Boche, we (who were the jockeys) each took a match and spurred our horses up the course. It was against the rules to use the hands or shake the shirt or in any way urge the horses except legitimately with the light at their tails and a given distance.

With all the Diggers cheering and a Froggie in our company dancing a 'pas seul' and a pommy asking to be struck rotten, the race looked a cert for the Boche. He was moving up like his bloody compatriots were at the time, and Ginger J., who was the most superstitious cow in our company, got morose about it.

He thought he saw in the victory of the louse another victory for the Boche, and became more and more blasphemous. It's not the blasted money, he kept saying, because a shell might declare the bet off at any time, but it's the principle of the thing. The Froggie, whose chat was second, was a bit with him. The Aussie was creeping up a formidable third, the Grey was practically out of the race; he had stopped to peck at a bit of BO on the shirt about the middle of the straight.

Bluey was bragging that the Boche was home and dried, and was even showing off by holding off the match from his tail. What followed was an accident, according to Froggie, but knowing

Ginger I have my doubts. Someone gave Ginger a shove and he fell up against the hand in which Bluey held the match. The Boche was at least four lengths in the lead with the Aussie crawling up neck and neck with the Froggie when Ginger bumped against the match, and the match went clean on to the tail of the Boche, and 'pop!' – the 'cert' exploded. Froggie sidetracked with fright and the Aussie won by a feeler!

Naturally Bluey demanded his money back and there was a prize argument on within the dugout, but 'the word' came that day, and I don't think anyone settled. Bluey didn't have to pay out, poor cow – the Boche got him.

The Queensland Digger, November 1934

Mantle of Beauty: Snow Hides War's Scars

By Lieutenant Stanley Herbert Delves

Our battalion entered Armentières within easy reach of the enemy's guns on 19 November 1916. To the left, shrapnel was bursting, and behind the lines our 'heavies' were busy, firing at long range.

By nightfall we had taken up our position – our company was placed on the right of Square Farm sector. All night we could hear the deep chant of the guns, and the shrill soprano of whistling shells, and now and again the rattle on the keyboards of machine-guns.

And so life went on there until 19 December, the morning of which broke fine and clear. Aeroplanes were overhead in expectation of a good flying day. Before midday, however, the sky darkened, and it snowed steadily, so that all the fields of Flanders became white.

There was a strange new beauty on the field of war, changed to a white enchantment. Away over the country on both sides of the lines every furrow in the fields was a thin white ridge; while the trees which were left stood ink-black against the drifting snow clouds. The old windmills which looked down upon the battlefields had been touched by the softly falling flakes, so that each rib of the sails, and each rung of the ladders, and each plank of their ancient timbers were outlined like a frosty cobweb.

Over Armentières, in the distance, the ermine mantle had fallen and changed the hideousness of shelled houses into a scene for rapture.

In the trenches the snow made white pillows of the piled sandbags, and snowmen of sentries standing in the shelter of the traverses. The roofs and timbered doorways of dugouts were so transformed by the snowflakes that they seemed the dwellings of fairy folk, or of Pierrot and Columbine in a Christmas hiding place:

and not of soldiers stamping their feet and blowing on their fingers and seeking to keep their rifles dry.

In its first gossamer of white the snow gave a beauty even to no-man's-land, making a lacework pattern of barbed wire; and carpeting very softly over the shell-torn tumbled ground, so that the ugliness of destruction and death was hidden.

The snowflake fluttered upon stark bodies there and shrouded them tenderly. It was as though all the doves of peace were flying down to fold their wings over the obscene things of war.

For a little while the snow brought something like peace. The guns were quieter, for artillery observation was impossible. There could be no sniping, for the scurrying flakes put up a veil between the trenches. The aeroplanes which went up early in the morning came down quickly to the powdered fields and took shelter in their sheds.

A great hush settled over the warzone, but there was something grim, suggestive of tragic drama, in this silent countryside, so white, even in the darkness, where millions of men for hundreds of miles were waiting to kill.

Behind the lines the joke of the snow descended upon the soldiers, quick to grasp a chance of fun. Previously they had been hurling bombs at the enemy in the Ypres salient. Now they bombarded each other with 'hand grenades' of white flakes which burst noiselessly, except for the laughter that applauded a good hit. This scene was legion. Everywhere soldiers led attacks upon their officers, and officers upon their soldiers.

The white peace did not last long. The mantle on the battlefield was stained by scarlet patches as soon as the men could see to fight again.

Reveille, June 1930

Stanley Herbert Delves was a nineteen-year-old student from Manning River, north of Newcastle, when he embarked as a private with the 34th Infantry Battalion in May 1916. He returned as a lieutenant three years later.

Shell-Hole Water

By A.J.H.

It is generally agreed that the coldness of the winter in 1916 on the Somme was the coldest coldness ever issued to the troops. Freeze! – Struth!! Snow! – Hell!! Rain! – Mon Dieu!! Mud! – Yow!! It was the frozen limit multiplied by two.

We used to chop our drinking and washing water with an axe. There was a large crump hole in front of our dugout and we chopped all our water from it during the winter, melting it in the dugout with Comforts' Cookers.

A ringer from Wollondilly reckoned that it was the best water that he had ever tasted. It was better than vin blanc, Belgique beer, or tea from the officers' mess.

All agreed that it was good. It was the only topic on which there was unanimity.

'That's one thing about this country,' continued the ringer. 'You can always rely on getting good, fresh water everywhere. It's a bit different to outback in Aussie, where I've sometimes had to pull two or three dead sheep out of a waterhole and then hold my nose while I drank the water.'

This encouraged some of the other Waybacks, and we had to listen to some tall tales about thick drinks that they had had when the water bag had run dry while they were on long rides out Behind the Beyond. After they had finished everyone was more than ever convinced that Comforts' Cooker heated ice-water from the shell holes of France was preferable to sun-heated water from the billabongs of Aussie.

In due course winter retired according to plan and spring arrived, as it has been in the habit of doing for many years. The little ice that was then in the shell hole soon melted.

And then one morning the ringer came in with an empty dixie. He was prominently displaying a sad and sorry expression.

'I'm not having any breakfast this morning, boys. I'm feeling a bit crook. This is a rotten game!'

He threw the dixie in a corner with a vigour that would have induced any conscientious sergeant major to charge him with malicious damage to government property.

'There's two dead Fritzes in that crump hole,' he said disgustedly. 'They've been there since last summer by the look of them.'

I've not heard a discussion on the virtues of shell-hole water since!

The Queensland Digger, November 1944

Leaves from the Diary of a Digger

By Engineer Sergeant W.J. Neilson

I enlisted at Atherton on 2 March 1915. After a few days' home leave, I left for Brisbane, sailing from Townsville on the SS *Bingera*, bound for Enoggera Camp.

I was not long in camp before I got my bearings and sorted out what unit I wished to go away with – light-horse, infantry, AMC and lots of others. The light-horsemen looked the prettiest, those emu feathers in the hat, leggings and spurs appealed to me. One morning I was told to report for a riding test. I arrived alongside two chaps with straw boater hats. In the horse lines were two big upstanding black horses, and one chap was telling his mate one was good and to leave the other alone.

Before I could get the oil, I was called on to mount. I took one of the blacks but was no sooner on him when I said, 'Bill, you got the crow.' To walk was good, but when he said trot, away we went for a gallop. On pulling up, 'Jump off, we know him, you pass,' was all I got, and back to camp I went to become one of the ALH.

However, in a few days applications were called for anyone desirous of joining an NCO class, for which I qualified as provisional sergeant, and after serving in Fraser's and Bell's Paddocks, I was attached to the 4th Reinforcements, 4th Pioneer Battalion, located at the rifle range. We embarked on the SS *Itonus* at Pinkenba on Tuesday 8 August 1916 about 11.30 a.m.

Thursday 8 March 1917 was our first day in action. Around Bazentin, Longueval and Contalmaison there was hardly a foot of ground not torn up by shell fire. Delville Wood was a mass of battered stumps. It was here some South Africans put up a great stand. Old Jerry put his hands up to surrender and when these troops came forward they were mowed down like rabbits.

The snow was falling and we had to travel over four miles by duckboards, eight to ten men at a time, with a distance of twenty to thirty yards between each section to avoid heavy casualties. The work was in a valley putting down a light railway. I had a new arrival with me, Fred Fielding. There were corpses everywhere. Right where we were working was a Fritz with his leg hanging over a shell hole, the boot still on, and his mate alongside with his hands pointing to the sky.

This had no effect on us, nor did the shrapnel that was bursting over us all morning, but when the coal boxes started coming over (these are high explosives), see the old hands scratching gravel for a tunnel about 300 yards away. Raw recruits, we knew nothing about taking cover, and were the last to leave. There were a few casualties that day, one being a chap who joined up the day before. He voluntarily gave an Army Medical Corps chap a hand and was killed as soon as he reached the dressing station.

On 25 May 1917 the artillery became very active. The famous Battle of Messines was now on. The bombardment continued up to 7 June, when the New Zealanders hopped over and took Fritz's front line of trenches on Messines Ridge. Our battalion and the 45th and 47th Battalions went over at 4 p.m. but got knocked back with heavy losses. They went at it again on the morning of the 8th and got the position they were after. Fritz made three counterattacks but got repulsed each time with heavy casualties and losing a lot of prisoners. We were put out under heavy shell fire to build communication trenches up to the positions taken by the infantry. Our casualties were light but we were lucky.

7 August 1918 – we got orders to hand in packs and blankets – was this the end of the war? The barrage opened up on 8 August at 4.20 a.m. We advanced about twelve kilometres, taking all our objectives. We met with very little shell fire. I don't think we had a casualty, but on our left there was a Tommy division that wore

a red triangle. I think they got every shell that day that Fritz put over. Prisoners all day were passing through our ranks shouting '*Kamerad*' and going for their lives. We were stopped at one of Fritz's barriers. Before leaving they had a parting shot at a British tank only about 250 yards away. They got a direct hit, killing one of the men who was looking through one of the openings.

No orders for us the next morning so Simpson, who is on the trams in Brisbane, decided to come for a walk over the battlefield where this English regiment was copping it. As soon as we got on the bank we hadn't walked 200 yards before we were on corpses by the score. Some were piled seven and eight on top of one another. They must have been great fighters, for coming on to Fritz's front line, the Germans lay in the bottom of it. They, too, must have been great men. We then went to an excavation where seven lay dead alongside a trench mortar, one chap very young, with just his trousers on. It is impossible to believe that we could advance without a casualty, while 500 or 600 yards away, men were being mown down in hundreds.

On 2 November there was a big round-up on the Somme by the 4th Division for deserters. 'D' Company of our unit located one chap. He made off up the river, discharging his revolver as he went. Orders were given to fire on him. He dropped dead, being hit in the lower part of the back. On being searched he had two revolvers and a credit of 14,000 francs in Paris.

The Queensland Digger, April 1942

William Joseph Neilson, a teamster aged twenty-six, enlisted at Atherton, Queensland, in March 1915, joining the 4th Pioneer Battalion as a private. He was promoted to sergeant before returning in September 1919.

Bullecourt Tragedy: Retrospect

By Lance Corporal Bert Knowles

Shortly after midnight on 10 April 1917, in company with other members of the 13th Battalion, I trudged across dark, muddy country somewhere between Favreuil and Noreuil. Just south of Noreuil in a sunken road, we came to our cookers, where we obtained a very welcome drink of hot tea and a snack of bread and jam, whilst waiting for stragglers to come up and various other units to get into position for 'the greatest blunder' which the AIF ever had any connection with.

We all knew the plan of attack and the positions the various battalions were to occupy in the advance, and were especially warned to leave all diaries and papers behind; and also to conserve our rations and water. Our job was to hammer our way through the great Hindenburg Line and go northward to meet the Tommies, who were to get through near Arras, and so cut off the Germans between.

After our short rest we moved off again, skirted the ruins of Noreuil, and came to a railway cutting, which was to be our starting point. The 16th Battalion was in a sunken road in front of us, about 200 yards, whilst about 1500 yards ahead was our first objective. The 16th were to take that, we were to go over them and take the second line, after which both battalions were to go on through the village of Riencourt. We had the assistance of twelve tanks to cover our flanks and help us through the wire.

It was about 4.30 a.m. when we were in position and about 4.45 a.m. we received word to 'go over', as the 16th were on their way. Our formation, of sections of men in single file, was adopted owing to heavy enemy shell fire. As Lance Corporal I had charge of six men and a Lewis gun section behind them. In front, and slightly to my left, was Captain H.W. Murray, VC. He was strolling along as if death was something which came only with old age.

After we had crossed the sunken road from which the 16th had started, we walked into a barrage of machine-gun fire from the village of Quéant, on our right. I saw rows of men, in the semi-darkness, crumple up. My own section now comprised two men and myself.

Out of the gloom ahead came Murray's quiet voice, 'Get down 13th, until it passes.' We lay close to the ground in the snow for a while and listened to a noise like thousands of bees passing overhead. I saw a tank smothered with little sparks where the bullets were striking. Various coloured star shells, flashes in the rear, and overhead, where their shells were bursting, lighted up the snow-covered ground, which was dotted with dead and wounded.

I remember remarking to a chap lying close to me, 'How cold it is on the fingers, lying in the snow.' His reply was, 'I think it's bloody hot,' and another man laughed, a little hysterically, perhaps, but the man who spoke had a smile in his voice and I had to grin at the audacity of him to laugh and joke in the middle of such terrible slaughter. I began to wonder where it would all end, as I knew we must have lost half our strength, and the job not yet commenced. We had yet to go through two lines of wire and trenches, a fortified village, and hold out for two days.

I was brought back to realities by the same wonderful voice in front, 'Come on, 13th! The 16th are getting Hell,' and we did the next 200 yards or so at a jog trot. It was now almost daylight, and although there was still a mist, the drizzle of snow had ceased; also our artillery fire, and the enemy machine-guns were having it all their own way. Anywhere, where men were grouped together trying to penetrate the barbed wire, the machine-guns simply wiped out 50 per cent, with a swish; but men lay on their sides and hacked at the wire with their bayonets. Some few had cutters; others tried to cross the top, leaping from one strand to another. Many slipped and became hopelessly entangled in the loosely bunched wire. Many were shot down halfway through, and hung up on the wire in various attitudes.

A tank (the only one which got so far) penetrated the front line of wire, which was about four or five yards across, and became a hopeless wreck. I remember a chap standing near the front of it with a short plank, trying to lever a piece of iron from amongst the big cogs beneath the wheels, and cursing like a bullocky whilst the bullets were rattling like hail on the tank itself.

I managed to scramble through a gap which had been left by Fritz for his patrol to use. The machine-gun which usually covered these gaps was evidently put out of action by the 16th, who had, by this time, taken their objective. I then arrived at what looked like an unfinished portion of trench, about eighteen inches deep and eight or nine feet wide, in which many dead and wounded were lying – mostly 16th men. Others were lying along the far side, using their rifles over the top. Several of us found a narrow opening down into the main trench, where the few who were with me helped to bomb our way along to the 13th Battalion's objective.

For the next four or five hours things seemed to be a nightmare, throwing Mills bombs over a traverse of the trench or sap, waiting for them to explode, and then rushing into the next portion of trench with a bayonet, and shoot or chase out any Hun who was not wounded. Meanwhile we would help Lewis gunners over the top into shell holes on either side of us, so they could stop Fritz's carrying parties further back along the trench. This gave us a breather occasionally, in which to drag our wounded back out of range of bombs, empty our dead pals' cartridge pouches, and load panniers for the Lewis guns. Others would run back and try to collect a few more Mills bombs from dead and wounded in the rear.

We were 'in the air' as there were 1500 yards of flat ground behind us, covered by machine-gun fire from Quéant and Bullecourt on our right and left; also from the housetops and windows in Riencourt in front of us; while their bombers were literally showering us with egg bombs and 'potato mashers'.

Our only hope now was to hold on until dark, or until our artillery gave us a covering barrage, in order to let us get back or get up some more ammunition. Murray had sent volunteers back through that hailstorm of lead, asking for artillery fire and bombs. One or two got through and even returned, but still no help came.

The beginning of the end came when the Lewis guns ran out of ammunition. Gunners took the pin out of a Mills bomb, laid it on the gun, and left before the bomb exploded and destroyed the gun; other men pulled their guns to pieces and threw the parts in different directions. Still I never heard anyone talk of surrender, and we drove the enemy back with the bayonet on several occasions, even clearing two or three sections of trench, only to be sent back under a shower of bombs.

We were then back in his original front line, and still the flanks were being driven back. Captain Murray said, 'Well, men, it's either capture, or go into "that". Each man for himself.' We had not a bullet or bomb among the lot of us; and only thirty of 'A' Company got into the trench in the first attack, though we started with 166; the remainder were lying on the plain, which we now had the option of crossing a second time, this time in broad daylight, with the enemy ready to shoot down anyone showing his head.

Many of us preferred risking 'that' to being captured. Some climbed the parapet, only to be shot down like rabbits; others like myself found gaps in the parapet made by shells, and crawled through. I lay under the shelter for a few minutes to take my bearings, made a mental note of positions of shell holes between myself and the barbed wire, then dived into the nearest one, out of that, and into the next. I fell over getting through the wire and lay perfectly still among the dead. Lay there for a long time, almost clear of the wire. The bombing had ceased and I knew the fight was over. Thinking it a good opportunity whilst Fritz was souveniring and putting his house in order, I started my short dashes into shell holes again, getting further out of range all the time. Many bullets droned past me or dug into the earth around me.

I often wished during the next few months that one had hit me. I saw others doing the same as I was doing, some successfully, others being shot down. When I was out of range I stayed in a shell hole with two badly wounded men and intended to have a spell until dark – a snowstorm or our artillery would give me a chance to get one of them back with me, the other being a walking case. I do not know what time it was then, but nothing had passed my lips since about 3 a.m. I had not even had time for a cigarette. My mouth was full of dust, and a taste of cordite and smoke of explosives. I ached all over through heaving bombs, and dragging wounded men and bags of dirt.

My clothes were in rags, and thighs and arms were scratched with barbed wire. I fell into a kind of doze, and was awakened by a voice. Looking down on us was a party of Germans, one beckoning me to get up. He made me understand that I was to carry the wounded man, while the other, whose shoulder I had re-bandaged, was pushed along in front of me. The Germans must have wanted prisoners for propaganda or information, to trouble wounded men like that. Our guards received a cigar each and it dawned on me how pleased the military heads must have been over their victory. I don't think they were so pleased when they counted the cost, as our brigade died very hard that day.

They returned our cigarettes and money. I had a smoke and finished in a sleep which only comes so heavily to anyone in a state of acute mental and physical exhaustion. I had gone over the events of the day, and grieved over the loss of such a fine lot of pals. What the Fritzies would have in store for me did not worry me a bit. I was despondent that I had not died like hundreds of my mates before the wire at Bullecourt.

Reveille, April 1931

Lance Corporal Herbert Knowles was to spend the rest of the war as a prisoner of the Germans, first at Dülmen in western Germany, later at Heilsberg in northern Poland. He confirmed he was alive in a postcard sent in May 1917, and in a letter dated 3 March 1918 wrote: 'We are both enjoying good health, food and warm clothing. Thanks to the Red Cross Society.' He was repatriated to England in December 1918 and returned to Australia the following February. When he had embarked with the 13th Battalion in December 1914 he was described as a 26-year-old labourer, whose next of kin were living in Cheshire, England.

Intentions Misunderstood

By 'Robbo'

'Young man, are you fond of women?'

This startling question was addressed by our captain quartermaster, 'Old Jerry' Hazlitt, to 'Daveo', temporarily orderly in charge of the dressing station in the barn at Millencourt. Again boomed out the demand: 'Young man, are-you-fond-of-women?' and 'Daveo', always remembered by his big 'starting-out' eyes, snapped, 'I dunno what you mean.'

'Don't know what I mean? Then what's the meaning of this?' and Jerry strode across to the bag-covered window, ripped down the sack, and revealed a dainty pair of knickers hung across the window, making admirable curtains. You know the kind – two fancy bags on a strip of tape, each 'bag' with a dainty blue ribbon at the end, just in the manner you'd tie back a curtain!

Did 'Daveo' start then? My oath, he did – those big eyes of his were easily an inch out of their sockets. 'Don't know what I mean, eh? Umph,' and Jerry stamped off on his tour of further inspection, snorting.

How did they get there? Well, here's the story.

Anzac Day 1917 was approaching, and it was decided the Australians and New Zealanders in France should fittingly celebrate the occasion. Our division was just coming 'out', and as we were not going back too far, it was decided a sports gathering should be held in the grounds of an old chateau.

To add to the fund and try to make us forget the horrors all around, prizes were offered for impersonations of well-known characters. (Charlie Chaplin seemed to be the most popular.) Prizes were also offered for female impersonations.

My unit was settled down in Millencourt some little distance from the sports ground, and as we had good representation in the sporting events, it was thought we should also contribute to the amusements.

'Bill' Dickson, a living double for the Charlie so well known on the screen (he was always recognised by the French kiddies as 'Chaplain Charlie') naturally dressed the part, whilst it was suggested I'd make a good mademoiselle because I had curly hair.

To obtain the clothes was a job. Marie, in the estaminet, came to the rescue with a white lace frock and shawl, satin shoes with red roses, stockings, and a large hat which we trimmed with some flowers. But as for lingerie – '*Non, non, monsieur, pas lingerie.*' A wig was 'borrowed' unknown to its owners from a pierrot troupe conveniently close handy.

'If you're going as a girl, Robbo, you must be a proper girl, and undies you must have,' so a job was found for young McKinley in Amiens, and he was duly commissioned to buy all that was necessary. Too true, Mac got them, but he was 'stung' when he arrived back and 'pinched' for overstaying his leave.

The day of the sports arrived, and I never forget that long, hot walk on 'Charlie's' arm, with shoes miles too tight and heels miles too high – and the boys – well they just *would* make certain I was properly dressed! Even dear old General Holmes had to make certain, and then shout a French '*bière*', and that was the first of many.

All good days come to an end; the prize I got certainly never covered my expenses at the refreshment tents or estaminets, but the walk back to Millencourt was more comfortable than the previous journey, even if I did wear out the feet of Mademoiselle's stockings, carrying her shoes around my neck.

Well, of course, everyone knows how Anzacs collected souvenirs, and so my clothing, or some of it, was souvenired. Whether 'Daveo' souvenired the 'curtains' that Jerry objected to is not known, but curtains they became.

Sequel: One day in 1919 my wife received a small parcel, with a little note. 'Ask Robbo where he got 'em.' You bet she asked – and was satisfied, and I've still got the 'souvenirs' at home, but one blue ribbon is missing.

The Listening Post, April 1933

Memories of Passchendaele

By A.J.S.

Passchendaele, also known as the 3rd Battle of Ypres, began on 12 October 1917. The 3rd Australian Division under Major General John Monash and the NZ Division advanced with five British divisions at dawn. It was a futile attempt to capture German positions, fought in rain and the worst muddy conditions. Total casualties at Passchendaele are estimated at 475,000; about 275,000 British and Commonwealth and about 200,000 German. 38,000 Australians, 15,654 Canadians and 5300 New Zealanders fell there, either killed, wounded or missing. New Zealand lost 2735 men on the first day alone, 845 dead, wounded or stranded in mud – still the worst loss of life in one single day in New Zealand history.

War, from the point of view of the Digger, was not all humour, despite the fact that most incidents related wherever Diggers foregather touch on the lighter side. This is probably because we endeavour to relegate the tragic to the background, but memory persists. I am reminded of two incidents touching on the tragic during the fighting at Passchendaele on 4 October 1917.

A captured German 'pillbox', near the Zonnebeke railway line and to the rear of the cemetery, was being officially used as company headquarters, but unofficially it became a shelter and resting place for a miscellany of Diggers of various units. Machine-gunners, trench mortars and infantry crowded the narrow trench surrounding it.

Came a direct hit on one corner and immediately the place of shelter became a shamble. When the smoke had cleared, and the debris settled, we had opportunity to observe the damage. Some had been killed outright, others terribly wounded, whilst a fortunate few, myself included, had escaped with a severe shaking.

My attention was caught by a young lad about eighteen years of age. He was in a bad way. One leg was shattered and his internal injuries must have been frightful, but he still lived.

We did what little was possible to ease his sufferings while awaiting the stretcher-bearers. He smiled his thanks and queried: 'I'm sticking it all right, aren't I?' We reassured him and he lay still for a few moments, then commenced to rave and curse in delirium. Suddenly he stopped and in a quiet voice repeated a few words of 'Our Father'. Then just before the arrival of the bearers he relapsed into merciful unconsciousness. He had no chance, but he did his best to go out game.

Shortly after came another hit, but without the accompanying damage, our numbers having been considerably depleted. Only a solitary voice was raised in the cry for bearers: a big chap, wearing the colour patches of a trench mortar battery, lay in the trench. To the query: 'Where are you hit, Dig?' he replied, 'In the back; for God's sake hurry up the bearers, I'm bleeding to death.'

Two of us eased him over on his side and looked for the wound, but could see no external traces, only a large black patch in the centre of his tunic. Still he persisted that he was badly wounded, and, getting to his feet, though shaking from head to foot, declaring that he wasn't going to stay there and bleed to death, staggered off in the direction of the advanced dressing station on the railway line.

Subsequently he was evacuated as a shell-shock case, and returned to Australia a nervous wreck. A large piece of mud, coupled with overwrought nerves, was responsible for his breakdown.

The Listening Post, May 1937

Holocaust: The 3rd Battle of Ypres

By Captain F.C. Green, MC

Most of us store away in our memories dates which we honour according to the memories they bring. Every man of the AIF who served in France in 1918 lets his mind go back every 8 August to the day for which we had prayed for over two years – the day on which we would see the German Army on the run. Every man in the original 3rd Division remembers 7 June [1917] – Messines – and on 28 March many Tasmanians reflect on that bright spring afternoon when we went forward with neither artillery nor machine-gun support, with Amiens behind, and the victorious German divisions in column of route in front, and just a few green fields between us.

Even now it makes the pulse beat quicker, but October brings to most of us that separate Hell of memory, the 3rd Battle of Ypres.

August of 1917 was a month of almost continuous rain, and though the weather improved in September, the whole of the Ypres battlefield was such a morass that it took three weeks to dry sufficiently to resume the offensive. Phase 1 of the Battle was on 20 September, and Phase 2, known to the Australians as Polygon Wood, opened on 26 September. It was not until Phase 3, on 4 October, known as the Battle of Broodseinde, that the 40th Battalion took part in this offensive. We were allotted the final objective of the 10th Brigade – the top of the Broodseinde Ridge.

The worst half hour of the whole attack was waiting in the shell holes on the assembly point, for the enemy had also timed an attack on us ten minutes later than ours upon him, and his preparatory barrage came down upon us there. There was no greater test of discipline and steadiness under that ordeal, and it was a great relief when our covering barrage opened and we went forward.

The first few moments were amazing. In the half-light of dawn we saw, not the trench garrison of the enemy, but his attacking troops in front of us, demoralised by our barrage and unexpected attack. The leading battalions dealt with them, and they came through us in hundreds with their hands up. When the 37th Battalion reached its objective we leapfrogged through them, and later through the 38th and 39th on their objectives, and then made for the final objective – the top of Broodseinde Ridge.

This last ridge was a grim fight. Right along it was a line of concrete redoubts, barbed wire and machine-guns, and the fire from this stronghold was terrific. Wherever there was a gap in the enemy wire his machine-guns were concentrated. Cecil McVilly, winner of the Diamond Sculls and now chairman of the Charities Board of Victoria, got his company from shell hole to shell hole to within 200 yards of the enemy's position, when he was badly wounded; but his company went on yard by yard under the covering fire of Captain Ruddock's company. Sergeant Lewis McGee led the first rush for the top by sprinting across the open and capturing a big redoubt single-handed. A few minutes later we were in possession of the whole ridge with seventeen machine-guns and 400 prisoners. McGee was awarded the Victoria Cross for his bravery, but his grave is on the ridge.

How it rained! From the 6th until the 9th it never stopped, and on the 9th, Phase 4 of the battle was entered upon. From the line we had consolidated, the 66th British Division attempted to go forward, but practically no progress was made by them, and when Phase 5 began on the 12th, with rain still falling, the 40th Battalion attacked from practically the same position we had won eight days before.

This attack was almost a complete failure. Our objective was Passchendaele, but we were never within striking distance of it. When we attacked with a protective artillery barrage which was scarcely discernible owing to the fact that mud conditions prevented the guns coming forward, we met heavy machine-gun fire from the front and the high ground on the left flank known as Bellevue Spur, and were soon hopelessly bogged in the mud.

Battalions telescoped into each other and added to the confusion. The attacking troops on our left – the New Zealand division – never got through the uncut wire in front of them, and died in the mud where machine-gun bullets played on them like water from a hose.

Between us and Bellevue Spur, the enemy's stronghold, was the Ravebeck, a stream swollen with rain – whose banks had overflowed into the neighbouring shell holes, making an impassable barrier of about 200 yards in width. Our men leaping forward into the shell holes were stuck there; rifles and Lewis guns were clogged with flying showers of mud from shell bursts, and the casualties were appalling.

The remnant of the brigade made its way forward for about half a mile under heavy fire from the front and left flank. Communications with the flanks and even the rear were impossible under the conditions, and command had passed out of brigade and even battalion control. The senior officer on the spot took charge of such troops of the brigade as had reached this point, and set to work to make a defensive position there. This officer was Major L.F. Giblin, now Ritchie Professor of Economics at Melbourne University. He will always be remembered in the brigade as an officer of great capacity and calm courage.

The day passed somehow with intermittent rain and hail; even the enemy seemed sick of the slaughter, and the indescribable misery of the conditions. Darkness made these conditions even worse. All night icy blasts of wind and sleet swept our position, till the troops became too numbed to move, and fell about like drunken men in the efforts to restore circulation.

Realising that further advance was impossible next day, it was decided that if the enemy did not counterattack, the time would be spent in getting the wounded back and extricating those who were stuck in the mud. Accordingly, parties went out soon after daylight, and met with an unusual attitude on the part of the enemy. He allowed these parties to carry on their work, and in some cases pointed to where our wounded were lying.

It took hours to get the wounded out where every step was an effort, and many had to be packed up with equipment and dragged out of the mud, in which they had sunk to their shoulders. Many of the wounded had disappeared altogether in the mud; had died there, and were never found. Of the living only one man was missed; he was found next day by the enemy and dug out, ultimately reaching Germany as a prisoner.

The attack on 12 October was a severe defeat. Why it was undertaken when doomed to failure under the conditions has never been explained. It failed on account of the wet weather and consequent mud, which made it impossible to get artillery forward after Phase 3. The New Zealanders were faced with uncut belts of wire with machine-gun positions behind. Had they succeeded in getting through and capturing Bellevue Spur, we had a possibility of reaching Passchendaele. We had to advance 2000 yards to reach Passchendaele, and though after our attempt, attacks were made by the Canadians, the town was not captured until 6 November after six weeks of constant fighting.

Of the 40th Battalion, out of a total of 620 officers and other ranks who went into the Ypres offensive, only 123 answered the roll call when we came out.

Reveille, October 1930

Captain Frank Clifton Green, MC (1890–1974) was a 25-year-old married civil servant, employed in the Tasmanian Parliament, when he went overseas as a lieutenant with the 40th Battalion in 1916. He was highly respected, promoted to captain, and became the battalion's historian after returning home in July 1919. After transferring to Federal Parliament he rose to be Clerk of the House of Representatives in 1937. He was a close friend of Joe Lyons (former Premier of Tasmania) and John Curtin but never got on with Sir Robert Menzies. Green retired in 1955, returned to Hobart and died there in 1974.

Captain Cecil Leventhorpe McVilly, mentioned above, was an Australian champion sculler and competed in the 1912 Olympic Games, but was disqualified for causing interference.

Menin Road: September 1917

From a Soldier's Diary

18 September

We're off at last – in single file – slipping and sliding on the muddy sloping bank. Belgian mud is on its own for greasiness. It's quite dark now. The men talk in whispers, though there's really no need to. Like walking on tiptoes in a death room, where the dead can't hear.

Through the streets with broken buildings and heaps of rubble on either side. The flash of an occasional shell gives Ypres a weird, ghostly look. Passed the railway station on the right. Now the ruined Cloth Hall looms up on the left like a monstrous skeleton; next to it is what is left of St Martin's Cathedral. We pass through what they say is the Menin Gate. No sign of one. On to the Menin Road. Cobblestoned, where it isn't torn up by shell fire. Traffic of all kinds. Never saw anything like it. The road is jammed with it. Even trains on railway lines with snorting engines taking up guns and ammunition.

Military police on point duty directing the traffic. Not a nice job. The sides of the road heaped with junk, cleared off the road by labour battalions: broken guns, vehicles, dead men and mules and all sorts of things. The world's biggest junk shop. Troops and vehicles coming and going – mostly going.

Hellfire Corner! Jerry's pasting it with a barrage. A nightly performance. Gas shells! Masks on. We're a queer-looking lot with our masks on. Better than gas, though. On to the corduroy road. Masks off – thank goodness. Things begin to hum. Not only the shelling, but the putrid smell of dead bodies. Several got their packets already. Pretty bad, too, by the screaming. If this is a nightly affair in the Salient, what'll the hop-over be like?

Incendiary shells light up the whole countryside. Am hoping one doesn't fall near me. I'd rather go out with a bullet than be burnt alive. A kid next to me is whimpering – he's about sixteen. Pouring with rain now. Shell holes everywhere, full of water. And muddy! Struth! Well, we've reached the reserve trenches. There's a foot or so of water in them. Sleep in it tonight.

19 September

Got the word to move at last. Clamber over the parapet and file off through rain, mud, water and barbed wire. Machine-guns! Ah! Somebody's copped one. Don't remember ever seeing a night so dark. Shelling and machine-gunning nothing out of the ordinary. Don't think Fritz is a wake-up to the coming attack or we'd be getting a rasper of a pasting.

Slipped down the side of a crater, half into the water. Ugh! Somebody yanked me out just in time. Great cobbers, these fellows you hardly know, or perhaps never saw before. Tripped over some barbed wire and nearly took a header. Suddenly came to a piece of level ground, horribly springy under the feet. Like walking on a spring bed. It's a crater filled with dead bodies and covered over with earth. What a life.

Through the frontline trenches, past the crouching troops in them, and into no-man's-land like a lot of flitting ghosts. Down on our bellies we go with a sigh of relief. Our platoon is lucky. We've struck a little ridge. Fairly good cover lying on the slope behind it. There's a crater full of water with bodies in it at the foot of the slope. Ghastly, swollen things. I slipped and trod on one. Thinking it was a log of wood in the water, put my foot on it to steady myself. It belched!

It's light now and damned dangerous to wait much longer. Most of the boys are smoking cigarettes. An officer looks at his wrist watch, and raises whistle to mouth. But he didn't blow it. If he did, no one heard it. Exactly at 5.40 our barrage burst out. Jee-rusalem! Like the crack of doom! The ground shook. My eardrums throbbed and vibrated till I thought they would burst. We get up stiffly, our rifles with fixed bayonets slung over shoulders, fags in mouth, and over we go, walking and smoking.

Before they advanced a step some of the boys crumple up and slither down the bank to join the ghastly company in the pool. Machine-guns crackle and spray continuously. Earth, black smoke and bits of men spout skywards. Shrapnel patter viciously all the time. The rain has stopped. A bit misty. It's hard to see the pillboxes till you're almost on to them. But the mist'll clear up as the morning wears on.

One of our blokes is laughing like Hell. He just cleaned up a whole machine-gun crew with his bayonet, and is running about looking for more. Just did a little job of work myself, and nearly a goner. A Jerry fired at me from the gun-rest opening of a dugout and missed. Levelled my rifle at the opening. Up he came again. I got him through the head.

Rawlings and I had a narrow escape. A 5.9 [shell] burrowed into the ground under our feet. It didn't go off. A dud. Watched 'Sherry' trotting through the barrage back to Battalion HQ with a message. A shell got him. Up he went. Corporal Grant got through at next attempt. Bert Mac humming 'The Merry Widow'. Cheerful cove, Bert. Somebody said he saw Pat Farrell's body in the pool at the jumping-off tape. Pat always said he'd get the full issue. Smithy just killed. Our Officer Commanding, Jim Fletcher, hopped down for a yarn with Rawlings and me. We shared his flask of whisky. Told us umpteen prisoners taken and the stunt a complete success.

The Queensland Digger, September 1937

Extracts from the diary were published without the writer being identified, but he appears to have been a member of the 25th Battalion, which was part of the 2nd Division's first wave at the Battle of Menin Road in Belgium.

The Flag on Anzac House

By Lieutenant Joe Maxwell, VC

A few minutes after we had captured our objective on 20 September 1917, corps headquarters was informed: 'Objective reached. Australian flag flying on Anzac House.'

The Australian papers featured this episode, and months later we received glowing accounts of a Digger rushing forward holding aloft an outsize in Australian flags. Illustrated papers devoted a full page to feature the deed in colour – a deed which stirred the imagination of every patriotic Australian. The French and English papers also elaborated on the initiative and bravery of this lone Australian soldier.

It may interest readers of *Reveille* to know the facts:

Anzac House was the objective of 'B' Company (18th Battalion) of which I at the time was company sergeant major. It was an exceptionally strong pillbox, and our Officer Commanding (Captain Jack O'Donnell) decided it would make an ideal company headquarters. It contained a goodly supply of German schnapps, whisky and field dressings.

When a man was wounded he was promptly carried to Anzac House for attention. I particularly remember one fellow, whose arm was blown to a pulp by a whizz-bang [shell]. He was carried in on a stretcher, and, in addition to the wound, was suffering terribly from shock. Between groans he prayed to be allowed to die. We dressed his wound and poured about a pint of schnapps down his throat. A few minutes later he jumped off the stretcher, helped himself to another 'spot', and remarked, 'This'll do me for a Blighty,' and headed it in that direction.

Everyone in 'B' Company will remember little Teddie Bell ('Ding-Dong', as he was affectionately called) who was seventeen years of age. His people had sent him a parcel in which was an Australian flag of about four inches by three inches.

Teddie was a company runner, and during a break in his message carrying, stuck the flag in a tin of bully beef and placed it on the corner of Anzac House, from where it fluttered until blown to pieces by a shell later in the day.

In April 1918 I stood by a stretcher, in the 5th Field Dressing Station, on which little 'Ding-Dong' lay. My mind travelled back to the incident at Anzac House. But 'Ding-Dong's' shattered arm did not augur Blighty for him. As the evening shadows lengthened, he died. In the distance the rhythmic rumble of artillery seemed to sound a requiem to the spirit of one of the bravest little soldiers ever.

Reveille, June 1930

*Sydney-born **Joe Maxwell** was one of the most highly decorated Australians of WWI. He enlisted in February 1915 and saw action at Gallipoli before being posted to France. During the 3rd Battle of Ypres, Maxwell took command of a platoon, led it in attack, and rescued men from a position under intense enemy fire. For this action he was awarded the Distinguished Conduct Medal and was commissioned in the field as 2nd Lieutenant; he was promoted to Lieutenant in January 1918. Further actions led to the Military Cross and a Bar to the MC for another act of bravery. Maxwell was awarded the Victoria Cross after he took charge in an attack at Estrées on 3 October 1918. Pushing forward alone under intense fire, he captured the most dangerous machine-gun and killed its crew. Again single-handed, he silenced another machine-gun and captured about twenty German prisoners.*

Maxwell was a talented writer and in 1932 published his acclaimed war memoir, Hell's Bells and Mademoiselles. *Although his health deteriorated, he attempted to enlist for WWII. Maxwell collapsed and died of a heart attack in July 1967.*

***Edward 'Ding-Dong' Bell**, mentioned above, from Mascot, Sydney, died on 15 April 1918 at a casualty clearing station near Amiens, after being wounded in action at Hangard Wood.*

The Human Chain

By Ernest Herbert Wilson

Poison gas! The foulest thing the mind of man ever conceived. An insidious creeping horror; a vapour that eats into the lungs, and skins living men.

Mustard gas! What soldier, at the first whiff, has not held his breath and thanked God for a quick pair of hands, and his respirator? I know I did. And in this little recollection I have tried to describe what four soldiers of the 25th Battalion endured, when temporarily blinded by poison gas. They spent a lifetime in a night; holding hands, a human chain, wandering sightless under shell fire.

The battalion was trudging along the Menin Road in the dark, going into reserve trenches. Another Digger and I were carrying a dixie of cold tea which we intended to make hot when we reached the trenches; for a drink of hot tea was comforting on a cold, wet night. Suddenly my foot slipped into a small hole in the road, twisted, and down I went with a sprained ankle.

Here was a pretty pickle. I could hardly put my foot to the ground, and one man couldn't carry that big dixie of tea alone. Sergeant Bill Berkeley ('Old Bill') came back from the head of the platoon, bringing another man to help carry the tea, and he himself gave me a helping hand. I was limping badly, and our progress was naturally slow. The company, the battalion, the brigade passed us by, and we four followed at a snail's pace.

The battalion had long since disappeared, and strange troops were now passing us, going up to the line. Even they vanished in the dark. By and by we reached Hell Fire Corner. And there, at the cross roads, to our dismay, Bill had forgotten which road to take to the reserve trenches.

Hell Fire Corner was not a healthy place at which to stand in conference, arguing which road to take. However, a few shell bursts close by made up our minds for us. We quickly decided to turn to the left. But before we could move, a barrage of gas shells hurtled over with a sound like water swishing in a bucket, and burst.

In a flash, the gas enveloped us. Our hands streaked for our masks, but not quick enough to stop that fatal whiff of poison gas. With throats burning, and noses choked with mucus, the last thing I saw, before I went blind, was a man, maskless, clawing at a tree stump, and breathing in great gulps of poison gas!

We linked hands, and four sightless masked soldiers stumbled off the road into a black wilderness of shell holes!

To most people, the fact of being lost is terrifying. Imagine, then, what our feelings were, blindly clutching at each other in a world of darkness and danger. If one slipped into a shell hole filled with water, all slipped in. If one stumbled, the others held him up. A piece of shell case screaming by, and we fell flat together, still holding hands; fearful, that once broken, the chain would never live again.

Towards morning we stumbled into a field artillery funk hole, to the great surprise of the occupants.

Our sight was now gradually returning, and by daybreak we could see well enough to leave the funk hole. And there, a few hundred yards away, were the trenches we had groped for all night! It was a night of wretchedness I should not care to experience again.

The Queensland Digger, April 1936

Private Ernest Wilson was one of the older volunteers, aged thirty-five when he enlisted in December 1916 and embarked with the 19th Reinforcements, 25th Battalion. Listed as Ernest Hubert Wilson, a storekeeper from Bundaberg, he appears to have adopted Herbert as his second name. He returned to Australia in June 1918.

A Passchendaele Vignette

By '106', Nhill, Victoria

Many returned men are confronted with visualisations of war experiences. These incidents are reflected in their memories at oft-repeated intervals. Little affairs of everyday life remind them of 'something over there'.

A dreary rain-soaked roadside recalls the more dismal interludes in the life of a Digger. Speak of rain, mud, slush and cold, and I'm in that devastating sector facing Passchendaele, where we saw scenes that sickened us intensely; things at which our spirit revolted; we who were part and parcel of that great military machine which seemed to say 'stick to it'. Four days from the evening of 3 October 1917, one saw the war in all its hideousness, and it was only one of the many stunts of its kind during that awful autumn offensive.

It reminds me of an incident which possessed all the humour, pathos and horror of that terrible conflict in one infinitesimal act. We had advanced beyond one of the ridges; got through (some of us) a barrage of machine-gun fire, some rifle-fire, and shells. We seemed to encounter feeble infantry opposition. We passed by a collection of dead which told of our death-dealing artillery. Up to our knees in slush we struggled on.

We reached what we were informed was our objective. We linked water-filled shell holes together into an improvised sort of trench. Cold and miserable, we awaited orders for a further advance, or for the inevitable counterattack.

Prisoners were being taken freely; others were offering themselves up just as freely. Some sought refuge in pillboxes which we had not bothered to investigate. It was whilst gazing back towards our original lines that I observed that unrehearsed act to which I make mention.

A German in the familiar grey uniform and Fritz-style tin hat emerged from underground. He peered nervously around, appearing extremely agitated. He walked a few yards towards me, suddenly halted, stooped beside the form of a dead man, lifted him up (it was one of his own battalion) and laid him gently down again.

He then stripped him of all his clothing and once again raised the body to a standing position. He thereupon engaged in an exuberant display of affection towards the unfortunate victim, hugging and apparently kissing him. And then, with startling abruptness, cast him to one side, there to lie in his nakedness until his time arrived for burial. The perpetrator of this peculiar act then wandered aimlessly further behind our lines, seemingly having become bereft of his senses.

Whenever I think of Passchendaele, that little tragedy is outstanding. Others may have seen it. I wonder!

Mufti, December 1934

The Battle of Broodseinde Ridge: 4 October 1917

By Lieutenant F.E. Trotter

Crash! Crash! Crash! Crash! The throbbing, humming Boche bombing plane which had been hovering overhead dropped its menacing load just to the rear of where, in the darkness, we were trudging through the sticky mud of the marshland.

In quick succession, with frightful reverberations, the incendiary bombs exploded, a great sheet of flame poured from each, leaving a glow from the burning mass akin to the light of day, illuminating all the country round about, revealing the wanton, piled-up mess and wreckage of dead horses, dead mules, dead men, smashed and overturned Army Service Corps wagons and motor vehicles – ammunition, food supplies, bodies of men in a chaos of destruction.

We had worked around the shore of Zillebeke Lake, through one-time beauty spots, where in pre-war days had stood forests of trees. But now, in place of sylvan retreats and the birds calling to their mates, was the screaming of shells, the groans and curses of men; fallen trees were blasted from the ground by their roots or smashed to stumps, a great forest felled by a mightier force than ever a woodsman's axe had been. Thus we traversed up Helles Track and on to Westhoek Ridge.

An hour after midnight we departed from a kindly pillbox at Westhoek Ridge and began our journey up to the rendezvous at Zonnebeke, where the tape line indicated our hopping-off position at dawn. The machine-guns now sprayed their torrents of lead close to our feet or just above our heads; sometimes finding a target amongst us; but we were buoyed up with the comforting assurance that before long we would oust those gunners from their points of vantage.

Fritz was using his new 'daisy-cutter' shells, quite a lot too, taking toll of our lads even when the shells burst wide, for the red-hot masses of steel, spurting from the burst, travelled horizontal to the ground and mowed down those within their course.

At length we arrived at the front line, and took up our positions at the tape line, lying down in no-man's-land waiting for zero time at dawn, and the coming attack upon the German line. It was a starry night and we could see each other's faces quite clearly. As we lay there, the enemy began a desultory shelling, which developed into a light bombardment. Some time after, the Germans opened up their artillery and machine-guns to their fullest limit, belching forth a constant rush of bursting shells, which formed a solid curtain of high explosive shrapnel and bullets. And we were caught in the open like rats in a trap in the ferocity of this German barrage. There we had to stay – until zero – to carry out our programme – should we be spared. I do not think that I had to endure at any time such a pandemonium of bursting shells.

So close and numerous were the shells raining down, that it seemed that every yard of that ground on which we lay must be blown up. Shouting our loudest to each other was useless – the din was too great for us to hear. Shell hole joining shell hole. Holes blasted out, to be re-churned once again by a further shell in the same spot. Looking into the faces of my companions to see whether they were dead or alive, it seemed as though this prolonged horror had paralysed their nerves and turned them into living statues.

When it seemed that everyone but yourself must be dead – when the debris blown up by shells rained constantly down on you, and you thought the next moment, or the next, must be the finish, your imagination gets the upper hand and you wonder just how your end will come. Will it be like that fellow over there – torn limb from limb? Would it be like that chappie who shot himself because his entrails were all lying out on the earth? Would it be a blasting by a high explosive shell, or would we be riddled with shrapnel? Would a daisy-cutter send a red-hot piece of iron to slice the head off?

Suddenly the tension on the nerves was released. We started, and listened, with eager smiles, as though awakened from a nightmare. It was our barrage! Then came the relief of movement.

Dawn, fast growing to the light of day, we rose and hurried over to the German line. And now became apparent the reason for that severe punishment we had suffered from the enemy guns. We found the Germans lying massed on top of their line, waiting for their signal to advance on us. The Germans had planned to attack us, but we had beaten them to it by arranging our zero, six minutes prior to theirs – so that instead of storming over to our trenches in attack, they were surprised to find us pouncing down on them.

There were two distinct elements in their line – a foundation of Prussian Guards who fought bravely, neither giving nor asking for mercy – standing their ground and killing until they themselves were killed. Splendid soldiers! Too proud to submit, too brave to run away. On the other hand, there were lads who were utterly demoralised. These readily surrendered with upraised arms. Watches, and all kinds of personal possessions, dangling from their hands as barter for their lives.

I shall never forget the look of astonishment on the face of the German Officer Commanding when he realised the truth. When we came upon him in his pillbox, he bade us lay down our arms, and expressed disgust that we had not already been disarmed. He thought we were prisoners, captured by his own men, who at that moment should have been getting well on with their attack.

'But it is ridiculous!' he expostulated.

'Of course it's ridiculous,' agreed one of our lads, approaching the German officer with open jack-knife, 'and I'm going to cut off one of your buttons as a souvenir. Got any smutty postcards from Berlin?'

Thus one of the bloodiest battles of the war was turned to a joke; in the midst of this dramatic event, the Australians could smile, and see the humorous side of it.

The Queensland Digger, October 1937

Frederick Edmund Trotter sailed on the Hororata *in the fleet that left Albany on 1 November 1914. He was then a 26-year-old salesman living at Pleasant Hill in central NSW. He enlisted as a private but was promoted to lieutenant and in October 1917 was awarded the Military Medal for devotion to duty and assisting the wounded at the Battle of Broodseinde Ridge, east of Ypres.*

From a Dugout Door: Westhoek Ridge, October 1917

By Hubert Donovan

It is a grey, autumn afternoon in Flanders.

From the door of my dugout I get an uninterrupted view of a typical war landscape, of muddy, brown ridges, dotted with scraggy trees, a few half-demolished houses, and an odd pillbox or two. Above all hangs a pall of grey clouds, which distant shrapnel bursts stab with tiny pinpoints of flame. Away to the left stands the grey-blue outline of a large forest. To the right the battered walls of Zonnebeke church raised in stark ugliness. Three miles away, and immediately in front of me, looms the great, oft-disputed ridge of Passchendaele, marked by a few trees and the remains of a little village.

Nearer, at the foot of another ridge, runs a straight, cobbled road. I don't know the name of that road, but I know that if you follow it westward, you will eventually find yourself at Ypres; or if you traverse it in the opposite direction, it will take you through the German trenches, across Belgium, and perhaps to Berlin, provided you don't get shot in the meantime.

It is not a nice road; I never walk along it without experiencing a cold feeling in the pit of the stomach. Ugly things have happened, and will continue to happen on that road. Its sides are piled high with broken limbers and gun carriages, dead horses and mules, and, yes, a few dead men who, owing to the hurry and bustle of war, have been left unburied. It reeks of dead things and blood. I repeat, it is not a nice road.

At the present moment it is quite peaceful, and a line of mules laden with shells for the 18-pounders is slowly traversing it. Suddenly, the peace of the afternoon is disturbed by a lazy, gurgling, rustling sound, which each moment grows nearer and louder. Then, with a noise like that of a railway engine emerging from a tunnel, a big shell pitches beside the road, and with a terrific crash, sends up a cloud of smoke and dirt.

The debris and shell splinters patter to the ground, and the ammunition train quickens its pace. Again comes that gurgling sound, and a shell bursts right in the middle of the road. When the smoke clears, I observe a wide gap in the centre of the pack train. Some of the mules have broken loose and are wildly careering among the shell holes. Some have turned back; the rest are madly galloping ahead, with their drivers running beside them and clinging to the pack saddles. The road empties and the bombardment ceases.

Bang! A 60-pounder fires behind me. A shell screams overhead; the sound of its flight dies away to a whisper; a column of grey smoke suddenly leaps from the ruins of Passchendaele; rises higher, thins, and drifts southward on the breeze. Swift as a serpent's tongue, a sheet of flame licks the gloom of a shallow gully to my right, and with a thudding bang, an 18-pounder sends a shell whizzing towards the enemy's lines. Guns are firing all around me now, and the ridges ahead are spouting columns of smoke and dust. The evening 'hate' has commenced.

Half an hour later, the guns are still. Fatigue parties are stringing out across the mud on their way to the trenches or to the road to collect rations. A squadron of aeroplanes, like a flock of rooks returning to their nests, comes droning homeward. The first flare of the evening rises above Passchendaele and hovers like a little fairy lamp against the darkling sky. There is a hint of rain in the air. From the mouth of a nearby dugout issues a cheerful voice uplifted in song:

Who wouldn't be a soldier, eh?
Oh, it's a shame to take the pay.
Oh, oh, oh, it's a lovely war!

The WA Digger Book, 1929

There are no records for a **Hubert Donovan**, *but the author would most likely have been* **Hubert O'Donovan Kelly**, *service number 3388, who enlisted at Kalgoorlie as a private in the 16th Infantry Battalion, 11th Reinforcements, and embarked on HMAT* Benalla *at Fremantle on 1 November 1915. He returned to Australia as a corporal in February 1919, and later wrote and published a memoir about railroads.*

Gutzer Farm, Meteren

By Sergeant P. ('Topsy') Turvey, DCM, MM

Stepping from railway trucks at Hazebrouck in April 1918, we were formed up and marched off towards Meteren. What we saw during that night march I shall never forget.

Refugees of all ages and infirmity crowded the roads, and at times it was most difficult to pass them. They were heartbroken, and carried their few belongings slung over their shoulders. One old lady, on being told that we were Australians, exclaimed: 'God bless you, my boys.'

After tramping for some hours, a halt was called and word passed back for all officers and NCOs to come forward. Then Lieutenant-Colonel Don Moore briefly explained the position to us. A few miles ahead lay the village of Meteren, which had been occupied by the enemy that morning, but it was unknown whether he had advanced any further during the day. Between us and Meteren there was no line of defence. We were instructed to closely question any British troops met with and get them to join us, and to beware of spies dressed in British uniforms.

From now on we expected to come in touch with Fritz at any moment. The first batch of Tommies came along, and, on being asked what [units] they belonged to, one, acting as spokesman, said: 'East Yorks and West Lancs, and fed oop.' They had not seen an officer or NCO for days, and were in a bad way, but they willingly joined up with us.

On reaching a position about 300 yards in rear of Gutzer Farm, I was to take out my company Lewis guns and act as a covering party, while new trenches were dug. The night was slipping away fast, and we knew Fritz would attack at dawn, so every man had to 'step on it'.

While scouting for gun positions in the semi-darkness, I discovered the bodies of a young woman about twenty-five and a girl of eight – they had evidently been caught by enemy gunfire during the day. At the sight of those poor souls, I saw red and swore to take toll of Fritz if an opportunity came.

The digging operations being completed just before daybreak, my guns were withdrawn to the front line. But the position at Gutzer Farm appealed to me as an observation post, and I received permission from Lieutenant ('Dad') Jarvis to take a Lewis gun out there. Four men readily volunteered to come with me and carry ammunition.

We had scarcely got into position, and were gazing towards the village of Meteren over the undulating country, when we saw miles of infantry slowly but surely goose-stepping towards us. Officers on grey horses were riding up and down the column. It was really a wonderful sight.

I sent one of my men back to HQ with a message, and inside of a few minutes the most awful slaughter was going on. Our artillery had got the exact range. But in spite of terrible losses Fritz kept on coming ahead, so I decided to present him with 1150 rounds of small arms ammunition. It was like firing into a haystack – one could not miss. The Germans were about six deep in places. They became very much unsettled in front, but kept creeping up on both flanks. So I sent the other three back to the line while I emptied remaining magazines into Fritz. As I finished there were 'Hocks' uncomfortably close, so I grabbed the gun and bolted across no-man's-land, followed by a hail of bullets, and reached the trench without a scratch, though one bullet tore a hole through the back of my tunic.

The enemy now re-formed his shattered lines and very soon came across the open at us. Lieutenant Jarvis would not allow any firing until the Germans came well forward, and at that stage I saw the finest example of bravery in my whole experience.

A German officer, on foot, leading his men, yelled out something like 'Forwich, Forwich,' but a volley from our lines sent him and many others to grass. However, he struggled to his feet and again called on his men to advance. Another volley sent him in a heap, and it seemed that he was done. But, to our amazement, he gallantly struggled to his feet, and, lurching unsteadily from one side to the other to get his balance, called again, 'Forwich, Forwich.' This time he took the full count.

I also recall the bravery of Private O.A. Compton (of Goulburn). He had lost a brother at Anzac in 1915 and had sworn to avenge him at the first opportunity – and this was the first real chance he had of point blank shooting. With reckless courage he stood right up on the parapet and put in some good work, but it was not long before he was hit, mortally.

Soon the attack fizzled out and we began to feel pleased with ourselves. One NCO got out his shaving gear and had a clean-up. Lieutenant Jarvis produced his tin whistle and played 'Australia Will Be There' and some German selections. Little did we suspect what was soon to be sprung upon us.

Suddenly a fleet of huge Gothas [heavy twin-winged bombers] swooped down upon our lines, dropping bombs and machine-gunning us viciously. Under cover of this, the German infantry again attacked, but they were beaten men. Our losses were terrible – good old Sergeant Jack Mott went west with many others of our best men.

The Tommies with us were the finest lads one would ever wish for. Later we took up a collection and a fair sum was handed to each. It was with tears in their eyes and lumps in their throats when they eventually had to leave us. That party, and many others who similarly joined us, would afterwards have you know that they were 'Lesslie's Own', after our brigadier, General Lesslie.

Reveille, November 1934

Sergeant Percival Turvey, from Rylstone, NSW, served with the 3rd Battalion and was twice decorated, for gallantry and devotion to duty and for daring and skill as a Lewis gunner. He had enlisted in June 1915 after, the records show, being rejected initially as he suffered at that time from piles or haemorrhoids. He returned to Australia in March 1919.

The 'Emma Gees'

By Private A.H. Cresswell

It would be interesting to know what was the AIF record for number of shots fired continuously – that is, rapid fire – by any single No. 7.

I heard of a machine-gunner at Daisy Wood (Passchendaele) who fired so continuously from a pillbox that the cordite fumes from the gun killed both him and his No. 2. But the best I saw was at Morlancourt in 1918, under rather peculiar circumstances. We were in the Bunbury close support line and had fired a barrage for the night stunt. We had a fairly quiet time from midnight onwards, and after 'stand down' were peacefully sleeping when the sentry yelled: 'Stand to!' A few 'Minnies' were apparently giving the chaps in the front line exercise. As we raced to our guns we thought there must have been some mistake, but the sentries mounting the guns on tripods – the latter had, of course, been left in their positions – disproved this. I had hardly arrived at the Vickers before the officer, who was at the trench telephone, started repeating the fire directions, concluding with, 'Battery 5000 rounds rapid fire!'

Forty thousand rounds on one spot in ten noiseful minutes! Before it was half-finished my No. 2 was bleeding from the nose, and we were enveloped in an enormous cloud of dust. We had no blanket screen and had no time to fix condenser tubes, and the steam from the water boiling in the barrel-casing was blowing straight on to the fine dust of the parapet. Between belts the No. 2 gasped: 'Christ, we have drawn the crabs, he's ranging!' The last shot had hardly left the barrel before we fled, and, if we had given Fritz a lively ten minutes, certainly he gave that trench twenty. It was wiped out when we returned.

We puzzled long over this sudden outburst of ours, and eventually it came to light that an artillery observation officer, well forward, had spotted a German light battery moving back, and, as for some reason he could not immediately connect up with his own battery, he called for the nearest machine-guns.

When we made the push in August, the German battery was discovered, the horses still unburied, and no less than 300 bullet holes were counted in one gun wheel! The crews must have suffered badly – and this, without a single ranging burst or correction, says something for that forward observation officer's range-finding, and for the machine-gunner's accuracy.

Reveille, December 1934

Private Arthur Herbert Cresswell, eighteen, from Brisbane, was a member of the 7th Machine-Gun Company. He was mentioned in despatches for his service.

The Australian Night Attack at Villers-Bretonneux

By Lieutenant General Sir J.J. Talbot Hobbs, KCB, KCMG, GOC of the 5th Australian Division at the time of the battle

April 25th – Anzac Day – is not only famous for the landing at Gallipoli in 1915, but also for a brilliant success in the recapture of Villers-Bretonneux on the night of 24 to 25 April 1918, which is justly considered one of the finest of many feats of arms achieved by Australian soldiers during the Great War.

Early on the 24th, the Germans, after a furious bombardment of high explosive and asphyxiating shells, launched their infantry attack against the 8th British Divisional front and the right of the 5th Australian Division held by the 14th Brigade, and also two minor attacks on the left of the division held by the 8th Australian Brigade, with special Storm Troops and tanks. The 5th Australian Division easily repulsed the two minor attacks on their left front; the 14th Brigade on the right, heavily attacked, stood firm on its ground at Hill 104.

Villers-Bretonneux was captured from the 8th Division and a great part of the Bois L'Abbé was also seized. Thus the Germans completely overlooked the low ground and could sweep the whole space around Amiens with the fire of heavy guns. Heavy fighting continued during the day, but the offer of assistance from the 5th Australian Division was declined until about 3 p.m., when the 5th was placed under III Corps and the divisional commander [the author] was informed by telephone that a brigade of the 5th would be required to co-operate with the 8th British Division and the 13th Australian Infantry Brigade in recapturing the village and other ground lost.

The 5th Australian Divisional Commander's plan, briefly, was for the 15th Infantry Brigade (Brigadier General H.E. 'Pompey'

Elliott) and the 5th Divisional Reserve (who had been eating their hearts out since early morning at not being permitted to take part in the fight) to make a converging attack from the north-west, in conjunction with a similar movement of the 13th Infantry Brigade (Brigadier-General Glasgow) from the south-east. The 15th and 13th Australian Infantry Brigades were to link up on the railway line south of the Amiens–St Quentin road.

At the appointed time the 13th Infantry Brigade moved off to the attack in the misty moonlight. At the outset there was a hitch. As the brigade began to muster at the edge of the Bois L'Abbé, it came under fire from the German outposts among the trees. It was thought that the wood was clear. A picket of British and Australian scouts was pushed into the wood to engage the German riflemen, and the place of 'rendezvous' had to be fixed further back.

On moving forward, feeling their way along the south side of the Bois L'Abbé, the West Australians on the left of the brigade soon became engaged in hard fighting with machine-gunners among the trees. As they cleared the wood they stumbled on a nest of machine-guns in a hollow. The West Australians passed to the right of this nest, leaving the German gunners firing at nothing. They moved forward past Villers-Bretonneux supported by Queenslanders on their right. As they did so, some German machine-gunners saw their chance and ran to the edge of the wood to fire into the backs of the West Australians. The South Australian Battalion, following in reserve, came upon them and annihilated them, capturing all their machine-guns.

The advance swept forward over the plateau toward the objective line. The scene was a weird one. Machine-guns were firing from every quarter. Villers-Bretonneux was on fire. Finally, after heavy fighting in Monument Wood and incidents too numerous to mention, the brigade took up positions a little to the north-east of the village and obtained touch with the 15th Australian Brigade.

The ascent of the plateau side was now almost complete. 'A' Company of the 59th Battalion came under heavy enemy rifle-fire from positions just in front as it reached the first objective line. Without an instant's delay, the company charged in the direction of the opposition, and Major Kuring, the senior officer on the spot, gave in loud tones the order for a general charge.

A wild and terrible yell from hundreds of throats split the midnight air, and the whole line broke into a rapid run and surged irresistibly forward, bayonets gleaming thirstily in the moonlight. A storm of enemy machine-gun and rifle fire was poured into the oncoming ranks, but checked them not at all. A hundred enemy flares lit up the terrible scene in vivid light, in which the Germans read their fate too well. Shriek following shriek marked the toll of the deadly bayonets and good round Australian oaths were ripped out in quick succession. The German defences were arranged in a series of strong posts distributed in depth as far back as the second objective. They fought stubbornly but they were hopelessly outclassed.

One by one the strong post garrisons were captured or exterminated, and the 59th and 60th Battalions, now hopelessly intermingled but still preserving a general correctness of formation and direction, were resting triumphantly on their final objective. From the moment at which the charge was ordered, it had been purely and simply a soldiers' battle, in which victory had been gained by the great dash and fighting superiority of the junior officers, the NCOs, and men. To them, therefore, the praise.

The Queensland Digger, April 1935

Sir Joseph John Talbot Hobbs (1864–1938) was one of the outstanding Australian generals of WWI, much respected for his concern over the welfare of troops. English-born, he was a successful Perth architect and prominent member of the Anglican Church, whose early war service saw him command Australian artillery at Gallipoli. By December 1916 he was appointed commander of the

5th Division on the Western Front and his planning and leadership were the key to the recapture of Villers-Bretonneux. He did not retire from the army until 1927, returning to his architectural practice and designing the West Australian War Memorial. He died of a heart attack at sea in 1938, on his way to the unveiling of the Australian War Memorial at Villers-Bretonneux.

Machine-Gun Bullets 'Bugs' Says Yank

By C.J. James

I first came in contact with the Americans at Villers-Bretonneux. I was with a section of brigade observers on the eastern side of the village, and lived in the cellar of a chateau attached to a wool factory, in which we had our observation post. A section of American observers came to us for instruction, and they were under a sergeant who introduced himself as 'William Har'm Ham from Karns's City'.

William Ham's first enquiry was as to the whereabouts of all the 'goddarmed cellars'. We explained that they were 'napoo' as Brigadier Rosenthal had sent a picket through the village and destroyed all the grog. Bill said he would see for himself and we could not stop him. We explained about the machine-gun fire, showed him where not to go, and left him.

Late in the afternoon we began to get a bit anxious about Bill, and a search party was going out to find what was left of him, when there was the sound of very inebriated singing, and along came Bill staggering under a heavy load inside and two bottles of champagne outside.

We welcomed him like a long-lost brother, and he told us what he had been doing. He had apparently visited every hole in the ground he found in the village, and found only sour cider – much to his disgust. He then agreed that we were right about the village, so looked about for a possie outside.

He saw in the near distance what he described as a very pretty little house with a coloured roof, and walked over the open field to it. When he got there he found a party of men who abused him and said he would draw the crabs. They were an anti-tank section. They told Bill that there were no bottles there, but Bill went to see for himself, and digging down in a corner of the cellar, he souvenired six bottles of 'phiz', four of which he and the gun crew drank, before Bill thought of his cobbers doing a perish in the village. He staggered out across the field and arrived safely.

We wondered where on earth he had been, and asked him if he could show us the house. He took us out and pointed to what was known as 'the Doll's House', outside the village towards the enemy trenches and approached by no cover but by a field as clean as your hand, and under direct machine-gun fire. You wouldn't have got an Aussie to go there in broad daylight for Hindenburg's own Iron Cross.

I asked Bill if he didn't notice any machine-gun fire while he was strolling across. 'No,' was his answer, 'but I tell you, while I was going over, and coming back, there was millions of bugs flying around me – buzz, buzz – and I could not see where they came from.'

I could never forget Bill's face when we told him the 'bugs' were machine-gun bullets!

Reveille, October 1931

Charles John James was listed as a 25-year-old journalist from Coogee, NSW, when he embarked as a private with the 2nd Infantry Battalion Reinforcements at Sydney in February 1917. He was a Queenslander, whose father ran the Western Champion *newspaper in Barcaldine.*

A Billet in France – and a Vision

By Major G.V. Dudley, DSO, MC

It is pouring rain, one of those days when one wonders if life is worthwhile, more especially as the job has to be done of getting six 9.2 howitzers into action as quickly as possible. We had just arrived at this spot, about 500 yards from the railway crossing at Morbecque. It is early April 1918, but the weather is still cold, damp and windy.

The battery's place of action is a field where a labourer's cottage stands, and the battery commander at once requisitions this as his signal station. There are two old women, sisters, still living in the house, one of them bedridden, but war cannot allow sympathetic feelings to creep in. The guns having been mounted, they are at once registered, and at every shot the old walls shake and the windows are broken.

The strength of the signal detachment at the time was twenty-four, and in some miraculous manner the sergeant managed to get them all billeted in the cottage, as well as establish his and the battery wireless posts there.

One old woman huddles over the stove, but as the door opens and the swirl of cold air catches her, she shivers and groans: '*La porte – ouverte toujours; toujours entrer et partir, toujours sorti et retourner, je suis très misérable.*'

The guns keep her awake all night and the great flashes light up her room in a terrifying manner. She cannot keep a decent fire going as coal is scarce and very dear. As with coal, so with food. She does not know how she will keep going for the people of the village have all fled. She has had no bread for the last three days. But for some meat sent from the officers' mess; this with one or two eggs, which with a little milk she beats into a sort of pancake, was all the food she and her companion had partaken of for days. They will not leave, though the house will probably crumble up – that is if it is not previously hit by a shell.

The signallers provide the sisters with food and fuel, and they become quite talkative, especially about their own troubles. There is the usual list of the men of the family killed, wounded and captured. A son was wounded in the first gas attack at Ypres. He was in hospital for eight months – six at Châlons-sur-Marne, and two at Clermont, where he died.

'I visited him twice at Châlons and once at Clermont,' one sister said.

'What!' I replied. 'You made those big journeys?' (For she obviously has never been beyond the nearest village.)

'Ah,' she explained, 'it was to Mass I went – three apparitions in all, I saw there!' The old soul seemed to have had great comfort out of these 'visits' to her son.

As there were no civil authorities in the district it took some time to arrange for the transfer of these two unfortunate women, but one day a French ambulance arrived with two gendarmes and a most heart-rending scene took place; the bedridden sister screaming and the other crying piteously that she would never again see her son if she were taken from the house in which he was born.

Reveille, December 1934

Major George Vernon Dudley was appointed after WWI as Chief Protector of Aboriginals and Commissioner of Police in the Northern Territory.

Captain C.W. Somerset, MC: A Gallant Company Commander

By Lieutenant K.H. McConnel

Those who served with him – either in the 5th Light Horse Regiment or the 1st Battalion – will be indeed sorry to learn of the death of Captain W.H.R. Somerset, MC, at Toogoolawah, Queensland, at the age of forty-one. He was one of the finest company officers whom the war produced – a man who earned the affection and respect of everyone with whom he came into contact. Many of his exploits are comparable with those of other heroes better known perhaps by reason of the array of decorations which they received for their work.

Rollo Somerset was born at Caboonbah, a cattle station on the Brisbane River, the son of Henry Somerset, a well-known Queensland MP. He came from a long line of soldiering forebears and took to it as a duck takes to water.

When war broke out he joined up, like many other squatters' sons, with the 5th Light Horse, and it was my privilege to be closely associated with him throughout the war. Our experience on Gallipoli did not give much opportunity for him to show his fighting worth, but he was one of those who, though worn almost to a skeleton by the ravages of dysentery, not only held on till it was almost too late, but kept many others going with his example of cheery optimism.

After the Evacuation he was granted a commission in the infantry, being posted to the 1st Battalion. At our first spell in the trenches of Flanders, he was caught on patrol by a machine-gun and evacuated, wounded, but was back again in six weeks, having refused to be sent to Blighty. He soon attracted the notice of our commanding officer, General (then Colonel) Heane, and went into the Somme stunt as assistant adjutant, to become adjutant on the very first day as a result of the gassing of Lieutenant B.G. White.

In that Hell that was Pozières he went about doing his job with a big grin as if the whole show were a picnic, and had the luck to come through this stunt and Mouquet Farm the only unwounded subaltern in the battalion.

He was then posted as second-in-command to that wonderful little soldier – Phillip Howell-Price, DSO, MC and Bar – in 'D' Company, and in that capacity at Flers, though severely wounded in the leg, he won, with Lieutenant A'Beckett, his Military Cross by leading three times in succession a hopeless attack over mud and filth up to an uncut enemy wire.

Once again he refused to be sent to Blighty and was back again in a few weeks to face that ghastly winter; and in the follow-up of early 1917 he distinguished himself on more than one occasion by his quick wit. At Bullecourt he was in command of 'D' Company when the 1st Brigade went in to find and take over from what was left of the 2nd Division, a seemingly hopeless position, and to hold that position against thirteen counterattacks in three days.

There are few who know the real story of how Somerset and Moffatt, with what was left of 'B' and 'D' Companies, not only hung on to the block on the left flank, under continued attacks, but were also largely instrumental in checking the attacks from the right flank by enfilading fire from their Lewis guns.

In the middle of one of these attacks I was sent over by Captain Mackenzie (later Colonel A.K. Mackenzie) and found these two wonderful men with a handful of rifle grenadiers going for their lives pumping the old Mills bombs into Fritz; stick bombs flying everywhere, little Hell to pay, and Somerset and Moffatt laughing like schoolboys as one of them loaded and the other popped off the bombs.

'Get to Hell out of this, you big mug,' they warned me. 'As if there aren't enough flaming officers about the place!' Just then they spotted a few more helmets across the way. 'Ping, ping' went a couple more grenades, there was a howl from over the way, and another delighted chuckle from Somerset. But for their own modesty these two officers could hardly have failed to be decorated for their work in this stunt.

The next night, back in support behind the railway embankment, I was just starting off for the line with a party carrying Mills bombs when a 5.9 [shell] plumped right in the middle of us, wounding several of the party and sending the rest scooting for shelter. I was as windy as Hell and rather nonplussed, but there was old 'Somy' out in the open telling me not to be a bloody fool, pulling the Diggers out of their dugouts with a joke, and in no time he had us off on our journey.

So he went on right through the piece, a man who knew no fear and who bore a charmed life, though three times wounded. It is history how up in front of Hazebrouck, not long after the German breakthrough of 1918, the 1st Battalion, finding the enemy somewhat sleepy in its front, started to send out daylight patrols, resulting in the taking of 150 prisoners and the advancing of the line by several hundred yards without a casualty. Who had the bright idea of sending out the patrols? Rollo Somerset and Captain R.I.C. Macgregor, MC. This stunt was reported throughout the British Army as an example of initiative, but neither company commander received a decoration.

Captain Somerset went home just before the Armistice on 1914 leave, and was immediately plunged into the task of managing an estate. Caught by the cattle slump of 1920, he, in common with so many Queenslanders, found himself in a sea of almost insuperable difficulties, but he set his teeth, and with the help of a plucky little wife battled along ceaselessly for fifteen long and difficult years until his health finally broke and he took the long trail which so many of his friends have trodden before him. To the very end he placed his family and his duty first, and himself last, and he went as he had lived, a soldier and a gentleman.

Lieutenant Kenneth Hamlyn McConnel, of Cressbrook, Queensland, had been a nineteen-year-old student when first posted to the 5th Light Horse Brigade as a private, and later to the 1st Battalion.

*His colleague and friend **Captain Charles William Henry Rollo Somerset** was just a year older.*

Soldiers, Underwear, Goats and Pigs

By 'J. McR'

The story was circulated after the 1st Division went into action in 1918 at Strazeele that two members of the 1st Battalion, one dressed in a frock coat and top hat, and his companion wearing women's attire, took part in the hop-over. As a member of the 1st Field Ambulance, which had a dressing station at the brewery in Borre Village, between Strazeele and Hazebrouck, I well remember two wounded Diggers talking and laughing about that incident. I understand that the frock-coated one carried a walking stick, and his efforts to emulate the antics of Charlie Chaplin were quite creditable.

Many of the Diggers in that stunt wore women's undies, which they had souvenired from the deserted home, exchanging their own, as they had no time to wash their clothes for days. Nurses at hospitals where the wounded Diggers were admitted were consequently amazed and amused at the garments that came to light when uniforms were removed.

Some of the funniest incidents of the war took place at that time in the Hazebrouck sector. A Digger was seen leading a goat down the main road from Pradelles to Borre when Fritz began to send over some of his 'daisy-cutting' stuff. With kindly solicitude for the goat, the Digger removed his tin hat, tied it over the goat's head, and went on with the leading process.

Again, a padre who was attached to the dressing station at Borre, led a squad one night to a field where a lot of pigs had been impounded under a guard. Through a back entrance admission was gained to the pound, and a porker was duly assassinated. He was then placed on a stretcher and covered with a blanket. When challenged by the guard on the way back, the padre explained that 'a poor devil had been badly knocked at one of the billets'. As the area was under constant shell fire, this went down well, and there was pork at the dressing station for several days.

Reveille, January 1931

The author, 'J. McR', would appear to be **Private James McRorie MM** *of the 1st Field Ambulance, who, as a 24-year-old clerk, embarked from Sydney on 13 October 1915, giving as his next of kin his mother in Toowoomba, Queensland. McRorie was awarded the Military Medal for his actions over three days (25–27 September 1917), when he worked without rest or sleep as a stretcher-bearer 'under the worst possible conditions, showing splendid courage and devotion to duty, despite continual enemy barrages and intense shell fire'. His actions encouraged his comrades to clear from the battlefield 'numbers of wounded men' who otherwise could not have received medical treatment. He returned to Australia on 23 September 1918.*

Propaganda Led to Record Number of Prisoners

From a staff officer's notes

The abnormally large number of prisoners captured by the 1st Australian Division at the Battle of Chuignes not only surprised us, but for a time caused us to wonder whether we had caught the Germans in the middle of an inter-divisional relief. The fact that we had taken prisoners from three divisions on our front seemed, for a time, to lend colour to this view.

Our intelligence officers began to question the prisoners, who all maintained that the three divisions comprised the normal garrison of the area attacked. They were then asked why they were holding the front in such strength, and they replied that the existence of good accommodation in the deep dungeons of the Chuignes Valley, and the absence of suitable living quarters in the devastated area east of that locality, had resulted in the support and reserve regiments being quartered close up to the front line.

As this was in direct opposition to the instructions Ludendorff had issued for holding the line, copies of which had fallen into our hands on 8 August and subsequent days, we began to wonder whether those instructions had been modified or disregarded. Among our prisoners were two battalion commanders belonging to different divisions, and they both gave the same explanation, blaming the German press for misleading them into believing that the Australian Corps had 'shot its bolt' on 8 August and was not capable of further sustained effort.

It so happened that just before the attack of 8 August, Sir John Monash had issued a message to the troops, in which he had said: 'Because of the completeness of our plans and dispositions, of the number of troops engaged, and of the depth to which we intend to overrun the enemy's positions, this battle will be one of the most memorable of the whole war; and there can be no doubt that by capturing our objectives, we shall inflict blows on the enemy which will make him stagger, and will bring the end appreciably nearer.'

It also happened that the Germans had obtained a copy of that message and had published it in the German papers with a colouring calculated to mislead their readers. In a leading article the *Berliner Tageblatt* of 17 August 1918 (several copies of which we afterwards found in the Chuignes Valley) construed this message to mean that Sir John Monash had promised his troops a breakthrough which had failed; and that the Australian Corps had been shattered and had come to the end of its resources. The Australians, therefore, the article continued, need no longer be taken into calculation as an instrument of attack by the English.

Both battalion commanders alleged that they had been misled by that and similar articles published in other German papers into believing that the Australian offensive had spent itself and that no further attack by the corps was probable. It was because of this belief that their respective divisional commanders had temporarily disregarded Ludendorff's instructions for holding the front, and had concentrated most of their troops in the excellent dugout accommodation in the forward area.

Was there ever a more striking case of propaganda recoiling upon the heads of those who employed it? Published with the intention of deceiving the German public and keeping their morale up, it had the effect of deceiving the German troops holding the line opposite us, and had enabled the 1st Australian Division to establish a record unique in the war.

The Queensland Digger, October 1932

Airman's Bomb: Toll of Death

By Lieutenant Colonel G.E. McDonald

The 3rd Battalion AIF was with the support line on 8 August 1918, on that part of the flank where the 1st Brigade covered the very dangerous position at Chipilly. During the night which followed, we were moved across the front to Harbonnières, where in the dawn of next morning, the whole of the brigade advanced in Lihons, relieved the 2nd Brigade and took over the old French trenches.

It was during the night march to Harbonnières that the 3rd Battalion had an experience which will live long in the memory of those who were present. Moving off in the early evening, we had arrived at the recent German gun positions, when, some doubt arising as to which was the correct route, the battalion was halted in close formation on a track, while the acting commanding officer, Major Burrett, DSO, had a look around. The night was then fairly dark, only a pale moon peeping through the clouds from time to time.

Presently the too-familiar drone of a German plane was heard, and the sound left no doubt that the plane was flying low. The command was passed through: 'Stand still everywhere!' As the plane flew overhead, it was so low that the German aviator could be seen looking over, but as no one moved it was hoped that we had not been seen in the darkness. Circling around, the plane turned back toward the enemy position, the battalion still standing perfectly still.

Then it was found that we had been observed. Apparently the glint of the moonlight on our helmets had betrayed us, for the shriek of the first bomb was quickly followed by the rapid succession of the plane's whole complement.

When the first bomb burst, I was standing at the head of 'D' Company. Immediately the bomb burst I shouted for the company to scatter and lie down. The order was executed very promptly. Myself, I took a couple of paces off the track and threw myself down just as a bomb burst where I had been standing a moment before. The concussion caused me to bounce on the ground.

The last bomb fell just about where the end of the company had been halted, and caused the only casualty in 'D' Company. One man, believing that the bomb was about to fall directly on him, crouched on hands and knees, evidently with the intention of jumping further away, and the bomb killed him.

Quickly re-forming, the battalion was steadied up. It was then found that the casualties were numerous. The first bomb, falling amongst battalion headquarters, killed Lieutenant Fergusson [from Bathurst, NSW] and about seventeen NCOs and men, and the other bombs caused casualties throughout the battalion.

When the commanding officer returned, and we moved through the circle of casualties, the doctor and the padres stood on either side of the track and warned the men, 'Step softly over our dead,' who were lying just as they had fallen.

This shook the battalion rather badly, because we had been halted in a comparatively quiet spot, and especially because there had been no shell fire at the time. The suddenness of the whole affair was startling, and the battalion standing closed-up offered a very easy target to the enemy. But if the advance in the morning was a little more grim and silent than usual, it was not to be wondered at. These things must pass, however, for the enemy was still in front, desperately trying to bar our way and stop our advance.

'So pass the word for the Fighting Third.'

Reveille, August 1930

George Edward McDonald, aged thirty-two, was a master sign-writer from Oxford Street, Sydney. He was mentioned in despatches and returned in July 1919.

The Largest Single War Trophy

From a staff officer's notes

The 1st Australian Division established a unique record in the Battle of Chuignes, that of capturing the largest single trophy secured during the war – the monster 15-inch naval gun with which the Boche had shelled Amiens. It was captured by the 3rd Battalion of the 1st Brigade in Arcy Wood.

The gun, with its carriage, platform and concrete foundations, weighed more than 500 tons. It had a range of more than twenty-four miles; its shell weighed nearly a ton, and its barrel was seventy feet long.

A double line of railway several miles in length had been specially built to the site in order to install it, and for the transport of its ammunition. The gun was electrically trained and elevated, and the machinery for handling its shells and for loading it was electrically operated. To accommodate the operating machinery, dynamos, etc. as well as the ammunition, tunnels had been dug into the adjacent hillside, which also contained dugouts for the crew of the gun.

When we captured it, the gun and its mounting had been completely destroyed, and the muzzle lay buried in the ground. For a long while there were animated discussions among the artillery experts of the corps and divisions as to whether the gun had burst while firing or had been deliberately destroyed, although eventually the latter theory was generally accepted. It was not until some months afterwards, when I was at corps headquarters, that the full facts about the gun were obtained from a German prisoner.

According to his story, the Germans began to emplace the gun early in April 1918, with the objective of bombarding the important railway junction at Amiens and denying its use to the Allies. The gun was ready for firing the first week of June, and fired continuously for about three weeks, its maximum firing capacity being about thirty rounds a day.

Towards the end of June the original gun was worn out and it was decided to replace it. Another gun was obtained from Krupp's and its erection had been completed by the evening of 7 August – the night before our attack. It started firing again on the early morning of 8 August and fired thirty-five shells in all. Early next morning, as the gun was then within range of our heavy artillery, it was decided to destroy it. The crew was instructed to remove everything that could be removed, and then about 9 o'clock the gun was blown up.

After the Armistice, when I was at corps headquarters, the question arose of what was to become of this gun. Both General Monash and the then Australian Prime Minister (Mr Hughes) were very keen that it should be brought to Australia as a trophy of war, and the corps was asked to make the necessary arrangements. Now, it is very easy to make such requests, but not quite as easy to comply with them. The corps commander (Sir J.J. Talbot Hobbs) instructed me to have very careful enquiries made as to what would be required to enable the wishes of Sir John Monash and Mr Hughes to be carried out.

Instructions were accordingly issued to a senior officer of the Australian heavy artillery and a senior officer of engineers to go into the matter and submit a report as to the work required and the estimated cost of removing the gun to England.

After a thorough enquiry lasting some days, they reported that the railway line to the site had been destroyed by the Germans and would have to be rebuilt, and that several miles of new line would have to be built to connect with the railway line to Amiens, it being risky to attempt to take the gun over any of the temporary bridges over the Somme built to replace those destroyed by the Germans in their retreat. As the machinery used by the Germans to install the gun had been destroyed, it would be necessary to obtain special railway cranes from England to lift it and special trucks to carry it. These would have to be specially brought across the English

Channel on the railway ferry. Finally, they reported, there was only one crane in Australia capable of lifting the gun from the vessel bringing it out.

The estimated cost was so great (running into thousands of pounds) that the corps commander did not feel justified in authorising the expenditure. Nothing more was heard for some weeks, and then word was received that Mr Hughes was coming to corps headquarters for a few days. Sure enough, the matter was raised the first night Mr Hughes arrived, but all we could get out of him was a demand that the gun be sent to Australia. So matters rested until the night before he was due to return to London, when it cropped up again, largely at my instigation, because I wanted something definite settled about it. Mr Hughes was equally emphatic that the gun must be sent to Australia, but he could not be induced to put the instructions in writing or authorise the necessary expenditure.

For some time nothing was done as we at corps headquarters had our hands full getting rid of the horses, equipment and ammunition still with units, as well as repairing the damage to roads, railways, bridges, etc. destroyed by the Germans. When our work eased a little, the case of the big gun at Arcy Wood again cropped up. The suggestion was then made by Captain Kemsley, an Adelaide boy who held the position of staff captain on the administrative branch, that the site should be cleaned up, fenced in, and presented to the city of Amiens as a monument to the part the Australian Corps had played in its defence. This proposal was placed before the corps commander and approved by him.

On the suggestion being referred to the Australian authorities in London, they gave their consent. After the site had been cleaned up and the gun fenced in, it was formally presented to the City of Amiens as a souvenir of the Australian Corps.

The Queensland Digger, October 1932

Billy the Bantam:
A True Veteran

By Lieutenant Len Plasto

Unique among the regimental mascots of the AIF was the little bantam cock – 'Billy' – which, for nearly three years, was the mascot of the 13th Battalion.

Billy joined the 12th Reinforcements of the 13th Battalion at Liverpool camp in September 1915, in the charge of Private W. Symonds. He was issued with an identity disc, which he proudly wore throughout his military career. The disc bore the following particulars: regimental number, 4000; name, Billy Bantam; religion, R.C.; rank, bugler.

From the start Billy took his duties seriously and never failed to sound the 'Reveille'. After six weeks at sea on the *Suevic*, Billy arrived at Zeitoun camp, Egypt, in January 1916. There he won quick ascendancy over the camp's heterogeneous group of mascots, which included wallabies, opossums, dogs and snakes.

A fox terrier took a violent dislike to Billy and on one occasion rushed at the bantam with murderous intent. However Billy shaped up to his adversary so fearlessly that the dog thought better of his evil designs, and thereafter treated the bantam with great respect.

Billy was at last posted to his unit in March 1916, at Tel-el-Kebir. He took part in the desert march to Serapeum, perched on the packs of various members of his company. Despite his haughty and arrogant bearing, he was a most friendly little fellow, and was quite happy on the shoulder of any of the Diggers when the battalion was on the march.

In France, Billy, for the first time since leaving Australia, found himself among his own kind, and in the farmyard of his first billet at Steentje, near Bailleul, proceeded to assert himself. Cheered on by his company, he quickly disposed of two roosters three times his size, but a third and even bigger one took some starch out of Billy.

At Bois-Grenier, Billy did a tour of duty in the trenches, and treated shell and machine-gun fire with nonchalance. On the Somme he was left with the transport when the battalion took part in the attack on Mouquet Farm, and where his owner, Private Symonds, made the supreme sacrifice.

Billy was now permanently attached to the transport for 'rations and discipline' and came under the care of Private Tom Igoe. At first Tom was a little too liberal with Billy's rations, and an overdose of cheese led to Billy being paraded before the Regimental Medical Officer. Castor oil and twenty-four hours no duty were prescribed.

At Neuve-Eglise Billy was introduced to the late Mr W.A. Holman, Premier of NSW, who, on hearing of his fondness for cake, gave Igoe 5 francs to provide the mascot with a banquet. However, judging by appearances shortly after the Premier's visit, most of the donation was used in providing Tom with the wine that was white!

At Ribemont, Billy was stolen, and Captain Harry Murray, VC, threatened to turn out his company to recover the mascot. However, the resourceful Igoe, by a little amateur sleuth work, succeeded in regaining possession of his charge.

Billy's sojourn in France ended in a state of peaceful domesticity. Igoe, after a brief visit to Hazebrouck hospital, returned to the battalion with a bantam hen, and in the course of time Billy became a proud father. His wife and progeny accompanied the battalion on its journeys, but they did not march with the men, like Billy. Their conveyance was a bully-beef box, on top of a limber.

Tom Igoe left the battalion with the first batch of 1914 men, in October 1918. With him went Billy. The orders about taking birds and animals on the transport were strict, but Igoe, with considerable resource, smuggled Billy aboard in a bandsman's instrument case.

Eventually Billy landed in his hometown, and in 1929 died at Pyrmont – a true veteran of the Great War.

Reveille, 1935

2nd Lieutenant Leonard Patrick Plasto, *who had left Australia as a 21-year-old clerk from Ryde, Sydney, took on the task of Honorary Secretary, 13th Battalion Association, after returning in May 1919.*

An Australian Race Meeting in France

By Lieutenant Colonel A.W. Hyman, OBE, VD

War is war, but the momentous years of 1914–18 for men of the AIF did not mean that they were fighting all the time! Some days (and nights), for example, in Egypt, England and France were the happiest of their lives!

The 22 July 1918, at Allonville in France, will ever stand out as one of these – an occasion on which a real Australian race meeting was held under the very eyes of the Boche. His balloons overlooked our proceedings, but he very sportingly never fired a shell the whole day. He had often done so before (and afterwards) and had got many casualties.

There were perhaps 11,000 present, including generals, officers and men, who came from all armies – Australian, French, British and Canadian – and there was one woman! There were bookies in tall hats and military uniforms; crown and anchor 'kings', and punters, of course. There were three-card tricksters wherever you looked, and they were all there with the consent of the 'Heads'. It had, in fact, been decided to give the boys (as they then were) a real 'slap up' happy day, because for weeks past there had been nothing but strife and strafing! The Battle of Villers-Bretonneux had just been won by the Australian Corps.

This day of comedy began with a tragedy, for two officers were killed in the first race. Fortunately we were able to keep the fact from the crowd, as the field ambulance quickly appeared on the scene. After that the proceedings went forward without a hitch.

The mule races (the principal one of which was the Villers-Bretonneux Sprint) alone were worthwhile, for their drivers and riders had faith only in their own donks, and their sleek coats were good evidence of the affection between the men and their mounts; the rivalry was something to be remembered.

Other events were the Gallipoli and Bullecourt Hurdle races, and the Pozières Stakes. Each unit had its favourite, with jockey and jacket complete. Many francs changed hands that day, and there was much bragging and talk on all sides.

Among the arrangements were a tote, a judge's box, and a judge inside; the clerk of the scales was the writer! I was very serious that day. I used a huge butcher's scale, borrowed from the nearest Army Service Corps unit 'for weighing in and out'; soon I had a crowd of the curious round me and they stopped for the rest of the meeting. There was a clerk of the course with red jacket and black cap, got from Heaven knows where.

It was a beautiful spring day; a whole squadron of AIF planes flew down from the north to see the show and provided, at the same time, one of the features of the gathering. It will not be difficult to understand that in addition to money flowing freely, so did the vin blanc.

One airman bet another distinguished gentleman (who still flies and lives in Australia) 1000 francs that he was not fit to fly; that was enough! Soon we all saw one of the most thrilling sights. How our friend survived no one knows; even the spectators could hardly stand the strain of looking on. In the course of his antics this real 'bird' flew several times just a few feet above the heads of the crowd, which had the effect of taking their hats off, but not a man stirred. In the end, sheer exhaustion brought the flyer down, and he and his machine were carried home by lorry

It was the first time in history one saw a line of aeroplanes parked, as one now sees motor cars. Perhaps aeroplanes will be like that at Randwick some time or other! The laughter throughout was one long scream. It was, in fact, a real happy day for 10,000 AIF men and that one brave woman!

Arthur Wellesley Hyman (1880–1947) was a solicitor and member of the 2nd Light Horse Regiment who volunteered for the AIF at the start of WWI. He was transferred to the 7th Light Horse and promoted to captain. He took part in the landing at Gallipoli, served in Egypt and Sinai, and with the rank of major was posted to 4th Division HQ in France and Belgium for two years. Twice mentioned in despatches, in 1919 he served on Sir John Monash's staff in London dealing with repatriation. A diligent worker for ex-servicemen, Hyman was for many years a vice-president, and in 1926–27 and 1940–44, president of the NSW Branch of the RSL and a trustee of the Anzac Memorial in Sydney.

Essay on Two-Up

By D.G.S.

If General Birdwood had been asked to name the influence that did most to keep the AIF together, he would probably have talked glibly about discipline and love of Empire. It is odds on he would have missed the great truth, which was simply – two-up.

This was the ruling passion which cemented the different elements of the army and made a home of the most outlandish camp in France. Its votaries were of all grades. Even padres were known to worship at the shrine of two-up. Nor was the status of the Two-up King any mean one.

A man might have held all the decorations which the Allied Forces could give, and not yet command that profound reverence with which popular feeling regarded the man who, with a masterful twist of the coin, could keep a circle of sky-turned heads in breathless suspense for a matter of seconds. The name of that gifted man used to be whispered with awe and he was excitedly pointed out whenever he entered a public place.

Next to him, in veneration, came the smart ring-keeper – the man who would never allow the high-diddle-diddle to flag for want of eloquence and who saw that side-bets were prompt and did not mar the expedition of the toss. The good temper of the mob had to be maintained at all costs, so tactful suavity in a ring-keeper was an essential. Furthermore, his knowledge of human nature – particularly that brand peculiar to the AIF – had to be at least equal to the life insurance canvasser, or the man who sells inferior razor paste at the market. He had always to keep a keen eye on the bird with the roll of notes, without making his attention too obvious, and he also had to sustain a running fire of exhortations until the spinner became set. Above all, he had to keep warily on guard against the mob, for he who introduced a double-header was a person in league with the enemy. The man who could conduct a ring without permitting matters to degenerate into the nucleus of a free fight was a genius who did much to keep up the spirit of the nation.

Two-up used to be played at all times, and in all manner of places, and the interference of padres with the running of the ring was reduced to a minimum. The selection and maintenance of a rendezvous depended largely on the characteristics of the orderly officer. If he happened to be a sport who did not mind a bit of a fling himself, the ring might be set up at any central spot, even, perhaps, in the austere precincts of the orderly room itself. If, on the other hand, he betrayed signs of a hostile attitude, great care had to be exercised in the way of camouflage, or the appointment of a wakeful sentry.

The proximity of Fritz was not necessarily a barrier to the playing of two-up. As a rule it was advisable for an outpost, near enough to the enemy to hear him sneeze, to refrain from two-up unless it could arrange one of those beautiful truces that used sometimes to be possible in a quiet part of the line, opposite a docile species of Fritz. But there was usually nothing to prevent a good game back in supports or in reserve, although Fritz was often known to spoil a handsome 'trot' with an inopportune 9.2 [shell].

General poverty was the only bar to a game of two-up; yet even that was not insuperable. It was not unusual, towards the end of a pay period, when money was almost an unknown quantity, to see cigarettes introduced into the ring as a medium of gambling exchange. Sometimes an inveterate devotee was even reduced to the desperate expedient of parting with a girl's address, in order to get a bet.

Two-up was not often seen outside a military camp or position. During a policemen's strike in London, however, there was an historic game in the Strand, where a number of resourceful Aussies took advantage of the law's brief suspension and set the coin spinning, much to the interest of Flossie and the newspaper boys.

The romance of the ring was something the London novelists should have heard about. It was on a par with some of the stories of the early mining days in Australia. For the vicissitudes of two-up fortunes led to some strange developments. Many a glorious three months Absent Without Leave was due to nothing more than a successful 'trot', while it occasionally happened that a life's destiny was fashioned by the same cause.

Most of us could name a few married Diggers who might still have been in a state of single wretchedness had it not been for a consistent run of heading 'em. There is a case on record of a chap who tailed his way into matrimony – that is, who amassed the means of betting against spinners.

The WA Digger Book, 1929

Arrogance Rewarded

By 'Gosh'

There are some Diggers who have retentive memories and they will doubtlessly recognise this story, whilst those to whom the circumstances are unfamiliar will probably be interested.

Don Roach was a stretcher-bearer in 'C' Company, and with his unit was billeted in Renescure. Close to the company's billet was a pond, which by a strange act of Providence, was not polluted with the drainage from the yard in the farm quadrangle. Instructions were issued that the troops were not to wash at the pond, but they might take water for that purpose.

It was a wet day, and Don was walking by the pond on the slippery and muddy turf, when he slipped and fell. Naturally he put his hands out to save himself, and his hands became so caked with mud that he rinsed them in the water.

Just as he regained his upright position and was shaking his hands free of the dripping water, out of the billet stepped Sergeant Purnett. This sergeant was a man who had been invalided from the Imperial Army and had later enlisted with the AIF.

'Washin' eh? Washin' in the pool is it?'

'Well,' replied Don, 'not exactly that – just rinsed some mud off.'

That closed the incident for the time being, but next morning Don was ushered into the orderly room and charged before the commanding officer with disobeying an order – 'conduct to the prejudice of good order and military discipline, etc.'. Of course Don owned to exactly what did happen and the arrogant commanding officer sentenced him to twenty-eight days in No. 1 Field Punishment. In the clink Don was confined after a spotless record since Gallipoli, to the disgust of the battalion.

Grumblings and imprecations were continued until a climax was reached when the battalion was lined up to leave for the forward area. The prisoners were to march under guard and were to carry full packs, rifle, etc., to which decision Roach took exception. He was stung to the quick by the unjust punishment he had received and had now grown sullen in consequence; so he refused to move out unless he was allowed to march out with his stretcher-bearer's kit only.

As soon as this was known, up dashed the adjutant and ordered Roach to 'fall in', and meeting with no success, he issued orders for a limber to be driven up. The commanding officer then put in an appearance and with the adjutant arranged for Don to be tied with stout rope to the back of the limber. The choice-spirited commanding officer accompanied his command to the driver to move forward with a cut of his whip on the nearside horse.

Plunging nearly out of control, they dragged poor Don several yards forward until he lost his balance and fell. By the time the horses were evened up our stretcher-bearer friend was badly bruised and grazed. The medical officer rode up at this juncture, and having the humane disposition of most members of his profession, he overrode the commanding officer's objections and ordered Don to the ambulance.

The wheels of justice move slowly, so slowly that miles of red tape had to be unwoven before a plea from Roach could reach the general officer commanding. In fact, the Passchendaele battles were fought and won, the commanding officer was invalided home severely wounded, the adjutant was killed in the March offensive in 1918, and later the Armistice came.

Slowly these wheels of justice turned and yet with no less unerring surety. For although the Reaper was not able to mark the progress of Justice in the field and reap the life of the commanding officer in atonement for his inhuman actions, yet the sickle garnered this noxious weed quite soon after peace came.

The Listening Post, January 1925

It is apparent that real names were not used in this article. No. 1 Field Punishment was common in WWI. A commanding officer could sentence a soldier for up to twenty-eight days, during which the man would be tied or handcuffed to an object such as a gun wheel or a fence post for up to two hours a day.

Wounded and Taken Prisoner at Bullecourt

Diary of Private Cecil Arthur Crews

11 April 1917: Wounded. Lying in a shell hole all day. Very cold. Three companions, all wounded very seriously. Eleven o'clock, the boys retired – those that could get away. Machine-gun fire on every shell hole, those trying to get from our hole did not get very far, always got shot.

Four o'clock. German soldiers come out to collect more of our wounded, saying they expected our people to bombard their trenches. I was carried to their trench. Being full of wounded there was no room for any more of us. I was once again unlucky that day, having to lie in a half-broken-down trench all that night until ten o'clock the next day. One of the worst nights I had experienced. Snowing, the first four inches of snow in no time, then rain. Wet through and through. Very cold indeed. Three greatcoats over me, being my own and two belonging to my comrades that had died in the trench alongside me.

Treatment by the Germans was all that one could wish for. Given cigarettes whenever I asked for one, they even hunted amongst our dead for any rum they may have had in their water bottles, always bringing it along and saying, 'Good! Comrade.'

I was one of the last to leave the trench. Carried out by four Germans on an oil sheet lashed to poles, two carrying and two of them 'spelling', it was a long carry, right through our own barrage. I never expected to ever get through. They were brave fellows these stretcher-bearers, our own shells bursting all around us, they never stopped until they reached the centre of a French village.

Houses all around us were coming down, expecting any minute that the one we were in would come down on our heads. Things were beginning to get warm in the village and the Germans began to clear out. Some moved us into another room of the house, thinking we would be safer, then they too cleared out. Within a few minutes one of our shells came through the top storey of the house, we thought our time had come, it fetched the plaster ceiling down on us, covering stretchers and everything. We had just given up all hope, when a dozen Fritzies came running in and grabbed our stretchers and hurried us to the coach. They ran three-quarters of a mile with us, six wounded on stretchers, and one with several wounds hobbling ahead, being urged on by the Germans. His name being Comery, he lived in West Perth for a number of years and belonged to the 16th Battalion – one of the 'Old Boys'. We were quickly shoved into the coach, Comery riding up with the driver. Shells bursting all around us necessitated us getting a move on very quickly.

Arrived at another village and carried to an old coach house and there met many of our lads. Not long there when hot soup was brought around by Fritz. This went down OK, being my first meal in some considerable time. Whilst meal in progress, two German doctors do our dressings. My leg has an entrenching tool tied to it to prevent my foot from turning the opposite way. New dressings are put on and the leg strapped into an iron frame. Then we are carried across the road to another house. Here we had a bed of straw, and the Germans waiting on us hand and foot, attending to our every little want. Not long before I am fast asleep and less before I am roughly wakened by a Fritz saying, 'Come!'

Three of us placed in a cart, with a walking case up with the driver. No springs on the cart and it moves off across cobbles, which brings howls and curses down upon the driver. Something like ten miles that ride, passing every now and again through French villages. Most were uninhabited, others billeted German soldiers. Unpleasant conditions owing to heavy snow and rain. Wet through again.

13 April: The next morning we are fed with soup and coffee. Life seemed a little brighter. About three o'clock placed on stretchers and carried across to a hospital train. About six o'clock it began to move off; where we were going we did not know. It was a very slow affair. After three days we arrive at our destination, a place called Verden. Fifty of us are taken off here, the rest are sent on to Hanover. Army Medical Corps men meet us, all very old men with great covered-in vans. Arriving at hospital we are surprised there is quite a crowd to meet us, including six British Tommies. I am first off, carried to Number Three Ward and dumped on a bed and left to get my clothes off the best way I can. A Tommy places my belongings in a bedside locker, our clothes are tied and taken away for fumigation. It is eleven o'clock and I sleep. They had nothing for us to eat when we arrived so we are given a huge, hard biscuit, sent out from Russia for their troops imprisoned in Germany. They have to be soaked in water for about twenty-four hours to make them soft enough to get your teeth into.

15 April: 7 a.m. Breakfast. One mug of coffee. One very thin slice of black bread. Nothing to put on it. We make the most of it, though hard to get down. A sister comes around with a doctor, picking out the most serious cases, to be dressed and operated on. I am left until the next day.

16 April: Soon after breakfast an operating table is carried into the ward, as the normal operating rooms are being used for wounded Germans. Sisters start buzzing around the table getting everything ready for the doctor. Fourteen of us to have our wounds dressed. My leg is very painful as they move me. Old blood-soaked bandages are removed and paper ones put in their place. Leg back into the frame and back into bed.

The young fellow in the bed next to me (48th Battalion) is very badly hit through the knee and blood poisoning has set in. His leg is three times normal size and covered in a wire netting arrangement to stop it twisting. The doctor removes his dressings. It is just on dinner time and the sister tells the lad he is not to eat for the doctor is to take off his leg. The lad says all right and gives up his soup to another. Shortly they come for him and carry him to the operation room. He is away about forty-five minutes and is returned in a semi-conscious state. They give him a needle and he sleeps, but soon awakes to his troubles.

The chap next to him is Barrett who is wounded in the head and has shrapnel in his shoulder. The doctor took the splinters out of his head, but it is giving him trouble. I don't think he will be able to stand a hot climate again and in the mornings he is always very dopey.

Next to him was O'Neal, who had been wounded in the left arm and also left leg. They cut his left foot off a couple of days after we got here. He seemed OK for a few days, but then seemed to sink and became delirious. Lasted about a week. Died. I think he must have developed some kind of fever.

Next again is Emmery, who is having a jolly bad time. Ever since he came in he has had something wrong with his insides. He can keep nothing inside him and is not expected to live much longer. He has hardly any flesh on him, just a mass of bones. I don't think he can last much longer.

Next to him is a chap called Castles, being wounded in a very dangerous place, also a very painful place. He will leave this country minus something he brought into it and that won't be a limb (enough said).

Next to him, Bryant of the 16th. One of the 'Old' Battalion, invalided home from Egypt, returned to France by the same boat as myself. He lasted about six weeks here, then sent off unexpectedly, having annoyed one of the *unteroffizers* in some petty way. Across the ward were lads who were here when we arrived: Sergeant Evens, Corporal Spencer and Privates Riley, Lynch, Burgers, Gibson and Melia. All seem content. All were receiving food parcels and Riley offered to help us write to the Red Cross people to organise parcels for us.

About a month after letters were sent out, parcels arrived for us. There was great excitement whilst they were being opened. Biscuits, jam, army rations, dripping, tinned fruit and a case of Wild Woodbine cigarettes.

X-rays showed there was nothing in my leg. I was put to sleep and when I awoke my leg was in plaster. I was this way for two months. Then another operation. I felt very bad afterwards and I think too much chloroform was used. I could not shake the effects for a week, no sleep at night and I cannot close my eyes without great nerve jumps all through my body, especially in my bad leg. I don't eat or sleep for five days.

The leg in some way has come apart again, and the least little movement causes great pain. I get a needle of morphine. This has no effect. No sleep. The following night I am given two morphine pills and I sleep all through the night and the biggest part of the day. They wait for the operation cuts to stop discharging, then re-plaster me. I am comfortable, being now able to turn in bed. But the plaster is being soaked with discharge and when the leg is hot, it gives off a terrible stink. I keep the blankets tucked in around me (to lessen the stench).

They take me back to the operation room and it surprises me that they don't make a face when the bandages are taken off, for the stench is enough to take your breath away.

20 July 1917: My leg has been out of plaster now twelve days, the bone is properly set this time. Today I did my first trip outside, the foot gets very painful after hanging down for a while.

21 August 1917: My third day out, feeling very weak on the one leg. Saw my first German funeral.

22 August: Out in the sun for about one hour, too hot to stay any longer. One of the boys died in 2 Ward. Bled to death. Two days of bleeding then they took off his arm this morning; he never recovered consciousness.

The Listening Post, Autumn 1999

Private Cecil Arthur Crews, from Leederville, Western Australia, had earlier been wounded at Gallipoli, been sent home, and then embarked again to return to the 16th Battalion. His days as a POW ended before the Armistice, when he was repatriated via Holland to Britain for convalescence. In providing his edited diary to the RSL for publication in 1999, his daughter noted that his leg had been five inches short as the result of his wounds and he had worn a built-up boot for the rest of his life.

Prisoner of War

By W.H. Carson

After the repulse of the 4th Brigade, only two courses were open to the survivors, to surrender or to retire. About 800 commenced to retire, and of these only eighty-six succeeded in getting back. Large numbers remained in shell holes, hoping to make their withdrawal under cover of night; but Jerry did not wait. He made a strong counterattack, capturing about 580 of us.

After capture we were taken behind the Hindenburg Line and the wounded received treatment from the German doctors, who showed no discrimination between friend and enemy. Discrimination of this kind was to come later, but I must say that the first German doctors we met were gentlemen. We were then taken further to the rear, where, in contrast with the villages on our side – all destroyed by the German artillery – we found villages hardly damaged.

Line after line of strongly fortified entrenchments were passed, each as strong as the original front line of the Germans. To the number of about 600, we were parked in a church and 'fed', a small loaf of rye bread – deep brown. We were then searched, knives and razors and such-like dangerous implements were taken from us, and then began the usual questionings, but the knowledge reaped was nil.

Supper came later, a cup of coffee – of unknown make. No further food or bedding was issued and no blankets. The time was winter, the worst that had been experienced for many years, so it is left to the reader to gather what had to be endured by fit and wounded alike.

Next day we were divided up into parties for work on the roads leading to the line, housed in a barn, still no bedding or blankets, wet clothes and only one-third of a loaf of bread and a cup of coffee. This was stated to be reprisal for what we know to be a wrong statement – the working of German prisoners behind the front line.

My party consisted of thirty-two men, but after two weeks it had decreased to twenty. The remainder had died off in the night, frozen. It may be wondered how we slept at all, but it was the sleep of utter exhaustion, due to shortage of food and long hours of work. Some of us used to take it in turns to walk about for an hour and then wake the others to have their turn, and so on through the night.

After the two weeks had passed we were removed to a concentration camp with other parties who had been similarly treated, and whose numbers had decreased in the same way. We were then entrained to Fortress Macdonald, at Lille, and there placed in dungeons, 110 to a cell, each cell about fifteen feet by forty feet. The men, about 400, were kept here for twelve days, but the bread ration was reduced and they were not allowed to leave their 'homes' for any reason whatever. The reason, as stated, was a reprisal on the British, and the Hun interpreter told us that we were allowed to write home and make as many complaints of our treatment as we wished. Pencils and paper were provided, but we refused to write the letters, thus denying the enemy that satisfaction.

When the twelve days were up, we were taken out into the open air. The effect was peculiar, each man reeling about as if he were drunk. We were allowed to lie on the ground until we recovered. We were then removed to another barn, still without bedding, but there was a roof over this one. The first had had only half a roof. The weather also had improved a little.

The party remained here about three months, still as hard worked as ever and as poorly fed. The local French and Belgian women, although strictly rationed and ill-treated, often gave the prisoners loaves from their own meagre store, risking untold dangers in doing so. In time we again returned to Fortress Macdonald, but after twenty-four hours were taken to the German prisoner-of-war camp at Dülmen. Here, for the first time, we were officially registered as prisoners of war. Up to this time we had been simply 'missing'. The fate of hundreds can now be determined, but those who had died from neglect and ill-treatment will never be accounted for. We were here inoculated for all known and unknown diseases.

From now on matters began to improve somewhat, and at last we were given permission to write to the Red Cross in London. Our relatives were notified. That suspense was over. We were alive – though only just – and prisoners, and our names were placed on the ration list at headquarters for parcels. No amount of talking would ever convey the extent of the gratitude felt by the men when their parcels began to arrive.

A move was now made to a camp at Güstrow, and a proof was received there of the spirit which united all men, from UK or Dominions. They found on the arrival at the camp some British prisoners of war, captured at Mons and shortly after. These, hearing that a batch of prisoners was due who were badly off and half-starved, had been saving portions of their Red Cross parcels, and by the time the new arrivals came, had got a real feed ready. To the gratification of the new arrivals, a really Mark I type of army stew awaited them. I never thought the time would come when an army stew could taste so good. We ate till we could eat no more – like pigs – and we were glad no one was there to see us.

After we were filled, we lay down, with some bedding now. The Tommies placed at the side of each man a basin of soup and we kept waking up in the night to make sure that no one had taken our food. This was the effect a good English feed had on us. The consequences were bad next day, however, for many of us – the writer included – were taken to hospital suffering from the effects of the first decent feed for weeks.

On recovery the prisoners were detailed for work on farms near the camp, and conditions became better. The open-air work, the parcels from Blighty (AIF Red Cross) all improved matters, even though the parcels were locked up at night with a sentry to take care of them.

However, one bad interlude occurred, which was not to the credit of the civil doctors of Germany. It was a rule of the camp that in case of an accident to a prisoner, the nearest civil doctor was to be sent for. I had the misfortune to break my leg, and the civil doctor, who had a proper Hun hatred of all men and things British, set it in such a manner as to convey the impression that he did not intend it ever to get right again. I bore it as long as I could, but in the end got recalled to camp. The camp doctor regretfully told me that he was not allowed to use anaesthetic on a prisoner except in very extreme cases. I therefore had to lie and have my leg re-broken and properly set.

After recovery I was appointed an orderly to interpret for the doctor, having rubbed up my slight knowledge of the German language during my period of farm work. This was all right for a time, but the strain of the sights and sufferings soon began to pall and matters finally came to a head on the arrival of 150 Italian prisoners. These had undergone similar starvation treatment to that meted out to the Aussie prisoners at first. They were placed into two huts, and I, with the aid of many articles of food from Red Cross parcels that had been left and stored up, had prepared for them a real meal. It was, however, too late; through their sheer exhaustion the food did no good. Next morning, of the 150, only four were living. That finished it. Another prisoner, looking for a cushy job and with a knowledge of German, was introduced to the doctor and I got back to farm work again.

It was while the prisoners were at Güstrow camp that parcels began to arrive. I never knew so many things could be put into tins. Cheese, butter, soup, tobacco, cigarettes, toothpaste, spuds, vegetables and many other things besides. The parcels also contained socks, clothing, towels and everything that could be desired. The total weight was sixty pounds per man, per month, and in addition white bread was sent to us from the nearest neutral country. This was, to us, 'it', but soap was a good runner-up. The latter was absolutely unobtainable in Germany because all fats were required for explosives. The blockade was at this time being felt most strongly, and food of all kinds was greatly restricted.

On my return to farm work I was sent to another farm. At the new place I was the only prisoner working, quite 'posh' too, with a sentry all to myself. However my work proved so satisfactory that the German wife – no men being there except such as were incapacitated or too old to fight – thought it was great, and applied for another British prisoner of war for work. The answer came that no other British man was available, but she could have two Frenchmen. This was not 'according to plan'. Eventually the matter was got over by her taking the two Frenchmen and the writer going back to the farm at which he first worked.

Matters went steadily on until the abdication of the Kaiser, which was known in Germany some days before it got abroad. Then followed the Armistice, and at once the change occurred. All sentries were removed, the gates of the camp were thrown open and a British naval officer placed in supreme command. Delay, of course, was inevitable in repatriating the large number of prisoners. They were given two alternatives until such time as they could be recalled to sail for the UK. They could remain at work on their farms or remain there on holiday. The latter alternative was selected for a while, but this did not suit for long. They then decided to put in a few hours' work each day. Even this wore out eventually, and they decided that the next day they would walk back the thirty-odd miles to the camp. The next morning, however, they received the welcome order to re-join, and there was no delay; they went while the going was good. The gates were open and the ex-prisoners, as they now were, were at liberty to roam at will, only being placed on their honour to keep out of trouble. The result of this was that in no case was any trouble caused.

Eventually we were shipped off to Copenhagen, where we arrived on Christmas Eve. We had a very good time during our enforced stay in Denmark. The inhabitants seemed as though they could not do enough for us. English was spoken on all sides and we were invited into the houses and made as welcome as friends.

After a few days we again embarked for Hull and the care and attention we received soon helped to clear away the effects of our long incarceration.

The Listening Post, January 1935

Sergeant Wilfred Harold Carson, of the 16th Battalion, enlisted in March 1916 as a 23-year-old farmer from the Western Australian wheatbelt town of Kellerberrin. After his release as a POW he returned from the UK in May 1919. He married in 1923.

HMAS *Sydney*'s Fight with German Zeppelin

By Leading Signalman Arnold Mellor

HMAS *Sydney*, during the whole of her service in the North Sea from 1916 to 1918, was attached to the 2nd Light Cruiser Squadron, with the base either Scapa Flow or Rosyth [both in Scotland], but mostly the latter, in the Firth of Forth. On 3 May 1917, the 2nd Division of the squadron, comprising HMAS *Sydney* and HMS *Dublin*, and four destroyers, left Rosyth for a special reconnaissance sweep to a locality about 140 miles east of our base.

From 8 a.m. till noon on 4 May I was signalman of the watch. About 10 a.m. the *Dublin* reported she had been fired at with a torpedo, which passed astern. A few minutes later the destroyer *Obdurate* reported sighting a submarine. The *Sydney* and the destroyer steamed at full ahead to where the sub had submerged and let go depth charges. Captain Dumaresq, realising that the attack was not the work of a submarine working independently, immediately ordered the *Dublin* to extend further to starboard and sent the *Obdurate* to examine a vessel on the port bow about ten miles away. The cruisers now were at maximum speed, twenty-five knots, while the destroyers were well ahead, zigzagging at high speed, on the lookout for subs or other enemy light craft. Telefunken signals had been heard and the feeling was that enemy ships were out.

I was crouched on the searchlight platform of the port side of the signal bridge, watching the *Obdurate* examine what turned out to be a Dutch fishing trawler, when, to my astonishment, I saw a zeppelin rising over and beyond the destroyer.

For a few seconds I was too flabbergasted to yell the warning. Reporting airships was something new! Anyhow, my cry, 'Zeppelin in sight, sir; four points on the port bow,' brought into train all glasses from the fore bridge. The zeppelin (*L.43*), one of the latest built, looked wonderful in the brilliant sunshine – something like a silver pencil as she rapidly gained altitude. Through the powerful cruiser telescope I noticed volumes of water ballast dropping from her, as she made rapid ascent to get out of the range of the torpedo boat destroyer's quick firers.

The zeppelin, when it reached a height of about 15,000 feet, at about 10,000 yards distance, turned away from us and made off in a southerly direction. Captain Dumaresq then ordered fire to be opened with the 6-inch guns; these had been elevated to their highest, but even then the shrapnel shells burst well below the zep. Dumaresq, after about ten minutes' firing during the airship's run south, realised that the submarines and zeppelin must be working in collaboration, and rather than be led further on – either into a newly laid minefield or submarine locality – ordered a 16-point turn and steamed away. On this move the zep turned about and chased the cruisers, which was just what Captain Dumaresq was hitching for.

As the airship quickly overtook the cruisers, the *Sydney* ordered the *Dublin* and destroyers to scatter, to minimise damage from bombs, and to encourage the airship to engage the *Sydney*. While the other ships were moving away the *Sydney* opened fire with her 3-inch anti-aircraft gun. Captain Dumaresq had purposely refrained from opening fire early with the anti-aircraft to tempt the zep to come within range.

Although our anti-aircraft gun's crew worked rapidly and were ably directed, it was disheartening to see our shells going true for the airship and then turn. The airship, once she realised that our anti-aircraft gun could not reach her, made for directly over the *Sydney*. The pipe, 'Clear upper deck – everyone below' was ordered. Only the fore (and after) gunnery control stations, anti-aircraft gun's crew, signal ratings of the watch, and a handful of lookouts were officially on deck. I had been ordered aloft up the foremast to keep a lookout for torpedoes. The zeppelin was now directly overhead. Through the binoculars every detail of her could be seen. It was a wonderful sight – she was much lower than she was when approaching us, as she was now in the 'dead' area – the gun could not fire perpendicularly.

On a signal from the *Sydney*, the *Dublin* and destroyers opened fire on the zeppelin. The shells burst immediately under the airship, and she did the 'standing on its tail' act and quickly gained altitude out of harm's way. Now it was the zep's turn to retaliate.

With a whine and then a dull roar, the first bomb burst on the port bow, about fifty yards away. Within half a minute the second one burst, again on the port bow, but about thirty yards away. *Sydney* then altered course. The third burst on the starboard bow. Although within a few minutes three 250-pound bombs had missed us, they were remarkably well aimed and we anticipated a direct hit any minute. There was a lull for a minute or so, when three more bombs burst simultaneously – two to starboard, the other to port.

Sydney then quickly swung over and passed the spot where the two on the starboard had burst. Down came another two, which burst together, off the port bow. The coolness of Captain Dumaresq and his able navigating officer, Lieutenant Commander C. Pope, RAN, was wonderful. They were as unconcerned as if the heavy bombing was a usual peacetime 'evolution'.

Bombs were dropped with regular timing, in twos and threes. I spotted the track of a torpedo about 600 yards on the port quarter. Quickly tracing back whence it came I saw the feathered foam of a sub, just submerging. Although I frantically endeavoured to make myself heard, it was only by signs and pointing that those on the fore bridge understood my warning, my voice being drowned out by the wind and the roar of the bomb explosions.

The next ten minutes were intensely exciting. From my wonderful view 150 feet above sea level I could see the destroyers tearing about at full speed dropping depth charges. The zeppelin and a flotilla of submarines were working together. The sea for some miles around was traced with 'wakes' and disturbed patches where the depth charges had exploded. Three enemy submarines were destroyed, but no survivors were sighted.

The tenth bomb, the closest of the issue, burst on the starboard bow close to the bridge, and pieces embedded themselves in the 'splinter protection': pads around the fore bridge. The captain of the *Obdurate*, during the bombing, trained the 24-inch searchlight on the zeppelin, and signalled some very caustic remarks in German. As a reprisal the zeppelin dropped the last bomb at the *Obdurate*; it burst and covered the vessel with spray but it missed by ten yards or so. There were no casualties.

I again spotted another zeppelin low on the horizon. The *L.43* turned away from us and made off to join her. Both then sailed away towards the German coast.

Reveille, October 1932

Heroes All

'Jacka should have come out of the war the most decorated man in the AIF. One does not usually comment on the giving of decorations, but this was an instance in which something obviously went wrong. Everyone who knows the facts, knows that Jacka earned the Victoria Cross three times.'

— Charles Bean

Our Bravest Fighter

By Lieutenant L. 'Fats' McCarthy, VC

In 1924, The Listening Post *reported a discussion at the Royal Military College, Duntroon, about 'Who was the bravest fighter in the AIF?' The war correspondent Charles Bean weighed in, writing: 'I have often thought that, if it were the subject of an election, there is one for whom I would cast my vote, partly because I feel sure there was no braver, and partly because one would avoid the invidiousness of mentioning a living soldier.' His vote was for Percy Black, profiled here by Lawrence 'Fats' McCarthy.*

I was delighted to read recent references in your journal to the bravery of Major Percy Black. Although it would be difficult to say exactly who was the bravest fighter of the AIF, I am prepared to say that I know of none braver than the late Percy Black, and I am egotistical enough to state that my frontline services place me in a favourable position to judge.

I have fought alongside VC winners Murray, Jacka, Axford, Hamilton, Carroll and O'Mara, and I make bold to say that we all take off our hats to Percy Black as a brave soldier and leader in battle. It may be asked what particular formula can be used in allocating degrees of bravery. This question would trick me, but in spite of it I again assert that Percy Black is the bravest man I have known. I call to mind many of his glorious deeds and perhaps an exposition of a few of them would show why I make the above statement.

At the Gallipoli landing Percy Black was a private in the machine-gun section of the 16th Battalion, and he loved his machine-gun as many men love their dogs and other living pets, and he was a 'dead' shot.

On 2 May 1915 our position at Pope's Hill was tottering and Percy Black, realising the critical position, picked up his machine-gun and under heavy enemy fire rushed forward alone into no-man's-land, placed his gun, and mowed down many of the Turks. After two bullets pierced his ear, a few his clothing and water bottle, he was compelled to fall back to the trenches. In spite of his wounds he remained wonderfully cool and calm and made further repeated attempts to carry out his job. For this brave deed he was given the DCM and a commission. During the whole of the Gallipoli campaign he performed many such brilliant deeds of bravery.

At a stunt at Mouquet Farm I had charge of the company on the left of Percy Black, and here again he carried out a wonderful single-handed fight against the flower of the German Army, the Prussian Guards, who stood up and called on Black to come on. Needless to say, Black never required any such invitation, and he advanced and in the process inflicted heavy casualties on the enemy. He was later picked up on the top of Mouquet Farm dugout, with very severe head and throat wounds, which would send any other man back to Australia, but Black was no ordinary man, he was a superman.

At Bullecourt, Percy Black again displayed very fine initiative and leadership, but the pity of it all is that although many read of these wonderful deeds, they were only witnessed by a few.

During the attack on the Hindenburg Line, Black had command of 'B' Company, 16th Battalion. We took the first two lines of trenches with few casualties and according to plan, we were to attack the third line without the aid of guns or tanks. The odds were heavy against us and we felt that our doom was sealed. No one knew of the tremendous risks to be taken more than did Percy Black, but he was made of the wrong stuff to hang back.

'On!' he shouted, and was the first out to carry on the fight. A few yards only were covered when a well-placed Prussian bullet put an end to the wonderful career of this gallant soldier and gentleman.

The Listening Post, September 1924

*The writer, **Lawrence Dominic McCarthy, VC,** was born in York, WA in 1892, raised at Clontarf Orphanage in Perth, and enlisted in the AIF in October 1914. His large build led to the nickname 'Fats'. Private McCarthy was posted to the 16th Battalion, which landed at Gallipoli on 26 April 1915. Having been promoted to sergeant, he was among the last to leave Gallipoli on 20 December. In France, McCarthy was promoted to company sergeant major and then commissioned as a 2nd lieutenant. He was wounded at Bullecourt, awarded the French Croix de Guerre, and during the August 1918 offensive, performed outstanding acts of bravery. He and a sergeant attacked German machine-gun posts, capturing almost half a kilometre of trenches and as many as fifty prisoners. This action resulted in the award of the VC. McCarthy returned to WA and later moved to Melbourne, where he died at the Heidelberg Repatriation Hospital in May 1975.*

***Percy Charles Herbert Black, DCM, MC, DSO and Bar,** was born in Victoria and was a carpenter before turning to prospecting on the Western Australian goldfields. Having enlisted as a private in the 16th Battalion and first seeing action during the Gallipoli landing, successive promotions saw Black serve ultimately as a major on the Western Front. He was killed at Bullecourt on 11 April 1917, one of 640 casualties in the 16th Battalion that day. He has no known grave.*

On the Death of Captain Albert Jacka, VC, MC and Bar

By Charles Bean, Official Historian AIF

Jacka should have come out of the war the most decorated man in the AIF. One does not usually comment on the giving of decorations, but this was an instance in which something obviously went wrong. Everyone who knows the facts, knows that Jacka earned the Victoria Cross three times. In many cases there may be doubt as to what decorations should be awarded, but there could be no real doubt in these:

1. At Courtney's

In Gallipoli, when, on 19 May 1915, the Turks made their great attack on Anzac they succeeded in seizing a bay of the Australian line at Courtney's Post, the rear of which overlooked the Australian communications. Jacka, then a private in the 14th Battalion, first, taking his stand alone behind the next traverse, prevented them from extending their hold; then, calling some of his comrades to divert the attention of the enemy by bombs, at great risk, he made his way to the other side of the enemy, leapt into their bay, and, single-handed, killed them all. For this action he was awarded the Victoria Cross, the first Australian to win one in this war.

2. At Pozières

After the Australians had taken the German lines at Pozières on the crest of the Thiepval–Longueval ridge, the Germans, early on 7 August 1916, after heavy bombardment, counterattacked in force, overran part of the line, captured a considerable number of the garrison, and penetrated down the rear slope behind the Australian position. Jacka was then a subaltern in charge of one of the posts that was unexpectedly overrun. Germans appeared at the mouth of his dugout and, rolling a bomb down the stairs, killed two men. Jacka at once fired up the stair, rushed to the top, and found large numbers of the enemy in the rear of his position, sending away their prisoners. Although he had only two or three men with him, Jacka immediately attacked, fighting desperately hand to hand. He was wounded three times, but continued to fight, killing many Germans. The Australian prisoners at once revolted and attacked their guards. Some of the nearest units joined in. The tables were completely turned on the enemy: most prisoners were released, a large part of the Germans were captured and the line was re-taken. Jacka's third wound – a rifle shot through the neck – nearly cost him his life. He received a Military Cross, yet one would say that no action ever performed in the AIF quite so thoroughly deserved the higher award.

3. At Bullecourt

It became necessary on the night of 8 April 1917 to make a thorough reconnaissance of the strong wire entanglements protecting the Hindenburg Line at Bullecourt, artillery being inadequate to ensure that the wire should be properly cut. Jacka, then captain and intelligence officer of the 14th, was entrusted by his brigadier with this special duty. He penetrated the entanglement at two points and after bringing back a valuable report, went out to lay the tapes for the attack which was to be launched before dawn. The taping was just completed when a German patrol was heard. Jacka arranged with a Lewis gunner to cover him, and then worked around and approached them from the direction of their own lines. They were evidently an officer and his orderly, the latter armed with a rifle. On Jacka's calling 'Halt!' they hesitated and would not hold up their hands. Jacka pulled the trigger of his revolver, but as it merely clicked, he rushed in and seized the officer. The orderly dropped his rifle, and Jacka captured and brought in both. A few minutes later the two Australian brigades came out and assembled on the tapes on which they had to lie for several hours. Jacka's action saved them from imminent danger of discovery and destruction. For this action he was awarded a Bar to his Military Cross.

Jacka's action led directly to a result of great military value, the saving of two brigades from being cut up by shell fire and machine-guns. It may be necessary to prevent men from risking their lives in saving regimental flags or guns, or even the lives of individual men, but surely the saving of a division from heavy loss is an action worthy of encouragement.

It is to be hoped that Australia will remember Jacka as the man who, if he did not win it, earned the Victoria Cross three times – some who knew him say four times, having regard for his actions at Zonnebeke on 26 September 1917 as well. The mistake, wherever it occurred, lay somewhere within our own force, not with British. Naturally, perhaps, Jacka was not an easily controlled subordinate. Though he remained a captain, he was one of our greatest leaders.

Reveille, January 1932

Charles Edwin Woodrow Bean (1879–1968) was the outstanding Australian war correspondent and editor of the twelve-volume Official History of Australia in the War of 1914–1918. *Bean was a key figure in the establishment of the Australian War Memorial, and of the creation and popularisation of the Anzac legend.*

Albert Jacka was born on 10 January 1893 near Winchelsea, Victoria. He enlisted on 18 September 1914 as a private in the 14th Battalion, embarked on 22 December and landed at Anzac Cove on 26 April 1915. Having become a national hero by his actions, he received the £500 and gold watch that prominent Melbourne identity John Wren had promised to the first VC winner. Jacka's image was used on recruiting posters and magazine covers. When he returned to Australia at war's end he was greeted by a large crowd that included the governor-general. A convoy of eighty-five cars, with Jacka at its head, drove to Melbourne Town Hall, where men from the 14th Battalion welcomed their comrade. During the post-war years Jacka went into business; one of his partners was John Wren. He married Frances Veronica Carey, a typist from his office, in 1921 and settled in St Kilda. In 1929 he was elected to the St Kilda council and a year later he became mayor. He devoted most of his energies on council to assisting the unemployed. In 1930, his business went into voluntary liquidation and Jacka became a commercial traveller with the Anglo-Dominion Soap Company.

He fell ill, entered Caulfield Military Hospital on 18 December 1931 and died on 17 January 1932 of chronic nephritis. Nearly 6000 people filed past his coffin when it lay in state in Anzac House. Eight Victoria Cross winners were his pallbearers and he was buried with full military honours at St Kilda cemetery.

Boarding System: Jacka a Victim of the Anzac Legend

By Captain Ken Millar, MC

'Boarding' was a process by which wounded officers were required to appear, after hospital treatment, before a medical board at the AIF administrative headquarters located on Horseferry Road, London. This determined whether an officer was sent back into the front line, held in England for further treatment, or invalided home to Australia.

Outstanding gallant – man of super courage – Jacka is dead! His war-racked body is now at rest. May his brave soul meet its kindred in that special Paradise we used to speak about as being reserved for all good soldiers.

Only thirty-nine years of age, and dead from the effects of severe wounds, in the prime of life. Jacka was the victim of a wretched voluntary system of fighting a war – a system that sacrificed him for the aggrandisement of others – a system that sought to keep five divisions in the field when the personnel was only sufficient for three. If Jacka had been in the Imperial Army he would not have been *allowed* to go back to the line, time after time, with his wounds.

The wretched AIF system which prevailed of boarding an officer was to leave the onus on him to say how he was. Was there ever such a travesty of justice to wounded men – I mean to men of 'guts' and spirit, such as Jacka?

The procedure in that little room at the end of the passage in Horseferry Road is well remembered by many AIF officers – firstly a question from one of the medical officers, 'How do you feel?

Are your wounds better?' The whole atmosphere of the place was repugnant to a good officer.

Could anyone imagine Jacka, a frontline troop, answering those formal questions in any other manner than, 'Oh, I'm all right,' taking the ten days' leave, and making the best he could of it?

Jacka was the victim of a system that rushed good officers back to the line whether they were fit to go or not. The officers of my battalion averaged two and a half wound stripes at one time, and included some who were obviously not fit to be there. If one could walk and assert that he wanted to re-join his battalion, the wretched system pushed him back.

Jacka was an inspiration, not only to his own brigade, but to the whole of the AIF. He wasn't a 'one-fight, one-VC artist', but a VC every time he went into action. He had the greatest reception any soldier ever received on his return from the war in 1919, and in 1932, broken by his war wounds, he stood up unaided to every trial only because of his indomitable spirit.

Reveille, January 1932

Christopher Kenneth Millar (always known as Ken) left Sydney in October 1914, aged nineteen, and, after training in Egypt, went ashore at Gallipoli in April 1915. Wounded, he returned to Cairo for hospital treatment and then returned to Gallipoli, where he stayed until the Evacuation in December 1915. In April 1916 the 2nd Battalion was posted to France, where Millar was again wounded and sent to hospital in London. He was awarded the Military Cross for conspicuous courage at Pozières.

Women in the War

By Principal Matron A.M. Kellett, RRC

Modern woman – having seen to her man's equipment and wellbeing and having waved a smiling if somewhat strained farewell – looks around for something to do – and how much she finds to her hand! Knitting, sewing, packing, munition making, farming, gardening, nursing – women of all classes turn their hands to anything and everything.

During the Great War, what astonishing work was done by them! The great lady, unaccustomed to toil, waited on the sick and wounded and did the most uncongenial tasks in the hospital into which she had converted her beautiful home; the busy worker who earned her daily bread gave her precious time to the washing of dishes, waiting in canteens, scrubbing, clerical work, any of the hundred and one jobs which had to be done.

One calls to mind the work of the voluntary helpers, who, amongst their activities, included the most valuable (if perhaps the least interesting) work of rolling bandages, making surgical dressings and sorting into bundles the old linen which was more precious than gold to the doctor and nurse on the field.

That wonderful institution – the Women's Army Auxiliary Corps – had so many branches that it is impossible to mention them all – telephonists, wardsmaids, cooks, housemaids, laundresses, all branches of clerical work – their activities for the army seemed endless. Then there were the Women's Royal Naval Service who did similar work for the navy, and the Women's Royal Air Force whose work was entirely for the air force. There were women railway porters, bus conductors, postwomen, drivers of post vans, farm hands and window cleaners – all carrying out their duties in order to release men for active service.

One remembers also that splendid organisation – the Voluntary

Aid Detachment – which rendered invaluable assistance to the Army Medical Corps and the Army Nursing Service, both at home and on the field. Women ambulance drivers were ready at all hours to respond to the call, oft-times within the danger zone – their duty was not only to drive but to keep the ambulances clean and in good repair, a most difficult task in those days of mud and slush and broken roads.

Nor does one forget the excellent work done by the nurses of the Red Cross Society, which had its own hospitals and organisation. These nurses did similar work to that of the Army Nursing Service and endured like disabilities and suffered similar tragic happenings.

The work of the Army Nursing Service is well known – to be a member was like a privilege and an honour! At the outbreak of war nurses vied with each other to be first to enlist – the principal matron's task was made most difficult not by the scarcity of applicants, but by the limitations of the numbers needed. And how bitter was the disappointment of those for whom a place could not be found! In every theatre of war were nurses from all parts of the world – Australia, Canada, New Zealand, South Africa, Italy, France and America. Exposed to dangers of all kinds, in bitter cold and extreme heat, in clearing stations, hospital ships and on transports – wherever there were sick or wounded soldiers, there were also army nurses carrying out their duties fearlessly and cheerfully.

Particularly dangerous was the work of the munition workers, and many were the deaths caused by explosions, to say nothing of the disabilities caused by the different chemicals handled in their daily work. Amongst the Women's Army Auxiliary Corps death was frequent – there comes to my mind an air raid at Abbeville in which ten were killed by a bomb. And in Boulogne two Voluntary Aid nurses were decapitated when returning from a concert. A number of Canadian sisters were killed at Étaples, and there were numerous instances of deaths from various illnesses and on torpedoed ships. Most tragic of all was the torpedoing of the *Marquette* – numbers were drowned, amongst them ten army sisters, many others dying later from wounds and exposure; several others were permanently disabled.

In considering woman's work in wartime, special reference must be made to the organisation known as the Scottish Women's Hospital in Salonika, which was entirely staffed by them – doctors, nurses, orderlies, stretcher-bearers, domestics, drivers, registrar, commanding officer – all were women. This hospital and the British and Australian Nursing Services working in this malaria-infested area suffered unusual privations: there were few comforts and the cold was intense. Many have never recovered their normal health owing to the severe strain of their experiences.

But, while rendering to all these our sincerest admiration, one thinks of the women who gave their men to the war. They were the truest heroines, waiting, waiting for news and comforting themselves as best they might, helping in the less spectacular ways, unrelieved by the excitement and danger of life at the front. To them one offers one's homage and admiration.

Reveille, August 1927

Adelaide Maud Kellett (1873–1945) joined the Australian Army Nursing Service in 1907, embarked in October 1914, was theatre sister in the 2nd Australian General Hospital, Cairo, served on the hospital ship Gascon *during the Gallipoli Evacuation, and returned to Egypt to become temporary matron of Choubra Military Infectious Hospital. In 1916 she became matron of the 2nd Australian Auxiliary Hospital at Southall, England, and in July 1917 took charge of the 2400-bed 25th British General Hospital at Hardelot, France. After WWI she became matron of the 4th Australian General Hospital at Randwick and principal matron of the 2nd Military District. From 1921 until retirement in 1929 she was matron of Sydney Hospital.*

Figures tabled in Federal Parliament in 1932 revealed that 2861 nurses enlisted in the AIF, of whom 2139 embarked for active service in the UK, France, India, Salonika, Egypt, New Guinea and Africa. In addition 130 nurses were selected in Australia for service overseas with the Queen Alexandra Imperial Military Nursing Service. Twenty-one AIF nurses died on active service.

Reminiscences of an Army Nurse 1915-18

By One of Them

The background of these reminiscences is the general service of Australian Army Nursing Sisters. They were on the transports that went to Gallipoli to carry the wounded to Lemnos and Egypt. They were on the ship that went to the rescue of those on board the *Southland*. At Alexandria, Suez, Cairo and Lemnos they worked night and day in the hospitals. When insufficient beds were available for the wounded, they gave up their stretchers and slept on the floor. When Red Cross stores were not in hand, they bought comforts themselves and gave them to the troops. At all the base hospitals, casualty stations and ambulance trains in France, they worked unceasingly and cheerfully; on hospital ships and transports they did their part, tending the wounded and caring for the sick, often at the risk of their lives and health.

On 17 July 1915, I, with 239 other sisters, left Port Melbourne for active service abroad. The ship was the *Orsova* and besides Australian Army Nursing Service, there were on board four Army Medical Corps units, 1000 infantry for Egypt, and the 1st and 2nd Siege Brigade Batteries – soldiers of the permanent forces from Queenscliff and Thursday Island – men, who, after training in England, were destined for service in France.

When I remember the boys on the boat; how well and strong they were then – the fittest and best of Australian manhood, full of hope and courage – I cannot help but think of them as they were brought back – maimed, wounded, gassed, some crippled for life worse off than many comrades who did not return at all.

At Suez, the infantry and sisters of the Egyptian Unit landed and entrained for Cairo. I had been transferred to the staff of the hospital ship *Kanowna*. We watched the train steaming through the dry, weary, sandy desert and felt sorry that the active service of so many shipmates had begun in such a hot, sandy land. Five hundred sick and wounded Tommies replaced the infantry on board and nursing work commenced in real earnest. In the Mediterranean we tended our patients at night without a light – using a covered torch when it was absolutely necessary that we should see properly. Even the lighting of a match for a smoke was forbidden. At last Plymouth Harbour hove in sight. Orders were issued to be ready to disembark in half an hour, and we boarded the midnight train to London.

In England the nurses had their first experience of shrapnel wounds – wounds with green septic discharges, needing much syringing and care. A week before the call came to board the *Kanowna*, now fitted out as a hospital ship, I experienced my first air raid. Returning from the Strand, Sister C. and I had missed our usual bus. We took shelter and later we learned that the bus we were to take had been blown to pieces. Visiting the scene of the raid next day we saw a whole row of houses ruined in Russell Square, the top of a hospital shattered and other buildings badly burnt. The casualties and deaths were many, more than was generally admitted at the time.

At Malta more patients were taken on board and I was placed on night duty. Some of the men had fearful wounds necessitating frequent re-dressing. There we met for the first time the wounded men from Anzac, bringing a grim realisation of the frightfulness of war. Some of the wounded were very young. Too young, I thought, for the stern tasks of a soldier. One young lad had a look in his eyes that told more than words of the Hell he had had to endure. Others had such injuries that lifelong suffering seemed the only alternative to death. And yet withal, there was a general air of cheerfulness.

The next trip began when the boat returned from Brisbane and took on another quota of men and nurses for overseas. It was now approaching the end of December 1915. At Suez more wounded were taken on board and the boat turned back once again for Australia.

I remember one patient with a shrapnel wound in the head who would sit on deck at night. As often as I passed he would ask for an aspirin. He was dreading an operation on the boat, and expressed the fear that he would never see his mother and sweetheart again, the photos of whom he showed me several times a day. One morning he became unconscious and an operation (trephine) [an instrument for cutting bone from the skull] was the only chance of saving his reason, or indeed his life. The operation was carried out, but it was not successful, and he did not recover. He died with his head on a cushion given to me by an Australian lady who worked at home for the Red Cross.

A burial at sea of a soldier was always an impressive ceremony. There were many such sad scenes. The saddest of all I witnessed was one that took place just before Fremantle was reached. The mother was waiting on the wharf for this soldier, just after receiving word of his brother having been killed at the front.

There was a ward of TB patients plus a number of shell-shocked men, giving us three types of cases to look after – the wounded, the sick, and the mentally ill.

On 1 August 1916 I joined the *Miltiades* with two other sisters and set out for England again. We had some officers who had recovered from their injuries and were returning to their units, and a number of men for the 14th Battalion and the 6th Brigade. Reinforcements joined the boat at Fremantle for the 11th, 31st and 46th Battalions.

After the Gaza stunt, hundreds of wounded came in covered in dust, with only an iodine dressing on their wounds, placed there by the Field Army Medical Corps. Most were infected with vermin. Even as we cut off their clothes, gave them a wash and placed a clean dressing on their wounds, many passed beyond our care. The hospital was full of wounded and more and more tents had to be erected to accommodate incoming convoys. The operating theatres were kept going day and night. There was no let up. It was no uncommon thing for a nurse to work the whole of the day, and then to be called up at midnight to work again until the close of the next day.

For three weeks this went on, and the nursing staff was thoroughly exhausted, when a welcome relief came in a reinforcement of thirty sisters from Australia. The tired nurses were given two days off, and they spent it – in bed.

In 1917 I was ordered to join a nursing unit bound for Salonika. On landing, the nurses were taken in ambulances to the 52nd General Hospital, staffed by Canadians whom the Australians were to relieve. Hardly had they settled down before they were attacked by insects. The nurses discovered to their disgust that the biting was coming from bugs, and big ones at that. The huts, or rather the timber from which they were built, had come from Lemnos and other infected areas, and were simply riddled with these vile insects. The nurses undid their stretcher mattresses and placed them on the floor, leaving the beds well alone.

The wards were filled with British soldiers suffering from malaria, dysentery and wounds. In hospitals further up the line Bulgar and Turkish prisoners were amongst the patients. As it was summer the heat was most oppressive and flies and mosquitoes were troublesome. Food was short but the nurses were able to supplement their rations with oranges, lemons, nuts, etc. purchased from the Greeks. In the winter the nurses clothed themselves in all the woollen things they could put on, looking more like Eskimos than Australians. On top they wore a goat-skin coat, for nothing else was effective against the biting cold winds.

Mufti, December 1939–July 1940

'Ricki' Little of the Royal Naval Air Service

By Major B.C. Bell, DSO, DSC

I shall never forget Robert Alexander Little. He came from Melbourne and joined the Royal Naval Air Service in January 1916. I first heard of him while he was stationed at Dover. I was then on the coast of Flanders with No. 1 Wing, Royal Naval Air Service.

A pilot of the Royal Flying Corps had crashed into the cliffs near Dover during heavy fog, and Little had climbed down the face of the steep cliff to rescue him. Shortly after this Little was posted to No. 1 Wing in France, and served with me for two months before being invalided to England on sick leave.

Very small, but well-proportioned and athletic, Little had dark eyes, which moved very quickly from one object to another and took in everything at a glance. His movements too were quick and decisive. He obviously possessed all the necessary qualities that went to make a good fighting pilot. When he returned to France he was posted to No. 8 Naval Squadron, which was attached to the Royal Flying Corps. He soon found opportunity to prove his worth. It was not long before he was awarded the Distinguished Service Cross, and a few days later, a Bar to it for conspicuous gallantry in attacking and destroying enemy machines.

One memorable morning while on patrol with some of his squadron, his machine developed engine trouble, and gradually dropped farther and farther behind the others. Little should have returned to the aerodrome, but, in a reckless spirit, carried on about a mile behind the formation, well over the enemy lines. Before long three enemy scouts picked him out for easy game, and dived from above to shoot him down. He was suddenly in the middle of their tracer bullets, and as he kicked his rudder and manoeuvred to avoid this fire, the rattle of their machine-guns grew louder. He knew that it was madness to turn and run, so he decided to fight to a finish.

Suddenly his motor picked up to its full revolutions, and he was able to use the superior climbing power of his triplane. He succeeded in getting one of the Germans in his sights, and after a short burst, its upper wing crumpled and the machine spun to earth. By this time the other two men were again firing at Little, but one of them, overshooting his dive, gave the Australian an opening which he quickly grasped, and the second enemy machine went down in flames.

The third Boche decided to discontinue the fight, but Little's blood was up and he was after his scalp too. Closely followed by the rest of the patrol, which had seen the fight and was coming to give assistance, Little got the enemy machine in his sights and sent a long burst into it. The German pilot was evidently killed, his machine crashing to the ground.

They nicknamed him 'Ricki' in the squadron (after 'Rikki Tikki Tavi') and I also heard him called 'The Little Butcher' by somebody who did not know him. But Little's one object was to destroy every German in the sky. I once heard him say, 'I am sorry for those poor devils on the ground; it's up to us to do all we can for them.'

One day in September 1917 I motored over to his squadron and heard from the commanding officer something about one of Little's latest exploits. Three machines were out on morning patrol when one had to return home with engine trouble. Suddenly the other two pilots – Stanley Dallas (also Australian) and Little – observed over our lines a large formation of fourteen enemy scouts escorting two artillery observation machines. Their observers doubtless felt quite safe with so large an escort, but they did not reckon on meeting two such daring adversaries. Dallas and Little, feeling that the Germans must be on an important job, decided to upset their plans.

So they climbed away to one side, and as soon as they had sufficient height, altered their course to bring them into a good position to open the attack from behind. Then, diving down through the 'nest of hornets', and opening fire at close quarters, they scattered its formation and continued straight for the two-seaters. Little crashed his, and the other was driven down by Dallas before the amazed escorting pilots could believe their eyes.

But they at once dived after Little and Dallas, only to learn that they were up against two men quite out of the ordinary. Before long the Germans found themselves in trouble. The two triplanes attacked again and again until the enemy formation was completely broken up and forced to make for home, with the Australians closely pursuing them. At least four of their number were destroyed or forced to land.

Little's brilliant career continued. He was awarded the Distinguished Service Order on 11 August and a Bar to it a month later. When he had destroyed forty-seven enemy machines he was sent back to England for a well-earned rest. March 1918 saw him again in France as a flight commander in No. 203 (Naval) Squadron, Royal Air Force. Inside two months, however, he, too, was to pay the supreme sacrifice. On the night of 27 May, at the age of twenty-two, he was killed while attacking a German bombing plane.

Five days later Dallas sacrificed himself to save the life of a young British pilot.

Reveille, September 1935

Major Bertram Charles Bell (1893–1941) was born at Coochin Coochin station, Boonah, Queensland, and after being educated at Toowoomba Grammar School joined his brothers in managing the family properties. When WWI broke out Bell was visiting England and was asked to take the first 'Queensland' motor ambulance to France. He served for six months as an ambulance driver with the Red Cross and the Australian Voluntary Hospital, and then took private flying lessons. In May 1915 he was commissioned as a probationary flight sub-lieutenant in the Royal Naval Air Service and was posted to No. 1 Squadron at Dunkirk in July. His subsequent record credits him with shooting down at least six enemy. From April 1917 until the end of the war Bell commanded No. 10 Squadron, RNAS flying Sopwith triplanes and later Sopwith BR Camels. He left the RAF in March 1919 after refusing a permanent commission, and returned home to manage Coochin Coochin.

Robert Alexander Little was born on 19 July 1895 at Hawthorn, Melbourne, was educated at Scotch College and later joined the family business as a commercial traveller. Rejected with hundreds of others for the four vacancies at Point Cook Military Flying School, he sailed for England in July 1915, at his own expense. He paid for his flying training at Hendon where he gained his flying certificate and entered the Royal Naval Air Service as a probationary temporary sub-lieutenant on 14 January 1916. On 1 November he scored his first aerial victory and by March 1917 was credited with nine enemy aircraft shot down; he was promoted flight lieutenant in April. In early 1918 he took command of 203 Squadron. Little is officially credited with destroying forty-seven enemy planes, the most by any Australian pilot. He ranks eighth of all British Commonwealth aces, and 14th of all aces from both sides of the conflict.

'Breguet' Dallas: A Great Australian War Pilot

By Major B.C. Bell, DSO, DSC

It was about the middle of 1915 when I first went to No. 1 Squadron, Royal Naval Air Service stationed at St Pol, near Dunkirk. I had not been there very long before a fellow countryman named Roderic Stanley Dallas was posted to the same squadron. He was a tall, squarely built, kindly dispositioned fellow with a charming personality and a dry sense of humour. We became great friends.

One evening while he was duty officer, I played a practical joke which caused him to be nicknamed 'Breguet' Dallas for the rest of his life. It was his job, as duty pilot, to answer the telephone which was directly connected with the commanding officer's office. I had just been talking to Dallas before going over to the officers' mess. On my way I passed in front of the CO's empty office; the door was open; the telephone stood invitingly on the table. I walked into the office and violently rang the telephone. In a few seconds Dallas answered.

Copying the CO's voice as much as possible I said: 'Oh, is that you Dallas?'

'Yes, sir,' came the smart reply.

'A zeppelin has just been reported over the North Sea. Take off at once in the Breguet de Chasse and try to locate it.'

'Yes, sir.'

I put the receiver down and waited, for the Breguet de Chasse had no propeller on and so was out of action. In a few minutes the telephone rang.

'Sir, the Breguet is out of action. It has no propeller on it.'

'Never mind, Dallas, take it up at once.'

'But, sir,' the astonished Dallas replied, 'she is out of action.'

'Never mind, never mind, take her up at once.'

Jamming down the receiver I walked back to the aerodrome where old Dallas was hurrying about in his flying gear. The Breguet, minus its propeller, stood out in front of the hangar, while another machine was being wheeled out ready to take up.

'The CO must have gone mad,' said Dallas. 'He told me to take up the Breguet after a zep and I can't make him understand that she is out of action.'

'Never mind, never mind, Dallas, take her up at once,' I replied.

A slow smile came over his face as he realised that he had had his leg pulled. He rushed after me but was laughing so much that he couldn't run more than a few yards.

Stanley Dallas soon carved for himself a very high reputation, his quiet, unassuming manner and his determined, dauntless courage soon making him outstanding. He was transferred to the Somme area and there had an opportunity to get a lot of aerial fighting. His score of enemy machines rapidly mounted and his name became more and more widely known. He had shot down thirty or forty enemy machines and had well earned the Distinguished Service Order, Distinguished Service Cross and Bar.

He was then given command of a squadron of triplanes, and in a very short time his squadron had a splendid name. He personally led them on many occasions, and he used to make a practice of taking out the younger and inexperienced pilots and teaching them to know the lines. If they could not open their score, Dallas would manoeuvre them into position so they could get a German while he protected them.

Every officer or man who served with or under Dallas loved him for he had every fine quality. Tolerant, straightforward, always seeing the best in everybody, brave, thoughtful, and wise, combined with a keen sense of humour. He had no vices of any kind so far as I know, and I never once heard him swear.

One day he took a young, inexperienced pilot over the lines to give him confidence and teach him the cunning of aerial fighting. For once Dallas was taken by surprise by an enemy formation of eight scouts. The Germans dived on to them and in a very short time the young British pilot was in serious trouble with an opponent on his tail. Again and again he was saved by Dallas, who, disregarding his own safety, would shoot the German off his colleague's tail while being attacked himself. He thus saved the boy's life, but in doing so, he fell himself, riddled with bullets.

It so happened that Dallas had this day been promoted to wing commander, and a message telling him to proceed to take over command of a wing and not to fly any more, was on his table waiting for him to read on his return.

The news of his death came as a great shock to us all in the air service. We realised that we had lost one of our most gallant members, one whose high standard had been so helpful to us; and I realised that Australia had lost one of the finest men she had ever produced and one of her most daring airmen.

I am sure, if he had lived, Dallas would have reached the highest places in the air service. I can think of no one more capable for a great command, and none of his old comrades would have been surprised to see him head of the Australian Flying Corps.

Reveille, May 1935

Roderic Stanley Dallas (1891–1918) was born at Mount Stanley station near Esk, Queensland. The family moved to Tenterfield, NSW, and about 1898 to Mount Morgan, Queensland. In July 1907 Dallas joined the assay office of the Mount Morgan Gold Mining Co. At night he studied chemistry and technical drawing at the technical college. He paid his own way to England in 1915, and topped the entrance examination to be admitted to the Royal Naval Air Service. His first dogfight took place in December 1915, and his first kill came in May 1916 in circumstances that won him the Distinguished Service Cross. His official tally of thirty victories soon rose to thirty-nine, although in correspondence he claimed only thirty-two as certain. Unofficial estimates suggested there were over fifty. At his death he was 16th on the list of Allied aces and second only to R.A. Little among the Australians.

'Smithy' Scared by Airman's Bombs

By Air Commodore Sir Charles Kingsford Smith, MC, AFC

My recent air travels about the world have brought me into contact with brother airmen of all nations. Among them are several fine types of German commercial pilots, with whom I was one day chatting. One man in particular seemed keenly interested in learning that I was an Australian and had served in Gallipoli.

He recalled that in that campaign he was attached to the Turkish forces, and was employed in making himself a general nuisance to Australian troops at Anzac. Immediately my interest was aroused; more so when he stated that a certain type of night flying had come within his sphere of activities, and I begged him to show me his logbooks.

This was done, and I looked up his record of flights on a certain night of August 1915. One entry (even my poor German effectively translated it) read: '*11.30 p.m. – bombed lighters landing troops; unable to observe extent damage.*'

Little did my courteous German friend know that a youth of just eighteen years crouched shivering (more with fear than cold) on one of those lighters, cursing him with as much fluency as chattering teeth would allow.

I felt the occasion called for champagne. 'My friend,' said I, holding up my glass, 'I drink to your bad aim. Had it been a little better, your gracious words of praise of myself would have remained unsaid, and the casualty lists of the Australian papers sixteen years ago would have included the name of Sapper Charles Kingsford Smith.'

Among members of the 4th Light Horse Brigade, 4 Signal Troop, on the troopship Ajana *when she left Sydney on 31 May 1915, was an eighteen-year-old electrical engineer named* **Charles Kingsford Smith**. *He held the lowly rank of Sapper and after joining the war at Gallipoli was initially a motorcycle despatch rider. He transferred to the Royal Flying Corps, earning his pilot's wings in 1917, and soon after was shot down and had to have part of his left foot amputated. He was awarded the Military Cross and promoted to Captain. Fame came in 1928 when Kingsford Smith and Charles Ulm flew the* Southern Cross *in the first trans-Pacific flight from the USA to Australia. After further exploits, and having been knighted, Sir Charles Kingsford Smith and his co-pilot John Thompson Pethybridge were flying the* Lady Southern Cross *overnight from India to Singapore, as part of an attempt to break the England–Australia speed record, when they disappeared over the Andaman Sea in the early hours of 8 November 1935. Their bodies were never recovered.*

Towards Armistice

'Thousands learnt for the first time the meaning of the word "comrade". There were made friendships which endured until death. There men found that the manly qualities of the navvy were on as high a plane as those of more favoured workers in civil life.'

— Anonymous

Seeing Peter Pan

Author unknown

St Dunstan's Hostel for Blinded Soldiers and Sailors, at Regents Park in London, had about 150 residents by early 1916. The men were taught to overcome their blindness and were given instruction in many skills that would allow them to work in civilian life. The Australian soldier described here was one of several trained as a masseur; others were taught boot repairing, mat making, net making, basket making, joinery, poultry farming and market gardening.

During the war, some time in 1916, I was asked by a young Australian soldier at St Dunstan's – Signaller Edward Penn – if I would take him out the following Sunday.

'You know,' he said, 'I'm to return to Melbourne in a week or two, and I simply must see Peter Pan before I go.' We always 'see' at St Dunstan's. It seemed to help somehow.

Penn was just twenty, six feet two inches, and a lion for strength. He had one of the finest characters I have ever known, right in his ideas of what was right, but he had enough determination to fit out a whole platoon.

He was blinded at Gallipoli when he went ashore from one of the first boats to reach that ill-starred landing place. When he made his request to me, Penn had been at St Dunstan's about eighteen months, and was expecting his boarding notice at any moment – his training as a masseur having been completed.

The following Sunday we started out. It was rather early, I remember, with not many people about; full summer and the grass green and springy. The gardens had everywhere the wonderful blue haze that seems to linger there among the trees. We walked through the 'Notting Hill' gate, the only true way to visit Peter Pan.

When we reached the statue Penn put his hands upon it.

'Why,' he said, 'it's smaller than I thought. I shall know it all.'

Very carefully, with the delicacy of touch his training taught him, he felt it piece by piece, with little murmurs of delight.

'Just look at this tiny mouse,' he would say. 'See this lovely little fairy. Why, she is stretching up to speak to him!' Then again: 'You are quite sure I am not missing anything?'

Indeed, I thought he was taking in more than many with sight. He was very intent on this examination, but at last he was satisfied that nothing had escaped him. He turned to me and whispered: 'Surely there are a number of people near us.' As a matter of fact there were, but I had hoped he would not notice.

They had stopped as they passed, seeing this tall young Australian finger so carefully the statue that all London knows and loves so well. He was so obviously blind, and just as obviously full of sap and strength and vigour as the trees that grew above him. I can remember two women among the little crowd who stood watching in silence with the tears running down their cheeks.

'Ah, well,' he said, as we turned away, 'I don't wonder it draws a crowd. It's one of the loveliest things I have ever seen. I shall be glad to think of it when I am back in Australia.'

The Listening Post, July 1929

Watery Grave: Barunga's End

By J. Graham

The transport ship Barunga *was a former German ship, the SS* Sumatra, *which had been seized in the early days of WWI. She was torpedoed in 1918 while transporting a large contingent of nurses and wounded soldiers. There was no loss of life, as she remained afloat for about an hour after being hit, and the escorting warships were able to rescue all aboard.*

Bound for Australia, we left Plymouth on 14 July 1918, by the *Barunga*, on which there were 900 invalids.

All went well until 4.30 p.m. on 15 July, when, in the Bay of Biscay, we received a 'present' from a Fritz submarine – a torpedo – in the forward hold. The first and second bulkheads collapsed, but happily, the engine-room bulkhead held, so the ship floated for a time.

The explosion shook the *Barunga* from stem to stern, and threw everyone to the decks, particularly those in the hospital, where the nurses were attending their charges. Digger patients were tossed from their cots.

The nurses behaved magnificently and assisted the patients to the boats. Despite the dreadful possibilities – for the ship was rapidly sinking – there was not the slightest panic. We all lined up at boat stations, helping those who were incapacitated, on deck. We saw the submarine circling around the stern, half submerged.

The captain ordered rafts to be thrown overboard and boats were lowered. Three British destroyers came to our rescue; one destroyer circled round the sinking ship, dropping depth charges. The other two destroyers lay off so as to rescue floaters and swimmers.

The *Barunga* soon settled down by the head, and there was no time to save clothing or valuables. Many men had to jump overboard to reach the rafts or swim to the destroyers.

On board the *Barunga* the time had been passed with typical nonchalance. Four Diggers were playing bridge on the mess deck at the time the vessel was hit; others were playing 'housie'. The banker had accumulated thousands of pennies when the torpedo struck. He took the pennies and scattered them on deck, saying, 'Come on, Diggers, help yourselves. These are too heavy for me to get away with.' The last to leave the *Barunga* were the ship's captain and Colonel Burnage, officer in command of troops.

Throughout the work of rescue, first attention was given to those who were incapacitated. Shell-shock cases suffered terribly. Many of us who had been floating about for over an hour were completely exhausted when rescued.

The *Barunga* sank with a final shiver, and then the ships, having completed the work of rescue, turned their bows homewards. Next morning we were landed safely in Blighty, kitless and in all kinds of attire. We all appreciated the whole-hearted generosity of the naval men, who supplied us with warm dry clothing, hot coffee and food.

Reveille, June 1930

Last Days at Weymouth

By 'Hazeldene'

There were three camps at Weymouth, and every returned invalid soldier – or almost every one – passed through one or more of these camps before embarking. It was there they had to face their last medical board, and, incidentally, the Bogey Man. Ask any returned soldier does he remember Colonel Ryan, and you will see a reminiscent look pass over his countenance; he is thinking of the Bogey Man, and how near he came to being sent back to France.

After the final medical board, if declared unfit, the soldier knew that it was only a matter of time and he would be on his way back to Aussie.

For weeks we had been on the tiptoe of expectation; each day there were rumours of a boat roll, but many times we were doomed to disappointment. Eagerly we watched our sergeant major as he came on parade, to see if his hand held the long expected boat roll. Again and again our hopes were dashed to the ground.

At last, when one day he came surrounded by NCOs, we knew by the excitement amongst the latter that the long-expected had arrived. For once, at least, the sergeant major had our undivided attention. He commenced to read: 'The following men will answer their names and fall out in front; they will be on J Carrier.'

We waited expectantly, 'Here, sir,' on the tips of our tongues. But we were doomed to disappointment – our names were not on the roll. In the vernacular of the troops, we had 'come a gutser'. We went back to our huts, cursing our luck, to follow the daily routine of hobbling on with crutch or stick to a never-ending succession of parades. On every hand you would hear some habitual grouser remark, 'Stiff luck, Digger, missin' that last boat roll. I'll be glad when we are finished with this joint.'

For a week we waited, each day expecting T boat roll. Then on a memorable Monday the sergeant major commenced: 'The following men will constitute T boat roll. Private Jones.'

'Right!'

'You'll be "right" in clink if you don't answer properly. Private Smith.'

'Here!'

'Answer properly, that man! There's an officer on parade. I'll crime the next man that doesn't answer correctly. Private Brown.'

'That's me.' (Then hastily) 'Here, sir!'

At length the roll was completed. To our joy we were on the list, and it was someone else's turn to leave the parade with a bitter feeling in the heart. For two days we were on parade incessantly. Medical, kit, and other inspections followed one another in quick succession. Then, on an eventful morning, we arose at 3 a.m., partook of a hasty breakfast, and fell in at daylight. There was joy in our hearts as we passed through the gates of the camp, while the guard stood aside without asking the old familiar question, 'Where's your pass?'

As we went through the streets, many a man, and many a girl, too, even at the early hour, stood on the footpath to wave farewell and bid us '*bon voyage*'; and many a man broke from the ranks to say a fond farewell to the girl he was leaving behind.

On the station we were regaled with tea and cakes, provided, I believe, by the Red Cross, and distributed by the colonel's wife (Mrs Spencer Brown) and a number of other ladies. We steamed out of the station to the strains of 'Auld Lang Syne', played by the depot band, after the popular camp commandant (Colonel Spencer Brown) had personally said farewell to us.

We travelled by train across Dorset, and among the beautiful hills of Devon. It was a bright sunny day, and everything looked fresh and green. By four o'clock we were all on board the troopship. It was the time long dreamed of; the end of a perfect day.

Next morning we weighed anchor and slowly steamed out to sea, passing three of England's old wooden vessels, now used as training ships. As we passed, the band on board a cruiser struck up, 'We All Go the Same Way Home'. We were accompanied by two or three other transports, a cruiser or two, and a number of destroyers. Overhead an airship sailed majestically, and two seaplanes circled and dipped like two gigantic albatrosses.

It was farewell to Old England, which many of us did not leave without regret. The way we had been treated by the ladies of Blighty after our return from France will long remain in our memory.

The WA Digger Book, 1929

I Never Knew His Name

By E. St Ives Bilston

As an atom is to this earth so is this earth to be compared to the universe. Not feeling in the mood to challenge this statement, I will take it for granted that what the astronomers say is correct. Anyhow, I can meet my scientific friends as far as saying that the world is not very wide, and I quote an example as proof of my contention.

At noon on 13 September 1915, I, with others, was detailed to go into the 'supports' at the Apex, Gallipoli, and relieve the New Zealanders. As I approached my possie I saw an NZ man stripped to the waist engaged in the exciting pastime of chasing 'chats' on his shirt. As I arrived he secured an abnormal-sized catch from a seam, and greeted me with the remark: 'This is what you will have to put up with here.' We became good pals. Within a week or two his unit proceeded to Lemnos for a rest, and we parted.

Having been issued with 'iron rations' on 8 December 1915, I was sent to Heliopolis Hospital. Being in Cairo on leave one day, I collapsed on the footpath, and awakened to consciousness to find a man in uniform standing over me. It was my chum of the supports again. He assisted me to a tram and we parted once more.

We met again in London at Horseferry Road. Our troubles were similar: we had both lost our pay-books owing to HQ taking them from us for audit purposes and being unable to find them again.

Nearly two years ago I caught the slow express to a single-cylinder place called Dinninup. I had the compartment to myself, and dozed off, and when the train was at a weird halting place called Qualeup I dreamed that some good Samaritan was holding a steaming hot billy of tea alongside my nose. In awaking I found that my dream was true, for sure enough, the tea was there, held in the grip of my NZ friend. The surprise was a pleasant one.

Some months ago I caught sight of him again, just as the train was moving off the platform at Pinjarra. He looked down on his luck. He was staring vacantly ahead, and had on a battered old NZ Army hat. Strange as it may seem, I never knew his name.

The Listening Post, May 1923

Private Euliseus St Ives Bilston was a 43-year-old married farmer from Doodlakine, 220 kilometres east of Perth. He enlisted in January 1915, embarked with the 28th Battalion five months later and returned to Australia in June 1916 after being wounded at Gallipoli.

Our Park of Memories: Blackboy Hill

By 'Non-Com'

When WWI began in 1914, Blackboy Hill, sixteen kilometres north-east of central Perth, was unoccupied, covered in light scrub and close to a railway line. It was ideal for use as an army training camp, as men could be transported easily by train to Helena Vale (now Midland) station and marched to Blackboy Hill. Some 32,000 volunteers passed through the camp during the war years. When the Western Australian government decided in the 1950s that the site should be developed for housing, the RSL lobbied to have a memorial built there. Today that is the only reminder of the military camp, the rest of the land having been built over by houses and a school.

Blackboy Hill! Its once well-worn slopes now covered with pasture; its bell tents and marquees 'returned to store'; but here and there a wooden hut still stands as a reminder of days – and men – that are gone.

The birth of the old camp! When the first thousand marched in! No kindly quartermaster to greet them with a beaming smile; to issue tunics, breeches and the equipment which was to be carried and cursed later on. It was a case of getting under cover that first day and, marvellous to relate, the evening saw order out of chaos, and eight long rows of bell tents where the morning had seen only the virgin bush.

Comrade 'Stew' was introduced that day. It turned out a long acquaintance which never developed into friendship. Indeed, while Stew may have its virtues, familiarity with it in the army bred contempt. The bosom of Mother Earth that night was hard and cold. The oil sheet and two army blankets, which comprised 'the issue', were indifferent substitutes for the cosy bed at home, nor did they ameliorate to any extent that chill midnight-to-morning air, which was always a feature of Blackboy Hill.

The whereabouts of that first thousand now! It would be interesting to know. The majority sleep on Gallipoli, in Belgium, or France, or have paid the last penalty back here in the Golden West. A few only were lucky. All carry some souvenir!

Some splendid men 'fell in' at Blackboy Hill: Percy Black, the Southern Cross miner who was a rock to lean on at Anzac, and died – a major, and mourned by the AIF – at Bullecourt; Wally Hallahan, the Kalgoorlie boy who saw Gallipoli and France from start to finish, and was killed leading his company through the wire of the Hindenburg Line in his unit's last 'stunt'; Harry Murray, the south-west sleeper-cutter, who finished up a lieutenant-colonel, and the most decorated infantry soldier in the British Army; McIntosh, the timber worker, who survived Gallipoli and France and flew back to Aussie with Parer 'by bus' – an epic flight in a plane only held together by wire and string, and the cheery courage and resource of its pilots; Sammy Taylor, the rough diamond among the 'sar-majors', who, after two years turning out soldiers at Blackboy, died in no-man's-land, in a night raid in France in '17; Meysey Hammond, the north-west pearler, who lost an arm, 'wangled' his way back to his unit and was killed later at the head of his company; Captain Peter Lalor, the smallest man, surely, in the AIF, a grandson of Peter Lalor of the Eureka Stockade. Killed during the first day at Anzac, waving his grandfather's sword, he was one of the very few men who died sword in hand in the Great War; 'Pink Top', the Perth fruit seller. Entertaining and enterprising at his fruit stand in Wellington Street, just so was he in camp and in the field. He lies peacefully in an Anzac gully; Pope, the insurance agent, who won both crosses when he and his platoon were ordered, at Lagnicourt, to hold their outpost 'to the last man'. A ring of eighty German corpses surrounding the silent garrison testified to their grim adherence to orders when the post was recaptured by Australian troops the next day; Simpson, the 'man with the donkey'. Surely no greater story was ever told than the simple record of this man's deeds on early Anzac. For him the cross of sacrifice!

The list is not complete. It never will be. Those who revisit Blackboy Hill will have their own special memories. The Hill will always have an attraction for those who once bore the heat and burden of those hectic days. That picturesque spot, so quiet now, was the rallying point of Westralia's finest manhood. There thousands learnt for the first time the meaning of the word 'comrade'. There were made friendships which endured until death. There men found that the manly qualities of the navvy were on as high a plane as those of more favoured workers in civil life. Blackboy Hill was the great destroyer of prejudice – the melting pot in which each entrant soon found his own level.

The WA Digger Book, 1929

The King Is a Sportsman!

By 'Jay Bee', 4th Battalion

The Prince of Wales referred to here was Prince Edward, then twenty-four years old. He succeeded to the British throne in January 1936 – a month before this tale was published – as Edward VIII, and abdicated in December of that year.

After the Armistice, the then Prince of Wales spent a month amongst the Australian corps. His time was spent in visiting units and mixing very freely with both officers and men.

His month was practically expired and he had seen almost every unit in the corps with the exception of the 4th Battalion. We of the 4th had our headquarters at Lansprelle Chateau, Acoz. We heard the Prince was to leave the corps on Thursday, and when Tuesday night came and still no word of a visit from the Prince, the colonel – Cecil Duncan Sasse – being thoroughly bored with life, decided to take a chance and make a long delayed trip to Brussels. Sasse had been a regular British officer, something of a dandy, but decidedly a hard case.

So on Tuesday evening Sasse and Freddy Newth, adjutant, set off for Charleroi en route to Brussels. His parting instructions to the second-in-command, Major Don Brown – a Duntroon boy – were something like this: 'It is obvious the Prince isn't coming to see us now, so if the brigadier happens to come along, tell him I have gone on a shooting party with the artillery. I will be back in a day or two.'

Less than an hour after he left, a phone message came from corps to say the Prince was coming at 10 o'clock next morning. Now here was a comic position for a young second-in-command to face! The colonel was entirely out of reach. The Prince would almost certainly be accompanied by the brigadier – of whom Sasse had a wholesome fear – there was no possible way of getting the AWL merchants back from Brussels since we hadn't the faintest idea where they would stay.

Next morning at 10 o'clock the Prince duly came along, accompanied by Lord Claude Hamilton and Major Hunn from corps. He was ushered into the smoking room, drinks were handed around, and for a few minutes there was a sort of breaking-in period of reticence and reserve on both sides.

Suddenly the Prince asked: 'By the way, Major Brown, where is your colonel?'

Don came out with his glib story that the colonel had gone away on a shooting party last night and we were unable to reach him.

The Prince expressed regret and then asked: 'And your adjutant? I suppose he is with the colonel, is he?'

Confusion reigns. Of course Brown agreed with this conjecture, and suddenly the Prince remarked severely: 'Well! That's strange, Major Brown! It may surprise you to know that I spent the whole of last evening with your colonel and adjutant in the Café Royale, Brussels!'

Brown was not equal to the occasion. He stuttered something and went red, pink and green behind the gills, and the incident looked like becoming serious when the regimental quack – Doctor Haines – gave a guffaw and ejaculated: 'By cripes! That's torn it!'

There was a howl of laughter – led by the Prince – and when it had subsided the Prince confessed that he had never anticipated any visit with such pleasure.

'Shooting party, by gad! It was one of the heaviest barrages I ever encountered!'

The colonel, of course, had advised him of the excuse that would be offered, so he came fully prepared for the fun. After that it was some party. When the Prince finally left us just before lunch the whole world was very rosy to every member of the mess.

Next evening the wanderers returned and we got the full story. Arriving at Brussels about 10 o'clock, Sasse and Newth had strolled down to the Café Royale to hit the high spots. As soon as they entered they saw Hunn, who came across and said: 'What the Hell are you doing here, Sasse? The Prince is going to your battalion tomorrow morning. You have no hope in life of getting back in time. I had better tell the Prince and see what he says about it.'

A few minutes later he returned with an invitation for them to join the Prince's party. 'He says he would much sooner see you here than at your battalion, so come along and join the fun.' From what Sasse and Newth could remember of the night, it was a very bright party, and when the Prince finally pulled out at 4 a.m. his last words to Sasse were: 'You must get back to the battalion as quickly as you can. If you catch the midday train I shall arrange for my car to pick you up at Charleroi and run you home. And you needn't worry about your brigadier. I will send Mackay a phone message as soon as I get back to HQ telling him I wish my visit to the 4th Battalion to be quite informal. I am certainly looking forward to hearing the yarn your fellows spin when I get there!'

Presumably there is something in the training of an heir apparent which prepares him for this sort of eventuality. It is certainly noteworthy that a young Englishman could mix with the hardboiled members of the AIF and never make a false step. This incident must be typical of many which occurred during his stay with the Australians, and he has since referred to that period as one of the brightest memories of his life.

Mufti, February 1936

The Quartermaster's Dilemma: Christmas 1918

By E.B.

Quartermasters in the different units of the AIF did not mind the practical work of that part of the outfit, but they had a great aversion to the clerical duties which that branch of the business entailed.

The official abbreviations and regulation short weight titles of the several articles of equipment sorely tried the Diggers, and at the handing over after the declaration of the Armistice, some amusing incidents occurred, especially in the attempt to juggle the equipment ledger with the articles on hand, in order to arrive at some approximate balance.

In the handing over of the equipment of a certain battery of the 11th Field Artillery Brigade one item on the list fairly puzzled the already overworked quartermaster sergeant, who could not reconcile it with the articles on hand, viz.: *Shov. Wood, 1.*

Search where he might amongst the collection for an article that to him would represent this item proved fruitless. He was in a real dilemma. In sheer desperation he confided in the battery artificer, 'What the Hell is this flaming Shove Wood?' he roared. 'Can't remember ever taking one over.'

'Don't know,' replied the artificer, 'never seen one – it's got me stonkered.'

That worthy (like the majority of the Diggers) was not lacking in initiative, and suggested making a contrivance that might be bluffed through for the missing item.

An old gun trail was accordingly procured, and with a pair of small truck wheels souvenired from a Froggy Farmer, a weird looking contraption was pieced together, oiled, and painted, and displayed for inspection with the rest of the gear.

Came the eventful day of the handing over at Bailleul: ordnance officer, with list of equipment to check up, and quartermaster sergeant standing confidently near at hand.

Officer: 'Everything OK, Sergeant?'

Quartermaster: 'Yes, sir.'

'Right-oh, let's run through the list. Carry on.'

All went jake until the item 'Shov. Wood 1' was reached. The quartermaster, seizing the opportunity to rush the item through, grabbed hold of the contrivance, saying: 'Here it is, sir.'

The officer gazed at the article for a moment, and then at the equipment list in his hand, but failed evidently to identify with any of the items.

'What the blazes do you call this?' he roared.

'It's the Shove Wood, sir,' replied the anxious quartermaster, 'handiest thing in the battery, sir, don't know how we'd have got on without it,' he continued, at the same time indicating the position of the item 'Shov. Wood' on the list in the officer's hand.

The officer burst out laughing. 'Why,' he said, 'the article mentioned on the list is an abbreviation of the item "Shovels – wood". There they are,' pointing to three shovels on the ground. 'You've got a surplus!'

The Queensland Digger, January 1926

Phantom Anzacs in the War Zone

Author unknown

Lively emotion has been excited among the peasants around Armentières, an area of the old battle front, by the appearance of Les Revenants (ghosts) garbed in the slouch hats and distinctive khaki of the Australian and New Zealand forces.

Almost every year since the Armistice there have been reports of these visitations, especially round about 1 November, the Day of the Dead in France. It is only this year that the reports have taken a form that makes it necessary to pay attention to them, in view of the fact that they are attested for by the clergy of the locality, and seen by the '*maire*' of one of the towns.

The first stories told of stray men in the familiar garb of the Anzacs who presented themselves late at night at estaminets and private houses around Armentières, claiming hospitality, which was never denied them, because the Anzacs have won a place in the hearts of the French peasants in the warzone that would prevent anyone being churlish with them.

One grim story told for the last ten years is of a giant Anzac, who appeared about midnight at a cabaret on the high road just outside Armentières for about a fortnight from 1 November onward. His coming was heralded by a quiet knock at the door, and when the proprietor or his daughter opened it, they found a white-faced man in the familiar garb of the Anzac, who pointed to a ghastly wound in his throat and signed that he wanted something to drink. The beverage was forthcoming, and though the proprietor and his daughter tried to engage the strange visitor in conversation, he would not speak.

After consuming his drink he placed some coins on the counter and walked out. Always the coins were the pre-war kind, which were in circulation during the war, but the amount left was generous enough to make allowance for the depreciation of the franc.

At first these stories were ascribed to the imagination of villagers who had had 'one over the eight', but they were so persistent that it became necessary to take them seriously, and this year the local priests and other persons of standing were called in to check the stories. From the eve of 1 November, watch has been kept in the area, and some of the stories vouched for by responsible observers are even more marvellous than those told originally.

One of the stories is of the appearance on one of the hills overlooking Armentières of a ghostly company of Anzacs, who beckoned to the observers to follow them, and after following for about two miles in the direction of the original German front line, the awed observers saw the Anzacs go over the top to attack the Germans. Ghostly figures appeared to put up resistance, but the phantom Anzacs gained the upper hand and took possession of the trenches. The awed observers pressed on to the trenches, but when they got there, the phantom Anzacs and their ghostly opponents had vanished completely.

The standing of some of the people who vouch for the truth of these stories makes it impossible to treat them with the scepticism usually given to such stories, and it has been decided to appoint a committee of scientists interested in the occult to proceed to the area concerned to study the phenomena on the spot, and to report to the French Academy of Science.

The Queensland Digger, May 1931

Abbreviations

AAMC	Australian Army Medical Corps
AANS	Australian Army Nursing Service
AFC	Australian Flying Corps; Air Force Cross
AIF	Australian Imperial Force
AMC	Army Medical Corps
CB	Companion of the Bath
CMG	Companion of the Order of St Michael and St George
CO	Commanding Officer
DCM	Distinguished Conduct Medal
DFC	Distinguished Flying Cross
DSC	Distinguished Service Cross
DSO	Distinguished Service Order
GCMG	Knight Grand Cross of the Order of St Michael and St George
GOC	General Officer Commanding
KBE	Knight Commander of the Order of the British Empire
KCB	Knight Commander of the Bath
KCMG	Knight Commander of the Order of St Michael and St George
MC	Military Cross
MM	Military Medal
NCO	Non-Commissioned Officer
OBE	Officer of the British Empire
RRC	(Lady of the) Royal Red Cross
2IC	Second-in-charge
VC	Victoria Cross
VD	Volunteer Decoration

Acknowledgments

This volume would not have been possible without the co-operation of the state presidents and CEOs of the several branches of the Returned and Services League of Australia, who made their libraries available to me and my colleague Richard Landels. The national president of the RSL, Rear Admiral Ken Doolan, and the Victorian branch CEO, Michael Annett, as chairman of the national organisation's marketing committee, have been of particular assistance.

The State Library of Queensland was generous in making available several decades of *The Queensland Digger* that had been lost from the RSL archives during floods.

I have made extensive use of the Australian War Memorial's resources in checking names, dates, facts and biographies, and am especially grateful to the AWM for providing ready online access to the WWI Nominal Roll, the Embarkation Roll, Red Cross files and unit histories. The *Australian Dictionary of Biography* has been a significant source of biographical detail.

Dr Brendan Nelson and Mark Small at the AWM were helpful in granting permission to use the H.S. Gullett extract from the *Official History of Australia in the War of 1914–18*, describing the incident at Surafend. Mark Small also assisted Richard Landels in his search for appropriate photographs.

My thanks go also to Mrs Audrey Adams, of Karrinyup, WA, for permitting the inclusion of extracts from the diary of her late father, Private Cecil Crews, and for providing us with a treasured family photograph.

At HarperCollins, the experience of Katie Stackhouse and Denise O'Dea has been invaluable as they guided this project enthusiastically to completion. I also thank my daughter, Alexandra, and her inherited love of books for providing a fresh pair of eyes, which proved very sharp in proof reading.

Ultimately, however, our biggest thanks go to the men and women of the WWI generation who recorded their experiences, and to the editors of the RSL magazines who so wisely published their stories, so that 100 years later another generation could read them and gain some personal insight into how Australians fought the Great War.

John Gatfield

About the editors

John Gatfield has spent most of his career as a journalist in television news, current affairs and documentaries, including thirteen years as the foundation anchor of Australia's first 24-hour news channel. A thoroughbred-horse owner and breeder, he is currently seen as a host on Sky Racing. Since 1995 he has also been an adviser to the RSL in NSW and editor of *Reveille*, the magazine of the NSW branch. He has been media director for the Australian team at three Commonwealth Games and worked with the Australian Olympic Committee at four Olympic Games.

Richard Landels has been in the publishing business for twenty years and has worked with the RSL in NSW and Victoria for the past fifteen years. He is currently the publisher of *Reveille*. He is heavily involved in the preservation and archiving of historic documents and the creation of useable digital libraries, working on projects with the RSL and other organisations.

Index

Individual military units are listed under Infantry, Light Horse, *etc.*

Printed in Australia
AUHW021349150922
369033AU00019B/134